Why Do You Need the New Edition of This Book?

Here are five reasons why the fifth edition of The Interest Group Society will help you succeed in your course.

1 The most current and comprehensive discussion of interest group politics. This fifth edition has been updated throughout to keep you informed of the latest developments in interest group politics. Coverage includes the explosion of business lobbyists and corporate spending, the appearance and impact of 527s, analysis of the legal limits of non-profit politics, and more.

2 In-depth assessment of the changes brought about by the 2006 elections. Up-to-date analysis in this fifth edition examines the effects of the new Democratic majorities–in both the House and Senate–on partisan lobbying, political action committee spending, and the relationship between parties and interest groups.

3 Expanded coverage of issues of increasing importance on the national level. New lobby reform legislation–passed by Congress in August, 2007–is affecting all aspects of lobbying, including spending, fundraising, lobby-sponsored trips, Congressional earmarks, and more. Examining the full implications of this new legislature, this new edition helps you develop a broader understanding of the context, meaning, and impact of emerging issues in interest group politics.

4 New material on technological advances affecting the issues and strategies of interest groups. Emphasizing the greater role of new technology on organization, mobilization, and grassroots efforts, this new edition will allow you to more meaningfully participate in discussion and debate of the important, technological factors that are reshaping the way interest groups interact with political systems.

5 Incorporates the latest data and statistics throughout. Grounded in thorough research, graphs and tables have been updated with the most current data on interest groups membership and PAC contributions, and incorporate examples and initiatives of new interest groups, lobbying shops, and grassroots movements.

PEARSON

Longman

The Interest Group Society

Fifth Edition

Jeffrey M. Berry
Tufts University

Clyde Wilcox
Georgetown University

PEARSON
Longman

New York Boston San Francisco
London Toronto Sydney Tokyo Singapore Madrid
Mexico City Munich Paris Cape Town Hong Kong Montreal

Editor-in-Chief: Eric Stano

Executive Marketing Manager: Ann Stypuloski

Supplements Editor: Brian Belardi

Production Manager: Stacey Kulig

Project Coordination, Text Design, and Electronic Page Makeup: S4Carlisle Publishing Services

Cover Design Manager: Wendy Ann Fredericks

Cover Designer: Bernadette Skok

Cover Art: Stephen Sweny/images.com

Senior Manufacturing Buyer: Alfred C. Dorsey

Printer and Binder: R.R. Donnelley and Sons

Cover Printer: R.R. Donnelley and Sons

Library of Congress Cataloging-in-Publication Data

Berry, Jeffrey M., 1948–
  The interest group society / Jeffrey M. Berry, Clyde Wilcox. — 5th ed.
    p. cm.
  Includes bibliographical references and index.
  ISBN 0-205-60480-3 (alk. paper)
  1. Pressure groups—United States. I. Wilcox, Clyde, 1953– II. Title.
  JK1118.B395 2009
  322.4'30973—dc22

                                                2008001025

Please visit us at www.ablongman.com

ISBN 13: 978-0-205-60480-7
ISBN 10: 0-205-60480-3
1 2 3 4 5 6 7 8 9 10—DOC—11 10 09 08

For Jessica and Rachel
Elaine and Neil

Contents

Preface

This new edition of *The Interest Group Society* comes in the midst of a period of great change in the interest groups in American politics. In the fall of 2005 and the spring of 2006, scandals sent lobbyists and policymakers to prison, and helped the Democrats recapture control of Congress for the first time in more than a decade. After some debate, Congress passed lobby reform legislation, and although the impact of these new rules is not yet clear, Trent Lott, a powerful Republican leader in the Senate, announced his early retirement in 2007 before these new rules went into effect, in order to pursue a lucrative career in lobbying. Meanwhile, the Justice Department continues investigations into corruption charges against several other members of Congress, and lobbyists. The story will end is still up in the air, but it is clear that the relationship between lobbyists and policymakers is likely to be carefully scrutinized for several years.

But it is important that students understand that all lobbyists are not corrupt, and that not all interest groups use extra-legal means to influence policy. More than 20 years ago, Jeffrey Berry described the myriad groups and lobbyists of the Washington, D.C., policymaking community, and that community has grown and become more complex in the years since. As I began revisions for this fifth edition, I find that many Berry's original insights are relevant today. Although they are an enduring part of American political life, interest groups today have more resources, represent more constituencies, and do more lobbying than ever before. We depend on them to speak for us before government and to ensure that legislators and administrators understand our needs and preferences. When we stop to think about the political issue that we care most about, we usually think of it in terms of interest group dynamics. We are truly an interest group society.

Of course, many things have changed as well, and this new edition highlights these changes. With the Republican takeover of Congress in 1994 came a new effort to more tightly integrate the policymaking and lobbying world. The K Street Project, conceived by Grover Norquist and implemented by Tom DeLay, placed many former Hill staff in key lobbying positions in corporations and trade associations. Over time, these lobbyists came to chair personal PACs of members and, in other ways, to renew and cement their relationships with their former bosses. The use of congressional earmarks exploded, giving interest groups new opportunities to seek special benefits from government. In 2007, Congress is attempting to limit earmarks, but it is not yet clear how successful they will be

Second, interest group involvement in elections has grown and has become more complex. Since the previous edition, interest groups have become involved in a new kind of "issue advocacy" spending, have spawned 527 committees that help coordinate coalitions and mobilize voters, and more generally have increased the level of their activity in elections. Interest groups have become more crucially involved in partisan electoral strategies and have forged closer ties with party leaders. Groups have become less bipartisan in their electoral support as the close partisan margins in Congress and growing partisan divides on policy have made each seat more valuable. And, in 2002, Congress passed a reform measure, the Bipartisan Campaign Reform Act, which has greatly reduced soft money and has influenced campaigns in other ways We have now had two full election cycles since the 2002 reforms, and the Supreme Court has recently overturned portions of the law, thereby allowing for a wave of new issue advocacy spending in the 2008 campaign.

I could not have completed this revision this quickly without the help of a number of people. Gregory Fortelny and my wife Elizabeth Cook provided much of the research needed to update this edition. Bob Biersack at the Federal Election Commission was helpful, as always. Chris Hull put me in touch with lobbyists when I needed certain key interviews. Many colleagues responded to queries about their current and past research. Many interest group leaders and lobbyists put up with my persistent questions, and colleagues such as Frank Baumgartner, Christopher Bosso, Michael Malbin, Paul Herrnson, Mike Bailey, and many others provided insights and often data. Jeff Berry provided his usual sage advice.

I am also grateful for the help of a number of people at Longman Publishers, especially Eric Stano and Donna Garnier, and Erin Melloy of S4 Carlisle Publishing Services.

Longman acknowledges the following reviewers who assisted in the planning for this revision: Kevin den Dulk, Grand Valley State University; Fred Meyer, Ball State University; James White, Concord College; and Charles Wiggins, Texas A&M University.

CLYDE WILCOX

The Interest Group Society

Chapter 1

Madison's Dilemma

> If you typed the word "lobbyist" into the Google News search engine last week [in January 2006], the first page of 8,670 search results would have included dozens of headlines that screamed out "Lobbyist's Guilty Plea Sends Out Shock Waves Through U.S. Congress," "Bush Campaign Getting Rid of Lobbyist's Money" and "Kennedy Among Leading Recipients of Convicted Lobbyist's Clients". . . . If Shakespeare lived today, perhaps he would write, "First shoot all the lobbyists."[1]

News stories about interest groups and lobbying in the past few years have focused on a widening network of scandals. In November of 2005, Randy Cunningham, a Republican Congressman representing San Diego, pled guilty to accepting bribes from lobbyists. Among the gifts he accepted were a Rolls-Royce, a yacht, a $7,200 Louis-Philippe commode, three antique nightstands, a leaded-glass cabinet, a washstand, a buffet, and four armoires. Lobbyists also paid more than $17,000 to repair the Rolls-Royce and provided a number of free trips on company jets. In exchange, Cunningham worked to steer lucrative Defense Department contracts to the clients of his benefactors. Cunningham promised to cooperate in the prosecution of others.

Ongoing investigations into charges of corruption had, by the fall of 2007, already sent to prison former lobbyist Jack Abramoff, former GOP Representative Bob Ney, and former U.S. Department of the Interior Deputy Secretary J. Steven Griles, and led to the defeat of other incumbent senators and representatives. Meanwhile the Justice Department was investigating charges that lobbyists had bribed other policymakers, including Alaska Senator Ted Stevens, whose home was remodeled by an Alaskan Oil and construction company. To many observers, these explicit cases of bribery were only symbols of a larger culture of corruption in the lobbying process.

In August of 2007, Congress overwhelmingly passed new lobby reform legislation. The new rules would strengthen requirements that lobbyists disclose their spending, require that they also disclose much of their fundraising activity on behalf of candidates, and require that all congressional legislation disclose special spending designations called "earmarks" that direct the government to spend money for particular projects.

---

[1] Jan Witold Baran, "Can I Lobby You? Don't Let One Bad Abramoff Spoil the Whole Bunch," *Washington Post*, January 8, 2006, p. B01.

The new rules were opposed by some lobbyists, but welcomed by others who believed that their profession was being debased by the behavior of a few corrupt colleagues. Citizens groups that lobby for government reform mostly applauded the new legislation, although some complained that it did not go far enough.

A troubling dilemma lies at the core of the American political system. In an open and free society in which people have the right to express their political views, petition their government, and organize on behalf of causes, some segments of the population are likely to pursue their own selfish interests. Farmers push Congress to adopt price subsidies, even though it means families will have to pay more at the grocery store. Manufacturers and labor unions press for tariffs and other trade barriers to protect profits and jobs. Consumers, however, will be saddled with higher prices as a result. Outdoor enthusiasts fight for increasing the number of parks and wilderness preserves, even though development of those lands might provide jobs for some who are out of work. In short, people pursue their self-interest, even though the policies they advocate may hurt others and may not be in the best interest of the nation.

The dilemma is this: If the government does not allow people to pursue their self-interest, it takes away their political freedom. When we look at the nations of the world in which people are forbidden to organize and to freely express their political views, we find that there the dilemma has been solved by authoritarianism. Although the alternative—permitting people to advocate whatever they want—is far more preferable, it also carries dangers. In a system such as ours, interest groups constantly push government to enact policies that benefit small constituencies at the expense of the general public.

This dilemma is as old as the country itself, yet it has never been more relevant than today. As lobbying has grown in recent years, anxiety has mounted over the consequences of interest group politics. Interest groups are said to threaten the integrity of congressional elections. Liberal citizen groups are blamed for slowing economic development with the regulatory policies for which they have fought. Labor unions are held responsible because America fails to compete effectively in many world markets, while tax cuts granted to businesses seem to increase their profits at the expense of huge federal budget deficits. Congressional "earmarks" that direct government spending to benefit certain groups has exploded, helping fuel large budget deficits that may undermine economic growth. Beyond the sins allegedly committed by sectors of the interest group community is a broader worry. Are the sheer number of interest groups and their collective power undermining American democracy?

It is important to remember that not all interest groups and lobbyists seek policies that enrich them. In December of 2005, some 300 religious leaders representing a number of churches, denominations, and interest groups knelt in prayer outside of the Cannon House Office Building, protesting cuts to Medicaid and food stamp programs that benefited poor families. Conservative religious leaders have protested abortion, same-sex marriage, and other policies—not seeking any personal economic benefits but instead representing the views of their constituents to government. Thus, interest groups can be thought to represent both efforts of individuals to pursue their own self-interest, sometimes by seeking narrow benefits that will enrich them at the expense of others, and also efforts by groups to represent the views of larger groups of citizens about the collective good. Some interest groups even lobby for reform of the lobbying process and urge government to enact stricter laws on lobbyists' gifts to policymakers.

Curing the Mischiefs of Faction

Although the founding fathers might not have anticipated the myriad ways that lobbyists seek to further their group's causes, they did foresee the dilemma of interest group involvement in politics. Contemporary discussions of this question inevitably turn to *The Federalist,* for James Madison's analysis in essay No. 10 remains the foundation of American political theory on interest groups.[2] Although, at the time he was writing, the country had no political parties or lobbies as we know them, Madison correctly perceived that people would organize in some way to further their common interests. Furthermore, these groupings, or "factions," as he called them, were a potential threat to popular government.

Factions were not anomalies, nor would they be occasional problems. Rather, as Madison saw it, the propensity to pursue self-interest was innate. The "causes of faction," he concluded, are "sown in the nature of man."[3] As any society develops, it is inevitable that different social classes will emerge, that competing interests based on differing occupations will arise, and that clashing political philosophies will take hold among the populace. This tendency was strong in Madison's eyes: He warned that free men are more likely to try to oppress each other than they are to "co-operate for their common good."[4]

Madison worried that a powerful faction could eventually tyrannize others in society. What, then, was the solution for "curing the mischiefs of faction"? He rejected out of hand any restrictions on the freedoms that permitted people to pursue their own selfish interests, remarking that the remedy would be "worse than the disease."[5] Instead, he reasoned that the effects of faction must be controlled rather than factions themselves eliminated. This control could be accomplished by setting into place the structure of government proposed in the Constitution.

In Madison's mind, a republican form of government, as designed by the framers, would provide the necessary checks on the worst impulses of factions. A republican form of government gives responsibility for decisions to a small number of representatives who are elected by the larger citizenry. Furthermore, for a government whose authority extends over a large and dispersed population, the effects of faction would be diluted by the clash of many competing interests across the country. Thus, Madison believed that, in a land as large as the United States, so many interests would arise that a representative government with its own checks and balances would not become dominated by any faction. Instead, government could deal with the views of all, producing policies that would be in the common good.

---

[2]*Federalist Papers* (New York: New American Library, 1961), pp. 77–84.
[3]Ibid., p. 79.
[4]Ibid.
[5]Ibid., p. 78.

Madison's cure for the mischiefs of faction was something of a leap of faith.[6] The structure of American government has not, by itself, prevented some interests from gaining great advantage at the expense of others. Those with large resources have always been better represented by interest groups, and the least wealthy in society have suffered because of their failure to organize. Still, even though the republican form of government envisioned by Madison has not always been strong enough to prevent abuse by factions, the beliefs underlying *Federalist* No. 10 have endured.

This view that the natural diversity of interests would prevent particular groups from dominating politics found a later incarnation in American social science of the 1950s and 1960s. *Pluralist* scholars argued that the many (that is, plural) interests in society found representation in the policymaking process through lobbying by organizations. The bargaining that went on between such groups and government led to policies produced by compromise and consensus. Interest groups were seen as more beneficial to the system than Madison's factions, with emphasis placed on the positive contributions made by groups in speaking for their constituents before government. Although the pluralist school was later discredited for a number of reasons (these will be outlined shortly), it furthered the Madisonian ideal: groups freely participating in the policymaking process, none becoming too powerful because of the natural conflict of interests, and government acting as a synthesizer of competing interests. Moreover, pluralists imagined that groups might form to pursue not only the narrow interests of their members but perhaps also broader conceptions of the public good. The ideal of multiple groups that offset each other's power remains contemporary America's hope for making interest group politics compatible with democratic values.

Interest Groups and Their Functions

One purpose of this book is to reexamine the fundamental questions raised by *Federalist* No. 10. Can an acceptable balance be struck between the right of people to pursue their own interests and the need to protect society from being dominated by one or more interests? Can we achieve true pluralism, or is a severe imbalance of interest group power a chronic condition in a free and open society? Is the interest group universe today balanced, as the pluralists had hoped, or is it dominated by narrow groups seeking their own benefits at a cost to the larger society?

Our means of answering this question will be to look broadly at behavior among contemporary interest groups. We will often follow research questions that political scientists have asked about the internal and external operations of lobbying organizations. Data for this study come not only from the literature on interest groups but also from interviews with interest group lobbyists, PAC officials, and party activists conducted by both of us at various times.[7] Although the topics addressed are varied, one argument runs

---

[6]There is an extensive literature on *Federalist* No. 10, but probably no analysis is more important than Robert Dahl's *A Preface to Democratic Theory* (Chicago: University of Chicago Press, 1956).

[7]Unless otherwise cited, quotations in the text are taken from these interviews.

throughout: Important changes have taken place in interest group politics in recent years, because of which renewed thought must be given to controlling the effects of faction.

On the simplest level, when we speak of an interest group, we are referring to an organization that tries to influence government. There are many civic associations that are not interest groups because they do not try to influence government personnel or policy. People often join groups because they share hobbies or other interests. Most of the time, groups such as the Boy Scouts, motorcycle clubs, soccer leagues, and charitable associations do not function as interest groups. But sometimes they do, at least for a time. The Boy Scout policy of barring gay men as troop leaders and gay boys as scouts has involved that organization in policy disputes at the local, state, and national levels. Soccer leagues frequently interact with local governments about their use of park facilities, and charitable associations lobby government about the tax deductibility of contributions. Even churches, synagogues, and mosques can function as interest groups if they seek to mobilize their members to oppose or support a government policy, a candidate, or a party.[8]

Interest groups are organizations that are not part of the government they are trying to influence.[9] Interest groups are often equated with voluntary organizations, membership groups composed of people with similar interests or occupations who have joined together to gain some benefits, yet the lobbying world is full of organizations that do not have members. Corporations and public interest law firms, for example, have no members, although they have constituencies they represent before government. Our focus here includes organizations that try to influence government policy through lobbying or electoral activity, regardless of whether they have members.

Interest groups are distinct from political parties because political parties run candidates for office under their banner, whereas interest groups do not. However, some interest groups do recruit candidates to seek the nominations of particular political parties, and a collection of interest groups can operate as a faction within a political party.[10] In the United States, many interests form groups that work within political parties. Although some environmentalists support the Green party, most are members of groups such as the Sierra Club or Friends of the Earth, which seeks to influence the Democratic party and, to a lesser extent, members of a more environmentally friendly faction within the Republican party. Religious conservatives in the United States have formed myriad political groups that seek to influence Republican nominations and policies, whereas in Israel similar types of groups have formed several distinct political parties.

---

[8]Churches and other religious groups have also sought direct government grants. See Diana B. Henriquez and Andrew Lehren, "Religious Groups Granted Millions in Pet Projects," *New York Times* May 13, 2007, p. A1.

[9]However, one level of government may organize a lobbying office or join a trade association trying to influence another level of government. Most states maintain lobbying organizations in Washington, and governors, state legislatures, counties, and cities have all formed special organizations to press for their collective interests.

[10]See Mark J. Rozell and Clyde Wilcox, *Second Coming: The Christian Right in Virginia Politics* (Baltimore: Johns Hopkins University Press, 1996). For an account of how the relationship between interest groups and parties varies by state, see John C. Green, Mark J. Rozell, and Clyde Wilcox, *Marching to the Millennium: The Christian Right in American Elections 1980–2000* (Washington, DC: Georgetown University Press, 2003).

This leads us to the distinction between *interests* and *interest groups*. Farmers do not constitute an interest group, yet the National Association of Wheat Growers, the American Farm Bureau Federation, and the National Milk Producers Federation are all bona fide interest groups. The critical distinction between farmers and any one of these groups is *organization*. Farmers are people in a similar occupation and they may share some views on what the government's farm policy should be. Farmers, however, do not all belong to an organization that acts on their behalf in attempting to influence public policy. People may share an interest or a concern without belonging to the same interest group.

The distinction may seem like an exercise in semantics; members of Congress may be worried about how "farmers" (rather than any particular organization) will react to legislative proposals. Political reality is that most interest groups represent only a part—possibly a very small part—of their potential membership. Government officials rightly care about what the larger constituency feels on policy issues as well as being attentive to specific interest group organizations. Just why it is that not all people who share an interest join an organization representing that interest is an important question, which we will address at length in Chapter 3. Interest groups are thus important not only because of their actual memberships but also because they may represent the views of even larger constituencies.

Interest groups are often also distinguished from social movements, although the boundaries are difficult to define because social movements are composed of interest groups.[11] Social movements are broad, decentralized, and diverse and may comprise several competing interest groups that offer differing ideologies, agendas, and strategies. The feminist movement encompasses the National Organization for Women as well as the Feminist Majority Foundation, The National Women's Law Center, and many other national, state, and local organizations. All share a commitment to gender equality, but they may disagree on specific issues and tactics.

When an interest group attempts to influence policymakers, it can be said to be engaging in *lobbying*. (The word comes from the practice of interest group representatives standing in the lobbies of legislatures, so that they could stop members on their way to a session and plead their case. In earlier times, when many legislators had no offices of their own, the lobbies or anterooms adjoining their chambers were a convenient place for a quick discussion on the merits of a bill.) Although lobbying conjures up the image of an interest group representative trying to persuade a legislator to vote in the group's favor, we should see it in a broader context. Lobbying can be directed at any branch of government—legislative, judicial, or executive. Interest groups can even try to influence those institutions indirectly by attempting to sway public opinion, which they hope in turn will influence government. Lobbying also encompasses many tactics including initiating a lawsuit, starting a letter-writing campaign, filing a formal comment on a proposed regulation, talking face-to-face with a member of Congress or a bureaucrat. Just about any legal means used to try to influence government can be called lobbying.

---

[11]See Paul Burnstein and April Linton, "The Impact of Political Parties, Interest Groups, and Social Organizations on Public Policy," *Social Forces* 81 (2002): 380–408.

Roles

In their efforts to influence government, interest groups play diverse roles in American politics. First and foremost, interest groups *represent* their constituents before government. They are a primary link between citizens and their government, forming a channel of access through which members voice their opinions to those who govern them. The democratic process can be described in the most eloquent language and be based on the noblest intentions, but in the real world of politics it must provide some means by which manufacturers, environmentalists, conservative Christians, construction workers, or whoever can speak to government about their specific policy preferences and have the government listen. For many people, interest groups are the most important mechanism by which their views are represented before the three branches of government.

Interest groups also afford people the opportunity to *participate* in the political process. American political culture leads us to believe that participation is a virtue, apathy a vice. A person who wants to influence public policymaking may not find voting or other campaign-related activity to be enough. Elections come only at intervals and do not render decisive judgments on most issues. If one wants a larger role in the governmental process, other ways of participating must be found. Pro-life and pro-choice groups, for example, offer members a chance to do something on an issue about which they feel strongly. If people care deeply about abortion, voting by itself is not likely to make them feel that they have done much to resolve the question. By contributing money to a lobbying organization—and possibly participating through it to do other things, such as writing letters or taking part in protests—members come to feel they have a more significant role in the political process. However, interest groups do more than facilitate participation. They actively try to promote it by stimulating members and potential supporters to take action on behalf of a particular lobbying cause. In the process, group members may develop important political skills.

Interest groups *educate* the American public about political issues. With their advocacy efforts, publications, and publicity campaigns, interest groups can make people better aware of both policy problems and proposed solutions. An inherent trait of interest groups is that they present only their side of an issue to the public, offering facts and interpretations most favorable to their position. For more than a decade, the national government has debated whether to permit drilling for oil in the Arctic National Wildlife Refuge in northeast Alaska. One lobbyist for the oil industry described its strategy in early 2001: "We'll use a range of arguments. National security, dependence on unreliable sources in the Middle East, cost of energy. The best way of winning is to make people concerned about the cost of filling up their gas tank."[12] Environmentalists, in contrast, mustered a range of arguments about the damage that drilling would cause to a pristine natural landscape and to caribou that breed in the area, and more recently that reliance on oil increases global warming.

Frequently, interest groups struggle to *frame* political issues. Public policy issues can be considered in different ways, each evoking different values. Although same-sex

---

[12]Roger Herrera, lobbyist for British Petroleum, quoted in "War over Arctic Oil," *Time Magazine* February 19, 2001, http://www.time.com/time/archive/preview/0,10987,98984,00.html (accessed January 2, 2006).

marriage had been debated by activists for several years, most Americans had not seriously considered the issue before the 2004 election. Gay and lesbian rights groups and civil rights groups sought to frame the debate around equality, arguing that it was fundamentally unfair to deny same-sex couples the same rights that heterosexual couples enjoyed. Christian conservative groups argued that same-sex marriage was a threat to traditional marriage and mounted a "defense of marriage" campaign. Neither side spent much time addressing the arguments of the other; instead, they promoted their own frame of the issue to the media and general public.[13]

A related activity is *agenda building*. Beyond educating people about the sides of an issue and framing the general debate, interest groups are frequently responsible for bringing the issue to light in the first place. The world has many problems, but not all are political issues being actively considered by government. Agenda building turns problems into issues, which become part of the body of policy questions that government feels it must deal with. Over the past two decades manufacturers and distributors of CDs, videocassettes, and computer software worked to get the government to pay attention to the problem of piracy of such goods in foreign countries. Their efforts paid off as the government began working on the issue and negotiated a major agreement with China in 1995, in which China promised to crack down on factories that illegally duplicated American goods.[14]

Sometimes agenda building is related to framing. In the 1990s, the National Federation of Independent Businesses (NFIB) beefed up its political operations behind an agenda that had as its first priority the repeal of the inheritance tax. To help frame the debate, the NFIB coined the phrase "death tax" to refer to the inheritance tax, and, when the media adopted the term, it helped catapult the issue onto the national agenda.[15]

Finally, interest groups are involved in *program monitoring*. Lobbies closely follow programs affecting their constituents and often try to draw attention to shortcomings through such tactics as issuing evaluative reports and contacting people in the media. They may also lobby agency personnel directly to make changes in program implementation or even go to court in an effort to exact compliance with a law. After the passage of the Bipartisan Campaign Reform Act in 2002, the Campaign Finance Institute commissioned a set of studies by scholars on the law's impact on the funding of campaigns. It also created a task force to study the financing of presidential campaigns, which reported that public matching funds for presidential primary election candidates had served the public good but that significant reforms were needed to retain the viability of the system for future presidential elections.[16]

[13]Paul Brewer and Clyde Wilcox, "Trends: Same-Sex Marriages and Civil Unions," *Public Opinion Quarterly* 69, no. 4 (2005): 599–616.

[14]Seth Faison, "U.S. and China Sign Accord to End Piracy of Software, Music Recordings and Film," *New York Times* February 27, 1995.

[15]Jeffrey H. Birnbaum, "The Forces That Set the National Agenda," *Washington Post* April 24, 2005, p. B1.

[16]Campaign Finance Institute, "So the Voters May Choose . . . Reviving the Presidential Matching Fund System," 2005, http://www.cfinst.org/.

Understanding Interest Groups

Important as the roles of interest groups are, these organizations remain misunderstood and maligned. Americans distrust interest groups in general but value the organizations that represent them. People join an interest group not simply because they agree with its views but because they equate those views with the "public interest." Groups that stand on opposite sides of the same issues are regarded with disdain. Intellectually, we accept the legitimacy of all interest groups; emotionally, we separate them into those we support and those we must view with suspicion.

The basis of any reasoned judgment about interest groups is a factual understanding of how they operate. This is not easy; though all interest groups have the same goal—to influence government—organizationally and politically they seem endlessly diverse. However, patterns are recognizable, and throughout this book such factors as size, type of membership, and resources are used to distinguish among basic forms of interest group behavior.

To place this analysis in perspective, we must step back to see how political scientists' perceptions of and attitudes toward interest groups changed in the latter half of the twentieth century. This is more than an interesting piece of intellectual history: A critical change in the thinking of political scientists helped broaden acceptance of the role of interest groups in public policymaking. That change, in turn, helped spur the growth of interest groups.

Pluralism

Early observers of interest group politics thought that interest groups formed easily and naturally and that, because of this, any imbalance in interest group politics would naturally lead to its own remedy. If one set of groups began to exert undue influence on the political system, then unorganized interests (called "latent interest groups") would organize and fight to bring politics back to a natural equilibrium. In *The Governmental Process,* published in 1951, David Truman makes a simple assertion: Politics can be understood only by looking at the interaction of groups.[17] He casts his lot with Madison, agreeing that "tendencies toward such groupings are 'sown in the nature of man.'"

A decade later, Robert Dahl published *Who Governs?*, a study of local politics in New Haven, Connecticut.[18] Dahl was responding to sociologists such as C. Wright Mills, who in *The Power Elite* (1956) had argued that America was ruled by a small stratum of wealthy and powerful individuals.[19] Members of this power elite were said to be the true decision makers in society, "democracy" being an effective illusion perpetrated on the

---

[17]David B. Truman, *The Governmental Process* (New York: Knopf, 1951). Truman traces the roots of a group theory of politics to Arthur F. Bentley's *The Process of Government* (Chicago: University of Chicago Press, 1908).

[18]Robert A. Dahl, *Who Governs?* (New Haven: Yale University Press, 1961).

[19]C. Wright Mills, *The Power Elite* (New York: Oxford University Press, 1956). See also Floyd Hunter, *Community Power Structure* (Chapel Hill: University of North Carolina Press, 1953).

masses. However, if the power elite thesis was false, as most political scientists believed it was, what was the counter theory?

Dahl examined three areas of local politics to see just who influenced policy outcomes. His crucial finding was that in the three areas—political party nominations, urban redevelopment, and public education—different groups of people were active and influential. New Haven did not have a small, closed circle of important people who together decided all the important issues in town politics. Dahl found policymaking in New Haven to be a process by which loose coalitions of groups and politicians became active on issues they cared about. Although most citizens might have been apathetic about most issues, many did get interested in the issues that directly affected them. Businesspeople were very active in urban redevelopment; teachers, school administrators, and the Parent-Teacher Association (PTA) were involved in school politics. Politicians courted groups as a way to build their own political support base. Consequently, not only were groups representing different interests active but their support was sought and their views carried weight.

Dahl argued that a realistic definition of democracy is not 50 percent plus one getting their way on each and every issue. Rather, as he wrote in an earlier work, the "'normal' American political process [is] one in which there is a high probability that an active and legitimate group in the population can make itself heard effectively at some crucial stage in the process of decision."[20] Through bargaining and compromise between affected groups and political elites, democratic decisions are reached, with no one group consistently dominating.

Critics charged that studies such as *Who Governs?* focused on too narrow a set of questions.[21] Social scientists using the pluralist framework did research on selected issues being debated by the relevant government authorities because they wanted to know who actually made policy decisions. On those issues, there may well have been participation by a number of affected interest groups, but critics argued that this did not mean that the governmental process was truly democratic. Instead, they suggested that the issues Dahl analyzed did not threaten to change the basic structure of New Haven society or its economy, no matter how they were resolved. In this view, only issues that do not fundamentally alter the position of elites enter the political agenda and become subject to interest group politics. However, elites combine to keep various issues, such as relative distribution of wealth among different segments of society, off the government agenda.[22]

Over time, the validity of the pluralist description of politics came into question. The civil rights movement that began in the 1950s made it all too clear that, for many decades, blacks had been wholly outside the normal workings of the political system. Eventually, it became clear that some groups are not as well represented in American

---

[20]Dahl, *A Preface to Democratic Theory*, p. 145. He later reflects on this sentence in *Dilemmas of Pluralist Democracy* (New Haven: Yale University Press, 1982), 207–9.

[21]The methodology of pluralism is best defended by Nelson W. Polsby, *Community Power and Political Theory* (New Haven: Yale University Press, 1980).

[22]A forceful statement of this position is in Peter Bachrach and Morton S. Baratz, "Two Faces of Power," *American Political Science Review* 56 (December 1962): 947–52. A further elaboration is provided by John Gaventa, *Power and Powerlessness* (Urbana: University of Illinois Press, 1980).

politics as others. In some cases, there are simply no groups representing large segments of the public. There are large and active groups taking pro-life and pro-choice positions on abortion, for example, but none advocating that abortion be allowed under some but not all circumstances—even though this is what the majority of Americans believe.[23]

In other cases, groups have unequal resources, and this persists for decades without any obvious countermobilization. The business community has long had more resources than consumer groups, for example. The National Rifle Association (NRA) and other pro-gun groups have long had more money, members, and clout than groups that advocate for gun control, although surveys usually show that a majority of Americans favor tougher gun control laws. Some types of groups form more easily than others, so that the interest group environment is not always, or even perhaps ever, in equilibrium. Thus, while it may not be the case that a single elite dominates all of American politics, neither is it true that all groups are equally represented and have equal resources to engage in politics.

Although pluralism was no longer seen as a valid description of the world, many in the 1960s took it as a reasonable prescription for the way that politics should work. In a way, pluralism was seen as a resolution to the Madisonian dilemma. If interest groups are not part of some type of balance in society, they present dangers. Failing a new resolution to the Madisonian dilemma, the solution has been to try to make pluralism a reality. Scholars, political activists, and policymakers have tried to justify and to improve interest group politics by proposing means to make it more balanced.

Some of those who have written about how to make America a true, pluralist democracy have focused on curbing what is seen as excessive privilege and influence of certain kinds of interest groups. Most conspicuous have been the arguments for reducing the role of interest groups in the financing of political campaigns, yet few believe that the power of business and trade groups is going to be brought into balance with other sectors of society merely by instituting campaign finance reform.

Instead, many critics focused on ways of enhancing the representation of those poorly represented in our interest group system. Political reformers sought to design government programs to require citizen participation in the programs' development at the local level.[24] Foundations sought to fund programs that might help develop interest groups to represent previously disenfranchised groups. Congress required bureaucracies to consult more broadly with interest groups in making rules to implement public policy. More recently, coalitions of interest groups sought to create still other interest groups that would help register and mobilize various segments of the population in elections.[25]

---

[23]Recently, organizations such as the "Third Way" have sought to reach compromise positions on abortion, but they have fewer resources than pro-life and pro-choice groups.

[24]See Jeffrey M. Berry, Kent E. Portney, and Ken Thomson, *The Rebirth of Urban Democracy* (Washington, DC: Brookings Institution, 1993), 21–45.

[25]Robert G. Boatright, Michael J. Malbin, Mark J. Rozell, and Clyde Wilcox, "Interest Groups and Advocacy Organizations After BCRA," ed. Michael J. Malbin, *The Election After Reform: Politics and the Bipartisan Campaign Reform Act* (Lanham, MD: Rowman & Littlefield, 2006).

Interest Groups and Civil Society

Although Madison focused on the potentially divisive aspects of interest groups in politics, interest groups may also play a positive role in social and political life. After touring the United States in 1831–1832, Alexis de Tocqueville wrote of the importance of the many political, moral, and intellectual associations that formed a key part of the public life.[26] In an influential study of the effectiveness of regional governments in Italy, Robert Putnam reported that government worked much better in regions that had a vibrant civil society—where individuals were involved in political and nonpolitical groups. Putnam argued that these regions were richer in social capital, which is comprised of social trust, norms of reciprocity, and networks of civic engagement.[27]

Scholars have posited three types of positive effects of interest groups. First, some types of groups can enhance the democratic capacities of their members. By being involved in interest groups, people can learn about issues and the political process, as well as think more clearly about their own interests.[28] By working with others, people can enhance their feelings of efficacy—the belief that they can make a difference in politics. Deliberating together with others may help them develop better political skills, such as the ability to make a strong argument, to bargain with others, and to build coalitions. Not all groups may be equally able to mold better citizens, however. In some groups, membership means simply writing a check, so those who are unhappy with a group's decisions may simply decline to renew their membership. In other groups, members meet face-to-face and discuss policies and strategies, and these groups may help develop members' civic skills.[29] Nonpolitical groups can also help them develop these skills; one study showed that churches are especially useful in helping socially disadvantaged individuals learn to be politically effective.[30]

Second, interest groups can help build social capital. Within groups, members may form bonds of friendship that involve shared identities, trust, and social relationships. Putnam refers to this in his book *Bowling Alone: The Collapse and Revival of American Community* as "bonding social capital." In the 1990s, Christian fundamentalists and Catholics came together to work in pro-life groups, and many reported that they had overcome previous religious disagreements.[31] But these civic virtues may not extend to those outside the group. As evangelicals and conservative Catholics discovered the

---

[26]Alexis de Tocqueville, *Democracy in America*, ed. J. P. Mayer, (Garden City, NJ: Doubleday, 1969).

[27]Robert D. Putnam, *Making Democracy Work: Civic Traditions in Modern Italy* (Princeton, NJ: Princeton University Press, 1993).

[28]Jane Mansbridge, "Does Participation Make Better Citizens?" Paper presented at the PEGS Conference, February 11–12, 1995, http://www.cpn.org/crm/contemporary/participation.html (accessed February 14, 2006).

[29]Gregory B. Markus, "Civic Participation in America." (Report of the Civic Engagement Study, Ann Arbor: University of Michigan, 2002). Markus argues that community-based organizations are best at developing political skills.

[30]Verba, Schlozman, and Brady, op. cit.

[31]Clyde Wilcox, "The Christian Right in Virginia: A Mixed Blessing for Democracy." Paper presented at the Conference on Civil Society in the United States, Georgetown University, June 1999.

values they had in common, they became increasingly convinced that they shared very little with liberals.[32]

In contrast, "bridging social capital" involves the development of trust and tolerance of those outside of particular groups. Some types of community associations are especially focused on building networks across racial, class, and other lines. In other cases, bridging capital may occur from overlapping group memberships.[33] Within a single group, such as the National Rifle Association, there may be people who are also members of the Sierra Club, the American Civil Liberties Union, or Focus on the Family. Truman suggested that overlapping memberships in interest groups help increase social trust and ameliorate the problem of "factions," and research has shown that individuals who are members of cross-cutting social networks have higher levels of political tolerance.[34]

Finally, interest groups can help government perform various functions better; some interest groups perform civic actions. The Sierra Club has group expeditions to help the National Park Service repair trails and other facilities. Government programs to help the poor are supplemented by programs by interest groups, and in some cases interest groups have contracts to administer programs. Public schools benefit from the activities of parent-teacher associations, which also lobby for increased funding for schools. Interest groups help control professional licensing, and to monitor government functioning. They provide spheres for public deliberation and enhance representation. In emerging democracies, the U.S. government helps fund the development of nongovernmental organizations (NGOs) to help perform some of these functions, but many countries lack this network of groups that can assist government.[35]

Many scholars have studied the impact of interest groups on civil society in recent years. In a rich analysis of the types of voluntary associations and their complex effects on democracy, Mark Warren has argued that some groups are far better than others at building social capital and that not all groups have a positive impact on democracy.[36] Some groups build trust among members by building distrust of other citizens. And membership in political interest groups is far more common among the better educated and more affluent citizens and therefore may magnify their advantages. But, overall, this research shows that the negative effects of interest group divisions are sometimes partially offset by the positive effects on civil society.

---

[32]Eric Uslaner, *The Moral Foundations of Trust* (New York: Cambridge University Press, 2002).

[33]For a good study of groups that build political skills and political capital among disadvantaged groups, see Mark R. Warren, *Dry Bones Rattling: Community Building to Revitalize American Democracy* (Princeton, NJ: Princeton University Press, 2001).

[34]Diana C. Mutz, "Cross-Cutting Social Networks: Testing Democratic Theory in Practice," *American Political Science Review* 96 (2002): 111–26.

[35]Marc Morje Howard, *The Weakness of Civil Society in Post-Communist Europe* (New York: Cambridge University Press, 2003).

[36]Mark E. Warren, *Democracy and Association* (Princeton, NJ: Princeton University Press, 2001). For a somewhat different view, see Nancy L. Rosenbaum, *Membership and Morals* (Princeton, NJ: Princeton University Press, 1998).

Conclusion

Critics of pluralism and those who extoll the virtue of groups for civil society have agreed on one thing: Expanding interest group participation by the chronically under-represented is at least a first step toward finding a new solution to the dilemma of *Federalist* No. 10. The past thirty years have seen an explosion in the number and activities of interest groups and the range of interests they represent. But this extraordinary growth in all types of lobbying organizations has raised a new questions about curing the mischiefs of faction.

In the remainder of this book, we will explore the role of interest groups in American politics. Chapter 2 examines the growth in the number of interest groups and tries to explain the underlying causes of the expansion of lobbying activity. Chapter 3 is devoted to the organization of lobbies, with the discussion emphasizing the origins, maintenance, marketing, and governing of interest groups. Chapter 4 analyzes the relationship between political parties and interest groups. In Chapter 5, attention turns to the way interest groups try to influence election outcomes.

In Chapter 6, the focus shifts to the lobbyists who represent interest groups before government. Chapter 7 considers how interest groups try to influence people at the grass-roots level and how Washington lobbyists try to mobilize support among constituents as part of their advocacy campaigns. Chapter 8 covers direct lobbying of the three branches of government. Chapter 9 extends that discussion to coalition politics among Washington lobbies. Bias and representation in the American interest group system are the subjects of Chapter 10.

Chapter 2

The Advocacy Explosion

There is a pervasive belief in this country that interest groups are out of control. They have grown in number and influence while rank-and-file Americans have become disempowered. This view has prevailed for most of the last 30 years and is echoed constantly in the press. In 1986, *Time* told us that "at times the halls of power are so glutted with special pleaders that government itself seems to be gagging."[1] In 2006, Hendrik Hertzberg argued in *The New Yorker* that the Abramoff scandal was not an isolated instance; rather, "it's simply the currently most visible excrescence of a truly national scandal: the fearful domination of private money over the public interest."[2]

Bemoaning the growing lobbying industry, the *New Republic* noted in 1986, "What dominates Washington is not evil and immorality, but a parasite culture. Like Rome in decline, Washington is bloated, wasteful, pretentious, myopic, decadent, and sybaritic. It is the paradise of the overpaid hangers-on."[3] Twenty years later, the *New York Times* editorialized that "the founding fathers' vision of a citizen's basic right to 'petition the government for a redress of grievances' has turned into a multibillion-dollar influence industry that is far too loosely tracked and regulated. The lobbyists' symbiotic relationship with lawmakers is based on their inside track as Capitol buttonholers and the campaign money trail, where lobbyists help to ensure that incumbents are enriched and their gratitude secured."[4]

More than 200 years after Madison thought he and the other founders had developed a solution to the problem of self-interested factions, former Speaker of the House Newt Gingrich noted that "things have to be done to really rethink where the center of the political process is. Right now, the center is a lobbying and PAC system center, which is not healthy."[5]

Observers of the Washington scene produce a steady stream of books and articles warning that democracy is in peril. Jonathan Rauch argues that interest groups are at the heart of both economic decline and governmental decay. "As [the interest group industry] grows, the steady accumulation of subsidies and benefits, each defended in

[1] Evan Thomas, "Peddling Influence," *Time* March 3, 1986.
[2] Hendrik Hertzberg, "Abramoffed," (accessed January 16, 2006).
[3] Fred Barnes, "The Parasite Culture of Washington," *New Republic* July 28, 1986, p. 26.
[4] Editorial, "The Lobbying-Industrial Complex," August 26, 2005, p. A18.
[5] Jeffrey H. Birnbaum and Dan Balz, "Case Bringing New Security to a System and a Profession," *Washington Post* January 4, 2006.

perpetuity by a professional interest group, calcifies government. Government loses its capacity to experiment and so becomes more and more prone to failure."[6]

Political scientists have been more temperate in their language, but many scholars have found the growth of interest group politics troubling. Robert Dahl, who, as noted in Chapter 1, once championed interest group democracy, was more critical in 1994. "In recent decades," he writes, "both the number and variety of interest groups with significant influence over policymaking in Washington have greatly increased." At the same time, "The increase in the number and diversity of interest groups has not been accompanied . . . by a corresponding increase in the strength of integrating institutions."[7] A decade later, political scientist Allan Cigler, a leading expert on interest groups, warned of the dangers of increased lobbying. "We've got a problem here. The growth of lobbying makes even worse than it is already the balance between those with resources and those without resources."[8]

Americans of all ideological stripes believe that interest groups are at the core of government's problems. In 1964, 64 percent of those polled agreed with the statement that government "is run for the benefit of all the people." Only 29 percent agreed that government is "run by a few big interests looking out for themselves." In 1995, a mere 15 percent agreed that the government was run for the benefit of all, while 79 percent agreed that government is run by a few big interests. In 2002, after the 9/11 terrorist attacks focused public attention on the war on terror, a majority of Americans had shifted back to believing that the government was run for the benefit of all, but within two years this pattern had reversed itself, and a majority of Americans again believed that a few big interest groups dominated politics.[9] In late 2005, as stories of lobbyists bribing members of Congress dominated the media, a Time/CNN poll showed that almost half of Americans thought that most members of Congress were corrupt.[10]

In short, there is a widespread popular perception that interest groups are a cancer, spreading unchecked throughout the body politic, corrupting and weakening it. Indeed, many interest groups seek to get more support from their members by arguing that they are helping oppose "special interests" on the other side. For example, the Concerned Women for America, a Christian conservative group, argues that it must mobilize to represent the views of its members against special interest organizations of feminists, as well as gays and lesbians.[11] Meanwhile, the National Organization for Women, a liberal feminist organization, argues that it must work harder to fight the influence of special interests such as the Christian Right on the same issues.

Not only citizen groups view themselves as combating special interest power. Corporations that became more active in elections in the late 1990s did so in part because of the

[6]Jonathan Rauch, *Demosclerosis* (New York: Times Books, 1994), 17.

[7]Robert A. Dahl, *The New American Political (Dis)Order* (Berkeley, CA: Institute for Governmental Studies, 1994), 8.

[8]Cited in Jeffrey Birnbaum, "The Road to Riches Is Called K Street: Lobbying Firms Hire More, Pay More, Charge More to Influence Government," *Washington Post* June 22, 2005, p. A1.

[9]The change in perception of the government in 2001 was because people were focusing on policies aimed at making Americans safe from a terrorist attack. As normal politics began to reassert themselves, the public began to again think about the way that government works with interest groups on other issues.

[10]http://www.cnn.com/2006/POLITICS/01/03/poll.congressimage/ (accessed March 14, 2006).

[11]http://www.family.org/cforum/fnif/news/a0037776.cfm (accessed January 16, 2006).

visible actions of organized labor, and many corporate lobbyists claimed that labor unions and other "special interests" dominated politics to create an antibusiness environment.

The Interest Group Spiral

The impassioned denunciations of interest group politics raise two important questions. Has there really been a significant expansion of interest group politics? Or are these the same kind of complaints that have always been heard in American politics?

The answer to both questions is yes. Surely nothing is new about interest groups being seen as the bane of our political system. The muckrakers at the turn of the twentieth century voiced many of the same fears that showed up in the 1980s in *Time* and the *New Republic*, and today in the *New York Times* or *The New Yorker*. Even if the problem is familiar, however, it is no less troubling. The growth of interest group advocacy in recent years should not simply be dismissed as part of a chronic condition in American politics. Although the complaints are not new, it is clear that the magnitude of interest group politics has grown explosively in recent decades. Many new interest groups have formed since the 1960s, and the diversity of groups has grown as well. Moreover, existing organizations have become more active in campaigns and lobbying.

Studies have shown that the number of interest groups grew dramatically in the 1960s and 1970s. Jack Walker's 1981 study of 564 lobbying organizations in Washington showed that approximately 30 percent of the groups active at the time had formed in the previous two decades.[12] A study by Kay Schlozman and John Tierney of a 1981 lobbying directory showed that 40 percent of the groups had been formed since 1960, with 25 percent formed since 1970.[13] Using a different approach, in 2005, Frank Baumgartner reported that the number of associations listed in the *Encyclopedia of Associations* increased from around 10,000 in 1968 to around 22,000 in the mid-1990s and remains relatively unchanged since.[14] The data in Figure 2.1 show substantial increases in many types of groups.

Existing organizations have established Washington offices or have moved their head-quarters to the nation's capital to become more involved in politics. Before 1920, only one corporation had a permanent Washington office. In 1978, there were 175 corporations with DC offices; by 2004, the number had grown to more than 600.[15] Equally important, many corporations expanded their in-house lobbying operations and hired additional professional lobbyists. Businesses have also expanded their use of public opinion pollsters and

---

[12]Jack L. Walker, Jr. "The Origins and Maintenance of Interest Groups in America," *American Political Science Review* 77 (June 1983): 390–406.

[13]Kay Lehman Schlozman and John T. Tierney, *Organized Interests and American Democracy* (New York: Harper & Row, 1986), 75–76.

[14]Frank R. Baumgartner, "The Growth and Diversity of U.S. Associations: 1956–2004: *Analyzing Trends Using the Encyclopedia of Associations.*" Working paper, March 29, 2005.

[15]Ronald G. Shaiko, "Making the Connection: Organized Interests, Political Representation, and the Changing Rules of the Game in Washington Politics," in *The Interest Group Connection,* 2nd ed., ed. Paul S. Herrnson, Ronald G. Shaiko, and Clyde Wilcox (Washington, DC: CQ Press, 2005).

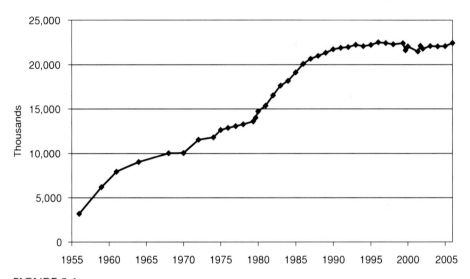

FIGURE 2.1
Growth by Sector.
Source: Frank R. Baumgartner, "The Growth and Diversity of U.S. Associations. 1956–2006.
Analyzing Trends Using the *Encyclopedia of Associations*" (2005).

media consultants, because many have concluded that they are unlikely to win political battles without the support of public opinion.[16]

A similar trend can be found in the number of trade associations that make their headquarters in Washington. These organizations, such as the National Funeral Directors Association and the National Independent Retail Jewelers, work on behalf of a single industry. Between 1970 and 1984, the proportion of national associations that made Washington their headquarters rose from 21 percent to 31 percent. During this time, many trade associations felt it was necessary to move to Washington so that they could focus more on lobbying, and Washington replaced New York as the city with the most trade groups. Since that time, the number of associations headquartered in Washington has flattened, but increasing numbers are now centered in the Maryland and Virginia suburbs of the capital.

Many corporations and trade associations have in recent years established additional offices close to Capitol Hill. FedEx and UPS both have townhouses near the Capitol, and the National Association of Realtors has built a glass tower nearby. The U.S. Chamber of Commerce has opened an additional office only a short walk from the Congress, in a neighborhood that includes the Sheet Metal and Air Conditioning Contractors National Association, the National Rural Electric Cooperative Association, and the Associated

---

[16]Mark A. Smith, *American Business and Political Power: Public Opinion, Elections, and Democracy* (Chicago: University of Chicago Press, 2000).

General Contractors of America.[17] These locations make it easy for lobbyists to quickly get to Congress when needed.

During the 1980s, many organizations also formed political action committees (PACs) in order to contribute to congressional candidates. PACs raise money from members of the group, then make donations to candidates for public office. Most are simply separate funds administered by existing organizations, such as AT&T, the AFL-CIO, and the National Rifle Association (NRA). Some organizations are separate in their own right, such as EMILY's List, which recruits, trains, and helps fund pro-choice Democratic women candidates for Congress.

PACs began to form in the mid-1970s in response to changes in federal law. Labor unions pressed Congress to allow PACs in the Federal Election Campaign Act of 1974, but it was corporations that quickly moved to form new committees. In December of 1974, there were 89 corporate PACs and 201 labor PACs, but six years later there were more than 1,200 corporate PACs and fewer than 300 labor PACs. In the fall of 2007, there were more than 1,500 corporate PACs, slightly fewer than 275 labor PACs, and slightly over 4,100 PACs overall. The number of PACs has leveled off since the 1980s, as new committees have balanced those that have disbanded.

The static number of PACs does not mean that interest groups have not become more active in elections. Existing PACs have increased their overall contributions to candidates, as we will see later in the book. Moreover, since the late 1990s, there has been a rapid growth in the number of special 527 committees that seek to influence elections without contributing money directly to candidates and parties. The name "527" comes from the segment of federal tax code that allows these committees. Liberal political activists have been especially active in forming new 527 committees, inspired by the control that Republicans had on both chambers of Congress and the White House. Conservatives also formed new 527 committees in 2004 and will doubtlessly form new ones in 2008.[18] Overall, the activity of interest groups in American elections has increased dramatically in the past decades.

Interest groups have also become more involved in lobbying national government. One measure of this is the number of members of the Washington bar. Washington law is lobbying law, and major law firms are hired by corporations, trade associations, foreign governments, and others to work with the government to try to solve specific problems. Figure 2.2 shows the increase in the numbers of lawyers in the bar, from 11,000 to around 63,000 between 1972 and 1994. In the next decade, with the GOP in control of Congress, the number exploded to more than 81,000—a 25 percent increase in only ten years. By March of 2007, the number had further grown to 85,762. The reason is that corporations are spending more money on lobbying than ever before. Retail giant Wal-Mart increased its reported lobbying expenditures from $140,000 in 1999 to

---

[17]Jeffrey H. Birnbaum, "Lobbyists Making Themselves at Home on the Hill," *Washington Post* July 24, 2007, p. A3.

[18]In some cases, 527 committees appear to be temporary campaign committees, rather than enduring interest groups. In a few cases, the 527 committees have been entirely funded by one or two large donors, who are mostly using them as a conduit for their electoral activity. See Robert G. Boatright, Michael J. Malbin, Mark J. Rozell, and Clyde Wilcox, "Interest Groups and Advocacy Organizations After BCRA"; and Steve Weissman and Ruth Hassan, "527 Groups and BCRA," both in *The Election After Reform: Money, Politics, and the Bipartisan Campaign Reform Act*, ed. Michael J. Malbin (Lanham, MD: Rowman & Littlefield, 2006).

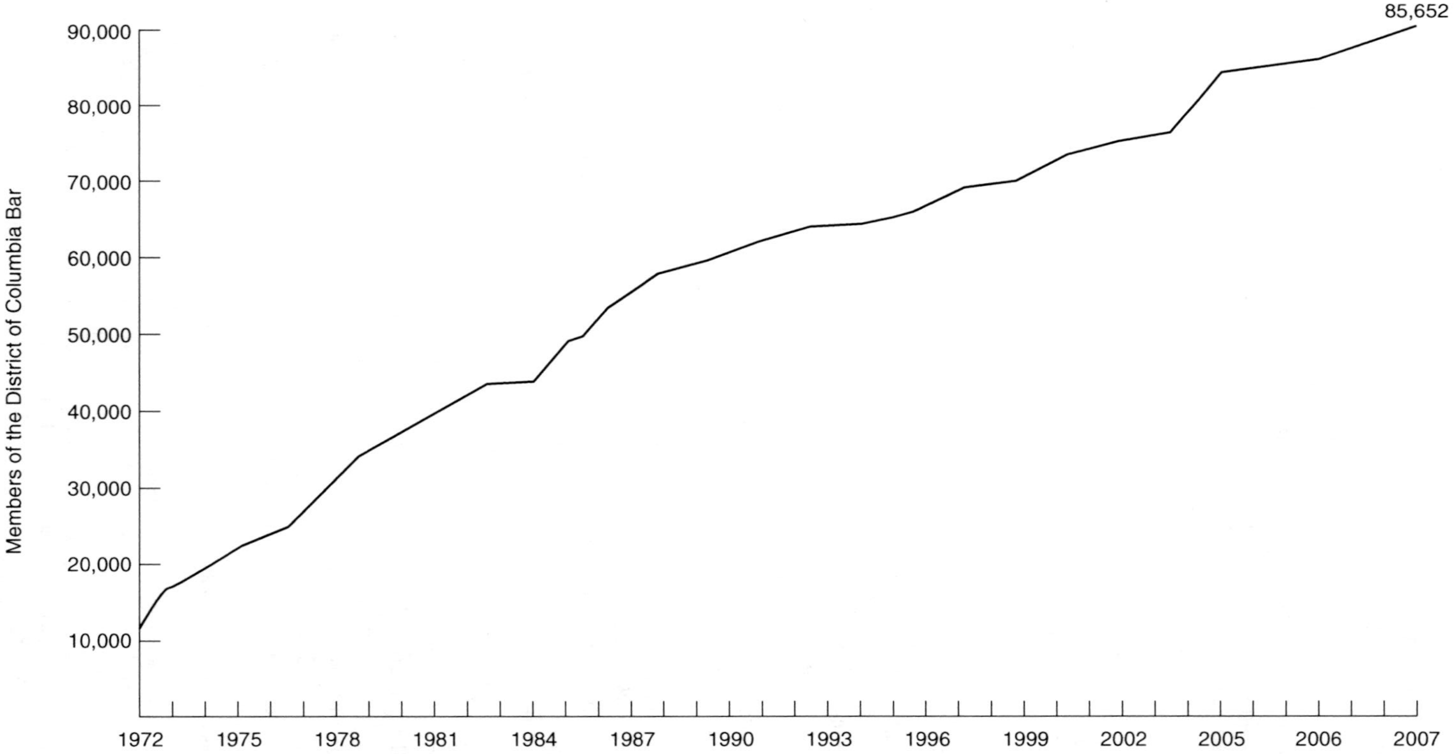

FIGURE 2.2
Washington Lawyers.
Source: Data provided by the Washington, DC, Bar Association.

$1,160,000 in 2004, a more than 700 percent increase in just five years. Computer maker Hewlett-Packard doubled its spending on contract lobbyists from 2004 to 2005. Google spent no money on lobbying before 2005, but increased this to $800,000 in 2006 and dramatically expanded its lobbying efforts in 2007.[19] Nearly every company that lobbied in Washington was spending far more money and effort in 2007 than a decade before.

Although the number of and activity of all kinds of groups have been growing, not all types of groups have grown at the same rate; in fact, some are declining. The number of labor unions did not increase during the past 30 years, and the number of labor PACs has decreased by 10 percent in the last decade. Moreover, as Figure 2.3 shows, the percentage of workers in the labor force who were union members declined from more than 32 percent in 1948 to only 12 percent in 2006.[20] Union membership declined for many reasons. Employment in manufacturing and mining, two highly unionized sectors of the economy, declined. Employers have also been more aggressive in trying to prevent their employees from forming unions. In recent years, the two most rapidly growing labor unions have focused on service employees, as well as on workers for national, state, and local governments.

In contrast to unions, there has been robust growth by health care lobbies. In the relatively short period between 1984 and 1991, health groups more than doubled in number. The primary reason for this is the increasing pressure on the federal government to rein in health care costs. When the government writes health care statutes and regulations, its

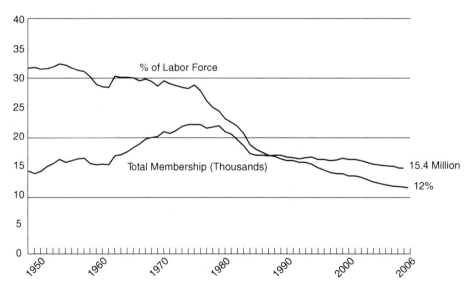

FIGURE 2.3
Union Membership (in Thousands and as a Percentage of the Labor Force).

---

[19]Kevin J. Delaney and Amy Schatz, "Google Goes to Washington with Own Brand of Lobbying," *Wall Street Journal* July 20, 2007, p. A1.
[20]http://www.laborresearch.org/charts.php?id 29 (accessed January 17, 2006).

decisions do not affect every part of the industry uniformly. What is good for teaching hospitals might be damaging to small community hospitals. A policy designed to help general practitioners might come at the expense of physicians who are specialists. With vast sums of money at stake every time government takes up health care reform, it is understandable that different sectors of the industry have enhanced their representation in Washington. Since 1991, the number of health groups has not increased substantially, but health-related groups have dramatically increased their political activity, as we will see.

In analyzing the development of interest groups, scholars must look at numbers of organizations, their memberships over time, and financial resources. By whatever standard used, however, we can be confident that the increase in lobbying organizations since the early 1960s is real and not a function of overblown rhetoric about the dangers of contemporary interest groups. The emergence of so many groups and the expansion of those already in existence fundamentally altered American politics. Let us look more carefully at the mobilization of different types of political groups.

The Rise of Citizen Groups

The growth of interest group advocacy in different sectors of society comes from many of the same roots. At the same time, the sharp growth in numbers of interest groups also reflects different sectors of society responding to each other. As one segment of the interest community grew and appeared to prosper, it spurred growth in other segments eager to equalize the increasing strength of their adversaries. This spiral of interest group activity began in large part in the civil rights and antiwar movements of the 1960s.

Movement Politics

The interest group texts of the 1950s barely make mention of citizen groups.[21] Today, citizen groups seem to be everywhere in Washington, and they are major participants in a wide range of policy areas. What catalyzed this change was the civil rights movement. The drive of African Americans for equality began to gather steam with the 1954 Supreme Court decision banning school segregation and the 1955 Montgomery, Alabama, bus boycott. In Montgomery, blacks refused to ride the segregated system (whites in front, blacks in the back), quickly depleting the financial resources of the city's transit system. Although it took a Supreme Court order to force integration of the system a year later, many other boycotts and sit-ins followed, increasing national awareness of discrimination. African American leaders organized many civil rights groups, which helped mobilize and coordinate movement activity.

Public opinion was not fully galvanized, however, until the early 1960s, when blacks began holding marches and demonstrations, many of which ended in confrontation with white authorities. Some ended in violence, with marchers being attacked by police.

---

[21]See V. O. Key, Jr., *Politics, Parties, & Pressure Groups,* 3rd ed. (New York: Thomas Y. Crowell, 1952); and David B. Truman, *The Governmental Process* (New York: Knopf, 1951).

The demonstrations, shown on network news telecasts, helped turn the public decidedly in favor of civil rights legislation.[22] The immediate outcome was the Civil Rights Act of 1964, outlawing many basic forms of discrimination, and the Voting Rights Act of 1965, which ended the exclusion of blacks from voting in many areas of the South.

Citizen group politics was also fueled by the anti–Vietnam War movement that took form in the mid-1960s. Its success was not as clear-cut as the civil rights movement's, because so many American soldiers continued to fight and die during years of protest. Many Americans became hostile toward the antiwar movement because they felt it was disloyal for citizens not to support American soldiers once they were committed to a military action. Most would agree, however, that the antiwar movement hastened the end of America's role in the war in Vietnam. This unpopular war helped push President Johnson out of office and brought pressure upon President Nixon to end American participation in the fighting. The antiwar groups spearheaded opposition to the war, and their periodic demonstrations were visible evidence of growing public anger over the fighting.

From the successes of the civil rights and anti–Vietnam War movements came the realization that citizen groups could influence the course of public policy.[23] This model of citizen group advocacy was soon copied by others suffering from discrimination who saw parallels between blacks and themselves. Hispanic farmworkers in California were organized for the first time by Cesar Chavez and his United Farm Workers union. Gays and lesbians would later organize into groups such as the Lambda Legal Defense and Education Fund, which works for civil rights for sexual minorities. Most conspicuous was the rise of the women's movement, deeply influenced by the citizen advocacy of the 1960s. Women saw the tools of these earlier groups as directly applicable to their own plight. Evans describes how the National Organization for Women (NOW) was formed:

> The lessons of the NAACP and its legal defense arm were not lost on the women who founded NOW: to adult professional women in the early 1960s the growth of civil rights insurgency provided a model of legal activism and imaginative minority group lobbying.[24]

Evans points out that many of those who became pioneers in the women's movement first gained experience working for those earlier causes.

Minorities and women were not the only ones influenced to organize by the civil rights and antiwar movements. Political activists began to look at the range of policy areas that interested them, such as consumer rights, environmental affairs, hunger and malnutrition, corporate responsibility, and access to media. Although the success of civil rights and antiwar groups inspired the formation of new groups in these areas, the protest orientation of these earlier organizations seemed inappropriate. Leaders of these new groups wanted to transcend "movement politics" with organizations that could survive beyond periods of intense emotion. The organizations that were needed could put the idealism of young, liberal activists in harness with financial support and policy interests of the middle class.

---

[22]David J. Garrow, *Protest at Selma* (New Haven: Yale University Press, 1978).

[23]On the influence of the civil rights and antiwar efforts, see David Vogel, *Lobbying the Corporation* (New York: Basic Books, 1978), 23–68.

[24]Sara Evans, *Personal Politics* (New York: Knopf, 1979), 25.

Public Interest Groups

Many of the new organizations in the late 1960s and early 1970s became popularly known as "public interest groups." They were lobbying groups without economic self-interest or, more precisely, "a public interest group is one that seeks a collective good, the achievement of which will not selectively and materially benefit the membership or activists of the organization."[25] The most prominent of the new groups were Common Cause and the Ralph Nader organizations. Common Cause, which focuses on opening up and reforming the governmental process, was founded in 1970 by John Gardner, a liberal Republican and former cabinet secretary in the Johnson administration. Declaring that "everyone is represented but the people," Gardner used full-page newspaper ads and direct-mail solicitations to build a membership of 230,000 in little more than a year, an astonishing feat for a voluntary organization.[26]

Ralph Nader came into the public eye in 1965, when his attack on the automobile industry, *Unsafe at Any Speed,* was published. Nader quickly became known as a consumer champion and, in his first decade in Washington, put together more than a dozen lobbying organizations. Many of his groups, such as the Public Citizen Litigation Group and the Health Research Group, have been major actors in Washington politics.

Many other groups, such as the Environmental Defense Fund, Zero Population Growth, and the Children's Foundation, started up as well. Older groups, such as Consumers Union, the League of Women Voters, and the Sierra Club, prospered, too, and devoted new resources to Washington lobbying. Indeed, public interest groups have existed for years, and the most recent wave of groups is in the tradition of American reform movements.[27] Public interest groups are distinguished from earlier reform movements, though, by the breadth and durability of the lobbying organizations. Some of the liberal public interest groups have developed into huge organizations, with large memberships and budgets in the millions of dollars (see Figure 2.4).[28] More important, these organizations have pushed their issues onto the nation's political agenda and have become major influences in the formulation of public policy. Indeed, one recent study suggested that liberal citizen groups are far more visible and active in politics than their numbers suggest and that they are "at the center of debate in Washington over public policy."[29]

Public interest groups of this era directly benefited from the growing force of the pluralist ideal. The lack of an acceptable alternative theory of democracy and the reality of interest group politics made pluralism a compelling idea, a goal toward which America should strive. As it became accepted that pluralist democracy did not, in fact,

---

[25]Jeffrey Berry, *Lobbying for the People,* 7.

[26]Ibid., 29–30.

[27]Andrew S. McFarland, *Common Cause* (Chatham, NJ: Chatham House, 1984), 23–37.

[28]On the evolution of the environmental movement in terms of memberships and budgets, see Christopher Boerner and Jennifer Chilton Kallery, *Restructuring Environmental Big Business.* Occasional Paper #146, Center for the Study of American Business, Washington University, December, 1994; Christopher Bosso, "The Color of Money: Environmental Groups and the Pathologies of Fund Raising," in *Interest Group Politics,* 4th ed., eds. Allan J. Cigler and Burdett A. Loosmis (Washington, DC: Congressional Quarterly, 1995), 101–30; and Mark Dowie, *Losing Ground* (Cambridge: MIT Press, 1995).

[29]Jeffrey M. Berry, *The New Liberalism: The Rising Power of Citizen Groups* (Washington, DC: Brookings, 1999), 25.

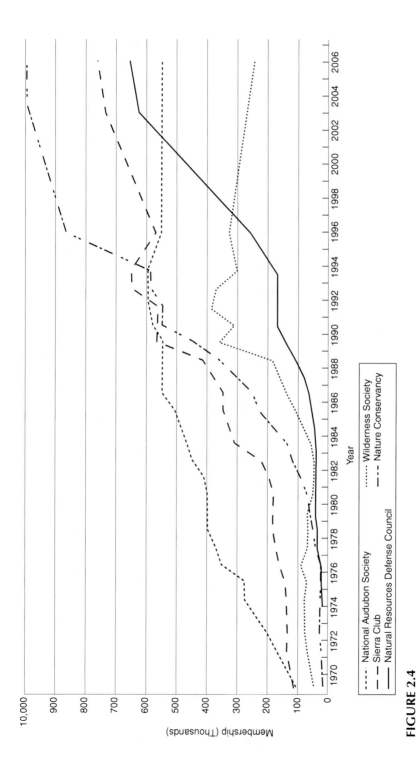

FIGURE 2.4

Membership in Environmental Groups.

Source: Data from Christopher J. Bosso, *Environment, Inc.: Grassroots to Beltways* (Studies in Government and Public Policy) (Lawrence: University Press of Kansas, March 16, 2005) (data updated by authors).

25

exist, how was its absence to be remedied? The solution was quite simple: The influence of existing groups had to be *balanced*.[30] Madison's words were echoed: Democracy could be achieved not by limiting the freedom of private interests to lobby but, rather, by "controlling" the "effects" of the one-sidedness. The Ford Foundation articulated this simple premise in defending their sponsorship of public interest law firms during the early 1970s:

> A central assumption of our democratic society is that the general interest or the common good will emerge out of the conflict of special interests. The public interest law firm seeks to improve this process by giving better representation to certain interests.[31]

The liberal public interest movement thus was built on a vision of how democracy could work, and the leaders of these groups came to a common conclusion as to how reform could be achieved.[32] Broad, sweeping reforms of the policymaking process were given only limited attention. Working through the political parties or initiating a third party was not given much credence as an alternative way of achieving their goals. The philosophy of the public interest movement of this period was that, no matter how much government was reformed, government by itself was inherently incapable of protecting the common good. Left to its own devices, the government would always be overly influenced by private sector groups. The only solution was continuing involvement by citizen groups in policymaking to balance the influence of other organizations. Making pluralism come true was the answer.[33]

Although the term *public interest group* has fallen out of common use, the pluralist logic remains active today in the formation of other types of groups. Foundations have helped fund organizations, such as the Center for Responsive Politics and the Campaign Finance Institute, that study the financing of campaigns in a nonpartisan manner and provide information and recommendations to the press and policymakers.

In addition, many liberal 527 committees in the early years of the new century have proclaimed their goal to organize and represent average citizens who are not part of the interest group system. For example, MoveOn.Org, a liberal group that is active in elections and lobbying, describes its mission like this:

> The *MoveOn* family of organizations brings real Americans back into the political process. With over 3.3 million members across America—from carpenters to stay-at-home moms to business leaders—we work together to realize the progressive vision of our country's founders. MoveOn is a service— a way for busy but concerned citizens to find their political voice in a system dominated by big money and big media.[34]

---

[30]Andrew S. McFarland, Public Interest Lobbies (Washington, DC: American Enterprise Institute, 1976).

[31]Gordon Harrison, The Public Interest Law Firm (New York: Ford Foundation, 1973), 8.

[32]On the ideology of the liberal public interest movement, see Michael McCann, *Taking Reform Seriously* (Ithaca, NY: Cornell University Press, 1986).

[33]Jeffrey M. Berry, "Public Interest vs. Party System," *Society* 17 (May/June 1980): 42–48.

[34]http://moveon.org/about.html. (accessed January 18, 2006).

Conservative Counterattack

While liberals were trying to balance interest group politics by bringing "the people" into the political process, conservatives were coming to believe that the liberals were so successful that they had *unbalanced* the representation of interests in Washington. When the Carter administration welcomed these lobbies into the policymaking process and appointed many public interest leaders to major positions in agencies and departments, conservatives began to mobilize in response. Conservatives worked to create their own think tanks, social movement organizations, and networks.

The 1973 *Roe v. Wade* decision energized opponents of abortion, most of whom were conservative. Many national, state, and local pro-life groups formed in the 1970s, and their membership and resources grew rapidly. These groups have used a number of tactics and strategies in working toward a goal to end most or all abortions. Some have sought a national amendment to the U.S. Constitution, others have focused on electing Republican presidents and senators to change the composition of the U.S. Supreme Court, still others have worked on changing national and state laws to make abortions more difficult to obtain, and a few have tried to change public attitudes about abortion, so that fewer women will choose to have them. In recent years, pro-life groups have been active in passing state laws to ban or restrict abortions, and in trying to influence Supreme Court appointments so that the Court would uphold these state laws.

Christian conservatives more generally organized around the themes of preserving traditional families and promoting religious values. These groups reacted to liberal policies and values that they believed led to an increase in crime, the divorce rate, illegitimacy, abortion, and other social ills. They sought to defeat the Equal Rights Amendment, to reinstate school prayer, to fight gay rights, and to maintain traditional gender roles. Many Christian Right groups that formed in the late 1970s, including the Religious Roundtable, Christian Voice, and Moral Majority, had broad agendas, which included many issues. Stop-ERA and Eagle Forum both centered their efforts on stopping policies that promoted gender equality. Other groups had less of a religious focus, including the National Conservative Political Action Committee (NCPAC), which sought to reduce taxes and support an anticommunist foreign policy.

Although many of the groups that formed in the 1970s did not long endure, new organizations, such as the Christian Coalition, Focus on the Family, and Citizens for Excellence in Education, formed in the 1990s. In the early 2000s, new organizations formed to oppose same-sex marriage. For the most part, these conservative moral groups got little support from the mainstream media, which were likely to feature public statements that made group leaders seem extreme in the public's eyes. Moral Majority founder Jerry Falwell blamed the terrorist attacks of September 11 on liberals and feminists, for example, while Pat Robertson of the Christian Coalition stated that feminism is a "socialist, anti-family political movement that encourages women to leave their husbands, kill their children, practice witchcraft, destroy capitalism and become lesbians."[35]

---

[35]Clyde Wilcox and Carin Larson, *Onward Christian Soldiers: The Christian Right in American Politics*, 3rd ed. (Boulder: Westview, 2006).

Conservative groups built their own networks to communicate their messages, unfiltered, to supporters. They developed their own magazines and newspapers, their own colleges and universities, and their own radio and television shows. Most important, they used white evangelical churches to mobilize members and supporters. Although churches are forbidden from engaging in explicitly partisan political activity, they can organize and work to support values and policies that are consistent with their teachings. The ability of Christian Right groups to pass out information in churches was a considerable asset, because the white evangelicals who constituted the target constituency of the movement are, for the most part, regular attendees. The Christian Right could assume that the people who would support them would be in a conservative church on Sunday morning, making it much easier to find and mobilize their base.

This was especially useful for organizations such as the Christian Coalition, which sought to influence policy by electing Republican officials. The group distributed tens of millions of voter guides in conservative churches in the 1990s and was often credited with helping the GOP win control of Congress in 1994. A spokesman for the organization succinctly articulated its strategy: "We think the Lord is going to give us this nation back one precinct at a time, one neighborhood at a time, and one state at a time."[36]

Business Fights Back

The rapid rise of liberal and conservative citizen groups frequently captures the public attention, for social movement group leaders frequently make extreme statements and use unconventional tactics. The dramatic growth of business lobbying is easily as important to understanding the role of interest groups. Business has always been well represented in Washington, but in recent years the community has become more active in response to challenges by liberal citizen groups and opportunities created by Republican control of government.

A Plague of Regulation?

During the 1970s and 1980s, business executives inevitably explained why they had opened a Washington office or expanded one already there by talking about what they saw as unreasonable government regulations. A Conference Board study revealed that, of the executives indicating a change in their government-relations work, 71 percent cited increased government activity as the reason.[37] The successes of consumer groups, environmental groups, labor groups, and other citizen organizations were part of the reason that business groups mobilized during this period.

The regulatory process is particularly conducive to interest group advocacy because it deals with the most complex and esoteric aspects of public policy. As technology has complicated policy in such areas as air and water pollution, nuclear power, telecommunications,

---

[36]Matthew C. Moen, *The Transformation of the Christian Right* (Tuscaloosa: University of Alabama Press, 1992), 108.

[37]Phyllis S. McGrath, *Redefining Corporate-Federal Relations* (New York: Conference Board, 1979), 1. See also, *New Laws/New Jobs* (New York: Golightly & Co. International, n.d.), 1.

and occupational health, the opportunity for regulatory advocacy has increased. Regulatory decisions in such areas must be made after considering relevant technical data—data often difficult to obtain and open to competing interpretations. No one has more incentive to collect industry data than the industries themselves. At its heart, regulatory lobbying is a process of interest groups bringing their data to policymakers and trying to make these data the information base from which decisions flow.

The growth in business lobbying during the late 1960s and 1970s was not just a response to an increase in the number of regulations being adopted but also a response to the changing nature of regulation. Many of the new agencies created during this time were given jurisdiction over broad problem areas, such as pollution or occupational health, rather than specific industries, such as broadcasting or securities trading. The breadth of regulatory authority for agencies such as the Environmental Protection Agency and Occupational Safety and Health Administration is immense, and many industries found themselves subject to their regulation. Businesses have found the new "social" regulation especially disturbing, "with its more detailed, multi-industry intrusions into areas of long-standing managerial discretion and its cost- and liability-enlarging potential."[38]

Since the late 1970s, however, there has been a move toward deregulation. In many industries, such as telecommunications and financial services, there has been significant deregulation. During the Reagan and Bush administrations, many regulations were relaxed, and the pace of new regulations slowed considerably. If businesses increase their lobbying efforts in response to regulation, it might seem logical for them to reduce lobbying in times of deregulation.

This did not happen, for several reasons. First, even at a time when government is relaxing regulations, the details of those regulations remain critically important to companies. If one set of regulations is relaxed more than another, one set of companies may gain financially at the expense of others. Indeed, companies sometimes need to hire more lobbyists just to keep track of the changes in regulations, so that their business can make changes to profit from them. Second, when government relaxes its regulations, businesses become encouraged to press for even more concessions. If the government has already lowered its requirements in this area, with additional lobbying it may relax them still further.

Finally, even in an atmosphere of deregulations, specific companies face regulatory issues. As Microsoft Corporation faced legal action from national and state governments for alleged monopolistic practices in the early 2000s, the company expanded from a negligible Washington presence to one of the top corporate lobbying operations. By 1997, Microsoft had spent almost $2 million on lobbying; in 2003, it spent more than $10 million. From 1997 to 2003, the company ramped up its political contributions, giving $4.6 million in hard and soft money contributions, divided fairly closely between the two parties.[39] Google's lobbying efforts in 2007 were sparked by a policy debate over regulating prices that Internet providers charge major Internet vendors.

---

[38]Edward S. Herman, *Corporate Control, Corporate Power* (New York: Cambridge University Press, 1981), 185.
[39]Shaiko, 2005, p 7.

Seizing the Initiative

During the late 1970s, as consumer and environmental groups organized and made gains, business leaders began to believe that more control was needed over the policy agenda. Business responded with a series of changes designed to help business regain control over the policy agenda in areas of concern. David Vogel describes this attitude:

> For nearly a decade, most of the issues placed on the political agenda affecting business were initiated not by business, but by those who represented constituents hostile to business. Environmental protection, occupational health and safety, consumer protection, price controls on energy, affirmative action, product liability, expansion of the welfare state, prohibitions on corporate overseas payments, corporate governance, campaign reform, restrictions on corporate compliance with the Arab boycott of Israel—not a single one of those issues originated with business. To be sure, business was successful in . . . influencing many of these areas, making them less threatening than their proponents preferred. But what is critical is that for most of the decade, business was fighting its political battles on terrain set by its opponents.[40]

In the 1970s, the business community devoted considerable attention to building its political muscle. Corporations established lobbying operations; set up Washington, DC, offices; and formed PACs. Trade associations moved to Washington and established PACs. Existing business peak associations, such as the Chamber of Commerce, expanded their role in coordinating the business community's political efforts. The nation's largest corporations formed the Business Roundtable, a lobbying group composed of around 200 chief executive officers (CEOs) from the nation's largest firms. The Roundtable used the CEOs themselves in lobbying efforts, often flying to Washington in their private jets to meet with top elected officials. Perhaps most important, the idea that government relations was critical came to permeate the corporate world, creating expectations that executives would contribute to company PACs and to politicians, that lobbying was a cost of doing business, and that coordinated efforts could pay off.

This impressive mobilization of business interests bore a bountiful harvest when the Reagan administration came into office in 1981. A sweeping tax bill passed that year significantly reduced business taxes. Numerous regulatory changes were made that pleased major industries. During Reagan's second term, however, a new tax bill helped some businesses while hurting others and badly split the business community.[41]

Although President Bill Clinton sought to appeal to business with a budget reduction package in 1993, the GOP swept the 1994 congressional elections, and business lobbyists worked closely with the Republicans and lobbied hard on behalf of the party's Contract with America. Congressional Republicans not only responded with a wide range of pro-business legislation but also granted unparalleled access to

---

[40]David Vogel, "How Business Responds to Opposition," 6. (Paper presented at 1979 annual meeting of the American Political Science Association).

[41]See Jeffrey H. Birnbaum and Alan S. Murray, *Showdown at Gucci Gulch* (New York: Random House, 1987).

corporate and trade group lobbyists.[42] Corporate PACs that had once divided their money equally between Democrats and Republicans began to primarily support Republicans. When George W. Bush won the presidency in 2000, the business community saw an opportunity that had not existed in more than a generation to rewrite tax law and regulatory law.

The Bush administration pushed through a series of tax cuts that benefited businesses and wealthy individuals. Congress frequently added even more tax cuts to the Bush proposals, sometimes in words that benefited particular companies substantially. For example, recall that Hewlett-Packard doubled its lobbying efforts between 2004 and 2005. Congressional action then saved the company millions of dollars in taxes by changing the treatment of certain profits earned by offshore subsidiaries.[43]

The Bush administration also relaxed a number of regulations and substantially slowed the pace of new regulation. Congress became involved in regulatory policy as well. Perhaps most important was the growth of earmarked contracts, in which Congress specifies that some of the money given to a particular agency must be spent to purchase goods or services from a particular company. These earmarks are often worth millions of dollars to particular companies—well worth the price of hiring some lobbyists.

The motive for business lobbying had thus shifted. Jeffrey Birnbaum, a longtime observer of interest groups in Washington, wrote in 2005,

> In the 1990s, lobbying was largely reactive. Corporations had to fend off proposals that would have restricted them or cost them money. But with pro-business officials running the executive and legislative branches, companies are also hiring well-placed lobbyists to go on the offensive and find ways to profit from the many tax breaks, loosened regulations and other government goodies that increasingly are available.[44]

Between 2000 and 2004, the number of corporate lobbyists doubled to more than 34,000, and the fees that corporate lobbying firms charged their clients in many cases doubled as well. Many firms doubled the number of lobbyists on staff in a few years and offered higher starting salaries, as we will see in Chapter 6. Nearly half of all lawmakers turned to lobbying when they left office in the late 1990s and early 2000s, usually substantially increasing their salaries in the process. "There's unlimited business out there for us," said Robert L. Livingston, a Republican former chairman of the House Appropriations Committee.[45]

During this period, the connections between lawmakers and lobbyists became tighter than ever before. House GOP leader Tom DeLay's K Street Project sought to pressure corporations and trade associations to hire Republican lobbyists, often with

---

[42]Stephen Engelberg, "100 Days of Dreams Come True for Lobbyists in Congress," *New York Times* April 14, 1995; and Jill Abramson and Timothy Noah, "In GOP-Controlled Congress, Lobbyists Remain as Powerful as Ever—and Perhaps More Visible," *Wall Street Journal* April 20, 1995.

[43]Ibid.

[44]Jeffrey Birnbaum, "The Road to Riches Is Called K Street: Lobbying Firms Hire More, Pay More, Charge More to Influence Government," *Washington Post* June 22, 2005, p. A01.

[45]Ibid.

close ties to his office. It also sought to pressure lobbyists to contribute only to GOP candidates, with the implicit threat that those who gave substantial amounts to Democrats might have less access to committee chairs.[46] As the web of connections between lobbyists and elected officials became denser, the potential for business gains from political involvement grew. Many companies dramatically ramped up their lobbying to find new opportunities; others did so to keep up with their competition.

By the fall of 2007, ongoing investigations of lobbying scandals had already sent two Republican members of the House to prison, along with a top lobbyist and top bureaucrat in the Bush administration. Moreover, Democratic party leaders, now in control of both chambers of Congress, promised to rein in earmarks. This might suggest that the tsunami of corporate lobbying had crested. However, corporations were hurrying to make friends with the new Democratic majority by hiring former Democratic members and staff as lobbyists, and by contributing to the reelection campaigns of powerful Democratic incumbents. In 2005–2006, corporate PACs directed 34 percent of their contributions to Democratic incumbents, but in the first quarter of 2007 after the Democrats took control, this increased to 57 percent.

A Labor–Liberal Alliance

When Republicans gained control of Congress in 1994, organized labor found itself on the defensive. Over time fewer workers belonged to unions, but this did not detract from their access to Democratic politicians. Now they found that Republican party leaders and even rank-and-file members refused to meet with labor lobbyists. Labor sought to use their resources more effectively in elections, to create a Democratic majority. Under the leadership of John Sweeney, the AFL-CIO focused on grassroots mobilization and tried a variety of electoral tools to influence election results.[47]

With the election of George W. Bush in 2000, other liberal interest groups developed a sense of urgency. Before the Bush administration took office, Vice President–elect Dick Cheney convened a task force to help set the administration's energy policy—the task force was comprised almost entirely of energy company executives and was convened by a man who later opened a lobbying firm, with the same energy companies as his major clients. Environmental and consumer groups were not part of the deliberations.

In the 2004 elections, labor and liberal groups combined to form many new 527 committees designed to register voters and get them to the polls. Whereas in the past, labor, environmental, feminist, and other liberal groups had cooperated in a loose alliance, these new 527s were formal coalitions in which each member group contributed funds or services and the overall strategy and message were agreed to by all groups. Seen in one way, the groups' efforts were very successful, for the total number of votes cast for Democratic

---

[46] Jim VandeHei, "GOP Monitoring Lobbyists' Politics; White House, Hill Access May Be Affected," *Washington Post* June 10, 2002, p. A1.

[47] Peter L. Francia, *The Future of Organized Labor in American Politics* (New York: Columbia University Press, 2006).

candidates increased dramatically. The Republican vote totals increased as well, and the labor–liberal alliance in 2005 sought to devise new strategies and create new groups to help win the 2008 presidential election. In 2005, environmental, civil rights, feminist, and labor groups cooperated in large experiments to study the best way to mobilize and persuade voters in the Virginia gubernatorial election, with an eye toward using these tactics in later elections.

In 2006, Democrats won control of both the U.S. House of Representatives and the U.S. Senate. Emboldened by Bush's low approval ratings and the large number of seats Republicans must defend in the U.S. Senate in 2008, liberal and labor groups are planning a major push in the upcoming elections. Funded with donations by wealthy liberals and by increasing amounts of small contributions raised through the Internet, liberal activists have established new organizations and revitalized existing ones.

Conclusion

By any standard, the amount of lobbying in Washington has expanded significantly. Interests previously unrepresented are now represented before the government by recently formed organizations. Interests that were already represented in Washington tend to be even better represented today.

Although the reasons for lobbying's rise in different sectors of society vary, some common threads appear in the broad movement toward interest group politics. Pluralist theory put forward the idea that interest group involvement in policymaking contributed to democratic government. Expanding governmental activity in the 1960s and 1970s, usually at the behest of interest groups, directly affected more and more constituencies and helped catalyze increased advocacy. Finally, as new interest groups form, they stimulate other constituencies to organize because new groups increase awareness about what various interests are doing, and, further, their formation threatens their natural adversaries.

While the advocacy explosion created new groups and expanded resources devoted to lobbying, this heightened competition among groups did not bring about a perfect balance of interests represented in Washington. Business was by far the best-represented sector of American society before this upsurge in lobbying, and its advantage has expanded in recent years. Business responded to the challenge of the public interest movement with ample resources and a fierce determination to maintain its advantages in Washington. It still faces potent competition from an array of liberal public interest groups, although its traditional rival, organized labor, is on the decline. The greatest restraint on business may not be its critics but, rather, the divisions within and between industries.

Chapter 3

Mobilization and Organization

Every year, new interest groups form, and some disband. In 2004, many election-oriented groups formed. Swift Boat Veterans for Truth ran ads attacking John Kerry's record in Vietnam, while Americans Coming Together (ACT) sent people door to door to register Democratic voters in swing states. In 2005, ACT disbanded, and conservatives formed the Judeo-Christian Council for Constitutional Restoration, which supported the appointment of judges who would oppose same-sex marriage and abortion and would allow for more public accommodation of religion in public life. In 2007, former Washington Redskin Ray Schoenke and real estate developer John Rosenthal formed the American Hunter and Shooters Association, which formed as an alternative to the NRA. In the fall of 2007, after a summer of record airline flight delays and lost luggage, one frequent flier founded the Coalition for an Airline Passengers Bill of Rights.

The impressive growth of interest groups described in Chapter 2 obscures a simple fact. Even in a bull market for interest groups, some types of groups are more likely to form than others. Among those groups that are formed, not all succeed. Some may be stillborn, not attracting enough money to go beyond initial fundraising efforts. Others may enjoy initial success, then find themselves in gradual decline, slowly losing members and income. Some groups that have been around for a long time will fold. All this points to significant questions about interest groups: How do groups form? Why is it that people join such organizations? What do groups do in order to survive?

Political scientists approach this question by asking what people expect to receive in return for dues or contributions and what leaders can do to make their organizations more attractive to potential members. This is not simply a matter of which marketing approach works best for which constituency. Groups that find and retain more members have more resources and are better able to represent their constituents' interests. If there is no effective way to mobilize potential members of a constituency, then its voice may go unheard in the policy process.

The resources collected by an interest group must be allocated among competing demands within the organization. Leaders must decide which issues are of greatest importance to their constituencies and how to apportion staff time and funds to those issues. These questions, too, affect the way an interest group is able to represent its members before government.

Competing Theories

Ideally, political scientists would like to be able to predict when and under what circumstances new interest groups will form. A theory of interest group formation should specify the factors important in this formation and should further specify which of these factors are crucial to a new group's success or failure. By examining successful groups and groups that have died, scholars have tried to isolate the critical determinants in their formation.

Pluralism and Interest Group Equilibrium

A starting point for serious discussion of interest group origins is David Truman's classic work *The Governmental Process,* which presents a pluralist vision of how interest groups come to form.[1] For Truman, interest groups are the product of two related forces. The first is society's growing complexity. As the economy and society change, new interests are formed, while others lose importance. The Brotherhood of Sleeping Car Porters was formed after the railroads developed. Although railroads transformed the American economy, they eventually declined, and the porters' union shrank along with them. New technology has created markets for new interest groups, such as the National Cable Television Association and The Cellular Telecommunications and Internet Association.

Evolving industry and society give rise to many new interests. Not all new interest groups, however, are directly linked to a new technology or profession. The second part of Truman's explanation, dealing with changing political and economic conditions, is more controversial. Truman states that people who share an interest but are as yet unorganized are brought together when they are adversely affected by a "disturbance"—an identifiable event or series of events that alters the "equilibrium" in some sector of society. The economic downturn in the 1870s disturbed the equilibrium of farmers, and that instability spurred development of the Grange. Truman writes, "Between 1873 and late 1874 the number of local Granges increased in number from about three thousand to over twenty thousand, paralleling an increase in mortgage foreclosures."[2] Disturbances do not need to be economic in nature. The formation of one group, such as the conservative religious organization the Moral Majority in 1979, can upset the balance of interest groups concerned with moral issues and can lead to the formation of another organization to balance it—in this case the liberal organization, People for the American Way. The terrorist attacks of September 11 disturbed the equilibrium in the American Muslim community, leading to the formation of new organizations, such as Muslims Against Terrorism USA and The New Dominion PAC.

The disturbance theory has an appealing logic: a cause-and-effect relationship between events and organizing. If people find that their political or economic interests are being adversely affected, they will organize to rectify the situation. This is the essence of pluralism: People organize when they have a stake in the outcome of controversies over

---

[1]David B. Truman, *The Governmental Process* (New York: Knopf, 1951).
[2]Ibid., 88.

issues. There are cases in which the pluralist theory appears to work well. When Massachusetts allowed same-sex marriages in 2003, conservatives responded to form a set of organizations to press to amend the national and state constitutions to bar such unions. When the Washington State Supreme Court declared that there was a legitimate state interest in barring same-sex marriages, the Washington Defense of Marriage Alliance formed to help promote the rights of gay and lesbian couples.[3] When elderly citizens come to believe that their Social Security or Medicare benefits might be cut, they are likely to respond to appeals from interest groups.[4]

Like pluralist theory more broadly, however, Truman's equilibrium explanation of interest group origins is deeply flawed. It is based on optimistic and unjustified assumptions about all people's ability to organize. Those who have resources can organize quickly when their advantages are disturbed, but people who are poor are repeatedly "disturbed" by adverse events, such as congressional budget cuts, but remain persistently unorganized. When Congress considered increasing taxes on managers of hedge funds (large funds that specialize in making profits for very wealthy investors), private equity funds dramatically increased their lobbying budgets, and formed groups the help coordinate strategy. When the U.S. Congress moved in 2005 to cut taxes for wealthier Americans and reduce spending on Medicaid, in contrast, the program that provides health care to the poor, the poor did not respond by organizing groups to reclaim their benefits; however, insurance companies were busy at the same time organizing to change health care policy to enhance their profits. Some interests are easier to mobilize, and some types of organizations are much easier to form than others.

Even when members of groups have suffered a disturbance, and have the skills and resources to organize, they do not always manage to do so. Over the past decade, workers at many companies have suffered cutbacks in their pension plans and health care benefits. Where unions have been in place, workers have protested these cuts. But in a number of cases, highly skilled and educated workers have failed to mobilize, in part because they believed that protest would be ineffective, and in part because their ideology conflicted with government solutions to the problem.[5]

Selective Incentives

Truman argued that people are social animals who naturally form and join groups. A very different perspective is offered by economist Mancur Olson's *The Logic of Collective Action*.[6] Olson says that people contribute money to interest groups because they receive some benefit in return. Olson argues that it generally makes sense for individuals

[3]Responding to a court logic that implied that the purpose of marriage is procreation, the Alliance filed an initiative that would require heterosexual couples to prove that they were able to conceive children before a marriage license would be issued.

[4]Andrea Louise Campbell, "Participatory Reactions to Policy Threats: Senior Citizens and the Defense of Social Security and Medicare," *Political Behavior* 25 (2003): 29–49.

[5]David Lawrence Madland, *A Wink and a Handshake: Why the Collapse of the U.S. Pension System Has Provoked Little Protest.* Doctoral dissertation, Georgetown University, 2007.

[6]Mancur Olson, Jr., *The Logic of Collective Action* (New York: Schocken, 1968).

to contribute to a group only if they get a selective benefit in return—that is, a benefit that goes only to group members. Individuals will not join or support groups that offer only a collective good, which can be shared by members and nonmembers alike.

Does it make sense for someone in business to contribute to the Chamber of Commerce to support its lobbying? If the Chamber succeeds in getting a tax ! ! favorable to business through Congress, then business executives will profit whether they are members of the organization or not. A general change in the tax law is thus a collective rather than a selective good. Olson feels, then, that it is irrational for people in business to support the Chamber solely for its political advocacy because they can be "free riders" and still enjoy benefits from its lobbying. The Chamber of Commerce also offers selective benefits for its members. Local Chambers of Commerce "are good places for businessmen to make 'contacts' and exchange information," and nonmembers cannot share this benefit.[7]

Olson makes some allowances in this general theory for cases in which selective incentives do not form the basis for a group's success. Individuals in labor unions are exempted because they commonly work in closed shops, wherein membership is mandatory. Groups with small constituencies, such as an industry with only a handful of companies, do not need a selective incentive because they can exert peer pressure on nonmembers. Visibly absent nonmembers can be singled out for not doing their part.

Olson's important contribution is in drawing attention to the importance of selective incentives. They can be powerful inducements for membership in large economic interest groups. For other types of organizations, the theory is considerably weaker. Few national citizen groups offer their members any real benefits other than ideological satisfaction. Selective benefits are not the principle reason that people join the Natural Resources Defense Council or the American Center for Law and Justice. Olson acknowledges that his theory works poorly for these "philanthropic" lobbies.[8] However, there are simply too many citizen groups, attracting too many members and millions of dollars, to be dismissed as anomalous or products of "irrational" behavior.

The pervasiveness of ideological lobbying also throws some doubt on the theory's adequacy when applied to business, farm, and professional organizations. Membership surveys show that an economic group's lobbying can be a significant incentive for those who join.[9] Even Olson's own example of the Chamber of Commerce is not wholly persuasive. When the Chamber became more active and visible in its political work, it saw its membership skyrocket. There may have been other causes for this, but its political vigor is surely one reason for that rise. Do businesspeople who join the Chamber of Commerce care less about the free-enterprise system than members of the Sierra Club care about the environment? It is difficult to answer with certainty, but business associations do offer members the opportunity to *mix* politics with business. And many business executives and interests have supported ideological pro-business groups, such as Club for Growth.

Olson claims that the lobbying activity of large economic interest groups is a by-product of other organizational activities that draw and hold members. Groups "obtain

---

[7]Ibid., 146.

[8]Ibid., 159–65.

[9]See Terry M. Moe, *The Organization of Interests* (Chicago: University of Chicago Press, 1980); and David Marsh, "On Joining Interest Groups," *British Journal of Political Science* 6 (July 1976): 257–72.

their strength and support" by offering selective incentives.[10] Viewing lobbying as a by-product may, however, underestimate how important political activities are in attracting and maintaining members.[11] The directors of Washington lobbies make a concerted effort to keep members informed of the political issues facing their organizations and of the lobbying work being carried out. Although many members of economic organizations would not join but for the selective benefits, those who run these groups clearly regard lobbying as an essential part of the organizations' appeal to members.

Olson's theory suggests that there should be few large national organizations providing primarily collective benefits; however, a quick look at the interest group universe reveals many large, powerful groups that do just that. The Sierra Club, EMILY's List, and Concerned Women for America all offer some limited selective benefits, but they are primarily ideological groups that seek collective benefits. All were organized by one or more individuals with a strong commitment to the cause.

Yet Olson's theory has clear application for the understanding of why some groups form more readily than others, and why some individuals are better able to organize to lobby than others. One recent study of lobby organization in the states reported strong evidence that collective action problems affect the ability of all kinds of groups to organize, and the free rider problem for most types of groups is serious.[12]

Entrepreneurs

Throughout the twentieth century, migrant farmworkers in California were poorly treated by farmers. Low wages, discrimination, and terrible working conditions gave farmworkers more than enough reason to join unions during periodic organizing efforts, but even the mighty AFL-CIO failed to organize them. In the late 1960s, though, a poor farmworker named Cesar Chavez succeeded in unionizing much of the California grape industry. The objective condition of the grape pickers was no worse than it had always been. The critical difference in the success of the United Farm Workers was unquestionably not an outside event but, rather, the inspired leadership of Chavez.

Political scientist Robert Salisbury argues convincingly that leadership is the main reason any group succeeds or dies.[13] Salisbury looked at farm groups during the same hard times in the nineteenth century that Truman did but came to a different conclusion. Salisbury points out that farm organizations began to decline before they had achieved their goals of high, stable commodity prices. If people join groups to overcome a disadvantage, why do they sometimes quit before equilibrium is restored? Salisbury reasons that individuals do not join interest groups strictly because of a disturbance but also because they see that benefits will accrue to them from membership. If, after joining, they feel they are getting their money's worth, they will continue to pay dues. If not, they will quit.

---

[10]Olson, *The Logic of Collective Action*, 132.

[11]John Mark Hansen, "The Political Economy of Group Membership," *American Political Science Review* 79 (March 1985): 79–96.

[12]David Lowery, Virginia Gray, Jennifer Anderson, and Adam J. Newmark, "Collective Action and the Mobilization of Institutions," *The Journal of Politics* 66 (August 2004): 684–705.

[13]Robert H. Salisbury, "An Exchange Theory of Interest Groups," *Midwest Journal of Political Science* 13 (February 1969): 1–32.

In analyzing membership surge and decline, Salisbury emphasizes the role played by each interest group's organizer, or "entrepreneur." He uses this term for the organizer because he likens the founder of a new interest group to a business investor who is willing to risk capital to start a new firm. In the interest group "marketplace," entrepreneurs will succeed if they provide attractive benefits or incentives to potential members. These benefits may be of three kinds.[14]

First, *material* benefits have concrete value. The goal of the Teamsters Union is to improve the economic lot of truck drivers and other union members. Second, *purposive* benefits are associated with the pursuit of ideological or issue-oriented goals that offer no tangible rewards to members. Those who join the Defenders of Wildlife do so because they have deep ideological convictions about the environment, not because they have an economic stake in changes in the laws affecting the preservation of wild animals. Third, individuals may join a group because of the *solidary,* or social, rewards. Those who join the League of Women Voters rather than other good-government groups may do so because of the network of local chapters where members work together directly, participating in politics. Many organizations offer a range of benefits and have members who are attracted by different incentives. Some people join the Sierra Club because of the discounted vacation packages offered by the organization, others because of the work the organization does to protect the environment, and still others because of the social aspects of local group hikes. We will discuss these benefits more fully.

Salisbury views entrepreneurs as motivated primarily by a self-interested quest for income and power. This is doubtlessly true in many instances, but in other cases it is too cynical. Ralph Reed may have been influenced in part by his own political ambitions when he helped found the Christian Coalition, but he was most likely also influenced by his views on abortion and the role of religion and politics. John Muir devoted many years of his life to the formation of the Sierra Club, primarily because of his dedication to preserving Yosemite Valley. Eugene V. Debs endured beatings and prison time in his efforts to organize railroad workers. In each case, the perceived sincerity of their vision helped them mobilize supporters.

There is much to Salisbury's theory, for the quality of leadership and the type of benefits offered unquestionably matter in a group's development.[15] Unfortunately, since Salisbury's work appeared, political scientists have not formed more explicit propositions about successful leadership traits and benefit structures for lobbying organizations. Still, Salisbury makes a convincing point: Interest groups operate in a competitive marketplace, and those that do a poor job of providing satisfactory benefits to members will lose to organizations created by more skillful entrepreneurs. Moreover, sometimes a group will acquire a new leader whose entrepreneurial skills will propel the group into greater prominence. Over the past few years, the Humane Society has become a much

---

[14]Salisbury uses the typology from Peter B. Clark and James Q. Wilson's "Incentive Systems: A Theory of Organizations," *Administrative Science Quarterly* 6 (September 1961): 129–66, in describing interest group incentive systems. We will also use the Clark and Wilson typology.

[15]Jeffrey M. Berry, "On the Origins of Public Interest Groups: A Test of Two Theories," *Polity* 10 (Spring 1978): 379–97.

more powerful and more political organization, thanks in part to the skills of the new president Wayne Pacelle.[16]

What can we say in summary about these three theories of interest group formation? In looking at all three together and assessing their arguments, what do social scientists know and not know about the origins of interest groups?

1. New interest groups evolve naturally out of changes in technology and the ever-increasing complexity of society. This evolution does not, however, explain why all groups form. Nor does it explain why one organization successfully comes to represent a new interest, while another fails.

2. Disturbances (wars, turns in the business cycle, and political events) can help new interest groups form by making potential members aware of the need for political action. Disturbances are not necessary for interest group formation, because many groups originate without one.

3. Interest group constituencies vary widely; some are much more difficult to organize than others. Business executives may respond readily to an organization that allows them to mix their concern for free-market politics with social interaction with other businesspeople. On the other hand, people who are desperately poor will be hard to organize under any circumstances.

4. Because interest groups operate in a competitive environment, leaders must make their organizations as appealing as possible to current and potential members. Selective incentives add to the attractiveness of membership, but entrepreneurs must put together a complex pattern of incentives.

Supply of Benefits

The work of Salisbury and Olson suggests that an organizer's chance of successfully forming an interest group is determined by the benefits offered to potential members. We will now go beyond the abstract notions of collective goods, selective benefits, and entrepreneurs to discuss more concretely the benefits leaders actually offer to their members.

Material Benefits

Any individuals or corporations who give their money to an interest group do so because they feel something worthwhile will result from the organization's activities. Consciously or subconsciously, potential contributors ask themselves one or both of these questions: (1) "If I donate this money, what will I get in return?" and (2) "If I donate this money, what will society get in return?" Material benefits are the tangible rewards that individuals or companies get in return for their donations.

The most common material reward one can get from contributing to an interest group is information. Nearly every group sends members some type of publication with articles directed at their interests. Many of the larger, well-endowed groups publish

---

[16]Jeffrey Birnbaum, "The Humane Society Becomes a Political Animal," *Washington Post* January 30, 2007, p. A15.

magazines. The purpose is to give individuals an attractive, polished publication with articles covering the readers' broad interests, rather than focusing exclusively on political issues. Only as a secondary focus does the American Bankers Association's glossy and sophisticated *Banking Journal* cover Washington politics. Other publications, such as *Bankers News* and *ABA Insider*, focus more on politics and are sent to subsets of members. The Sierra Club sends out a glossy *Sierra* magazine, which includes political coverage but also photo contests, stories about national and international wilderness areas, and listings of the club's sponsored hiking tours. The National Rifle Association (NRA) allows members to choose any one of three magazines—*American Hunter, American Rifleman*, and *America's First Freedom*—as a free benefit of membership. These publications vary in the amount of coverage they give to political issues.

The information in interest group publications and web pages is useful to members because it can educate them on developments in their industry or on issues they care about, and it can advise them of government actions that may affect their lives. It is difficult to generalize with any precision on just how important publications are to members and how the publications influence the decision to join or contribute. Yet, in reading through samples of different organizations' publications, one is led to the inescapable conclusion that most interest groups provide their rank-and-file members with far more information than they can ever want to read. A lobbyist for a food-industry trade association said, "We bore them with information." Although the intention is surely not to be boring, groups would rather provide too much information to potential members than too little.

The development of the Internet has allowed many groups to offer even more information to members. The NRA has an extensive web page loaded with political and nonpolitical information. One major section on legislation and politics allows interested members to learn more about national and state legislation. It provides them with direct e-mail links to national and state legislators and has links to more extensive action alerts and news stories, whereas other sections of the web page focus on shooting clubs, gun safety, programs for young people, information on hunting, and a wide variety of other topics. The site typically includes video and audio clips, and during election campaigns it often contains copies of media ads suitable for playing on computers. A dedicated gun enthusiast could spend days every week reading material on this frequently updated web site and can sign up for e-mail alerts that contain web addresses to new stories of interest. Many groups now have password-protected members-only sections that provide exclusive content to those who join the organization.

Information overkill by interest groups is not a bad membership strategy—far from it. Washington lobbies devote substantial resources to publications because these reinforce members' appreciation of what the national organizations are doing. Publications and web pages are periodic proof that members' money is well spent. For the circle of activists in any organization, publications and web pages provide useful information to help in their political work. For the larger segment of rank-and-file members of the group, they provide reassurance that someone is speaking on their behalf in Washington. Many members may not read the material provided by the interest group, but the volume of the information might persuade them to renew their membership.

Interest groups can also offer direct services to members. The U.S. Conference of Mayors assists individual mayors when they are in Washington to lobby the government.

Its staff is at the mayors' disposal to work on individual projects. Says one lobbyist, "There is constant contact. . . . I'd say that I personally speak to five or six mayors each day." Some organizations, such as the National Federation of Independent Business, have "caseworkers" on their staff to handle individual problems brought to them by member businesses.

Most membership services, however, are those provided without much personalized attention by staffers outside of the government relations section of the organization. The American Association of Retired Persons (AARP) offers a variety of services to its 35 million members, including a mail discount pharmacy, a motor club, a money market fund, and health insurance. The organization solicits new members primarily through promises of these selective benefits, and the organization's lobbying is a by-product of other activities that bring members into the group. When the organization surveyed its members, only 17 percent said they had joined because the group was concerned about the elderly. Twenty-two percent cited the group's publications as a reason, while 8 percent mentioned the health and drug benefits, 7 percent the health insurance, 5 percent the motor club, and 3 percent the money market fund.[17] Unlike most citizen groups, the AARP does not depend on the ideological fervor of its constituents to sustain itself.

The most important material reward is, of course, a change in public policy that directly benefits members. Individuals may well join groups that work aggressively to win material benefits for them, even if those material benefits also flow to nonmembers, if the benefit is great enough. If organizations seeking to block changes in taxation for hedge fund managers succeed, these managers will save billions in taxes over the next decade.

When groups promise quick benefits, however, they risk disillusioning members. The American Agriculture Movement, a protest-oriented group born in the late 1970s, worked for quick relief from inadequate market prices. After some initial government help, no other visible successes followed and, lacking other attractive material benefits, the group began to lose membership. Arguments over the strategy to be used to reinvigorate the organization badly factionalized it, and a splinter group of dissidents formed.[18] This suggests the importance of lowering members' expectations for rapid delivery of material benefits.

Purposive Benefits

When people join organizations pursuing policy objectives that are of no direct, material benefit to them, they are said to be attracted by purposive incentives. Thousands of organizations across the country offer members primarily one thing: satisfaction that they have done their part to make the world a better place. Whether a group's goal is to change U.S. foreign policy toward the Middle East, to protect endangered species, to stop abortions, to urge the United States to send troops to prevent genocide, to allow same-sex couples to marry, or to promote a more visible role for religion in public life, people join to further a cause, not their own material self-interest.

---

[17]Paul Light, *Artful Work,* 2nd ed. (New York: McGraw-Hill, 1995), 73.
[18]Allan J. Cigler, "From Protest Group to Interest Group: The Making of the American Agriculture Movement, Inc.," in *Interest Group Politics,* 2nd ed., ed. Allan J. Cigler and Burdett A. Loomis (Washington, DC: Congressional Quarterly, 1986), 46–69.

Why do people voluntarily join a group that relies on purposive incentives? Political participation is related to socioeconomic status: The more highly educated and wealthy an individual, the more likely he or she is to participate in all forms of political activity. Schools socialize children toward believing that participation in politics is vital and that all citizens must take some responsibility for the well-being of their community. As adults, people may acquire skills on the job that are transferrable to political organizations.[19] Joining civic organizations is part of the "American way," and adults who belong to any type of political organization believe they are fulfilling part of their civic responsibilities as well as advancing their own political views. Often they believe in a cause so intensely that they are willing to contribute money and volunteer time to help it succeed. Sometimes this intensity comes from critical events in one's life. Studies of activists on both sides of the abortion issue have found that personal experiences with abortions were a prime motivation for many.[20]

The benefit one gets in return for committing resources to a group primarily offering purposive incentives is the belief that one has made at least a small contribution to the betterment of society. Contributions to Amnesty International will be used to fight torture, human rights violations, and political imprisonments by authoritarian regimes. Donating to the group is a very direct way to link one's concern for the oppressed with political advocacy on their behalf. The degree to which an individual's contribution works to accomplish such a goal as stopping abuses of human and political rights is obviously rather negligible. Seen from Olson's theory, ending torture is a public good that will occur regardless of whether any individual member contributes $50. Donors adopt the attitude that, even though their own contributions cannot possibly be critical to the organization's continuing existence or success, the organization could not exist if everyone took that view.

Recently, American politics has become more polarized.[21] For those who care about issues, the stakes of legislation and elections seem higher than in the past. In a state of heightened group conflict, purposive benefits become more important. Joining the Sierra Club seems more important if you believe that Congress might soon pass legislation that would dramatically weaken clean air laws. Joining the NRA seems more important if you believe that your right to own a hunting rifle is endangered by liberal activists who are close to winning. Thus, ideological interest groups can offer even stronger purposive benefits when partisan and ideological cleavages are broad. Many organizations in 2007 have framed their purposive benefits as defensive—by giving to the organization you can help prevent the other side from imminent victory.

---

[19]See Sidney Verba, Kay Lehman Schlozman, and Henry E. Brady, *Voice and Equality* (Cambridge, MA: Harvard University Press, 1995), 313–20.

[20]Kristin Luker, *Abortion and the Politics of Motherhood* (Berkeley: University of California Press, 1984), 101; and Carol Maxwell, *Pro-Life Activists in America Motivation and Meaning* (New York: Cambridge University Press, 2002).

[21]Jon R. Bond and Richard Fleisher, eds., *Polarized Politics: Congress and the President in a Partisan Era* (Washington, DC: CQ Press, 2000); and Gary Jacobson, *A Divider, Not a Uniter: George W. Bush and the American People* (New York: Longman, 2006). See also Morris Fiorina, Samuel J. Abrams, and Jeremy C. Pope, *Culture War? The Myth of a Polarized America* (New York: Longman, 2004). Fiorina argues that the public is not polarized, but political actors including interest groups are polarized.

Solidary Benefits

Some people join interest groups because they enjoy social contacts with others who share their interests. The solidary incentive is a social benefit that accrues primarily from interactions with like-minded colleagues. Local chapter groups that provide opportunities for face-to-face interaction can offer solidary benefits that may be unrelated to the overall purpose of the group. Some people join groups primarily for these social benefits. Many members of the Audubon Society join local chapters in order to take part in birdwatching hikes, not because of the group's activism on wetland protection, and others join the Chamber of Commerce in order to socialize with community business leaders.

Solidary benefits are often related to ideology. Interest group members may especially enjoy the drama and excitement of working with people who share their political convictions. The activists in a political organization can form a community for the individuals who come to devote their time to it. In an organization such as Operation Rescue, which engaged in actions such as blocking abortion clinics, solidary incentives played a crucial role. The small number of activists who formed a chapter of the organization gave strength to each other by reaffirming the value of their protests. The support activists gave each other contributed to their own sense of well-being, and their belief that they were doing something important.

Social incentives can be important even for groups that are organized around economic issues. In the National Association of Broadcasters (NAB), busy corporate executives who run the member television and radio stations can gain social benefits from NAB activities. Like so many other national associations, it has a circle of activists in each state who accept the responsibility for grassroots lobbying. These broadcasters work to influence their own legislators in Washington. They do such work at the request of NAB staffers and derive the satisfaction of taking part in a coordinated advocacy effort to help the industry. Some status, too, can be gained by dealing with members of Congress and their staffs, who are receptive to talking with such important constituents. The NAB's annual convention offers further social (as well as material) inducements that give members a chance to socialize, do business, meet with Federal Communications Commission officials and members of Congress who appear there, and enjoy camaraderie in the collective fight for sensible government policy toward broadcasting.

The role of solidary incentives varies among interest groups. Solidary incentives may be at the core of the decision to join the Audubon Society, be one part of the decision to become active in Operation Rescue, but have nothing to do with the decision to donate money to the National Committee for an Effective Congress. When social incentives do play a role, they must still be combined with other incentives. Solidary benefits can only complement the avowed purposive or material goals of a lobbying organization.

The Mix of Benefits

Each organization has its own benefit structure, which affects its ultimate success in attracting and maintaining members. If entrepreneurs cannot offer appealing benefits to their constituency, the group will cease to exist. Yet the benefit mix offered by entrepreneurs is not the primary factor in organizational development. Although it is significant, it is difficult to explain the rise or fall of many interest groups in terms of specific benefit choices made by leaders. One reason is that the choices are fairly limited. The variety of benefits to choose from is not endless, and the benefits that can be offered may already be widely available. Nothing is novel about a new interest group publishing a top-notch newsletter, giving members a chance to work at the grassroots, or offering members the satisfaction of belonging and doing their part. Services not readily available elsewhere can sometimes be developed, of course, but cost and administrative feasibility are serious constraints on what may ultimately be offered, especially for modest-sized organizations.

Newly forming interest groups often find themselves in a highly competitive market with existing groups and must be quite adept at targeting their potential membership. Finding a particular niche to target may be far more important than the exact nature of the benefits themselves.[22] A new general business organization is a tough sell, given the substantial competition that already exists. In the 1980s, the American Business Conference was able to attract a membership by its focus on rapidly growing firms. No group had previously seen that constituency as a niche in the business interest groups marketplace.

In social movements, interest groups find niches sometimes based on ideology and tactics.[23] In the Christian Right, the Christian Coalition focused on electing Republican candidates to office, in some cases regardless of their positions on issues. Focus on the Family centered its activity around research, while Concerned Women for America built grassroots organizations that were effective in lobbying local governments. In the environmental movement, Earth First has used far more confrontational tactics than the Sierra Club, and thus appeals to more radical environmentalists.

In the final analysis, it is often hard for organizers (or political scientists) to know exactly which benefits or combination of benefits bring people into different organizations. In many groups, members receive a package, and it is not easy to determine which part of the package was critical in their decision to join or renew their membership. A single group can offer social, material, and ideological incentives to join. Asking members their most important reason for joining provides some clues as to the comparative value of benefits, but it may be the overall package that makes the group so attractive.[24] In time, the information an individual receives may turn out to be the most valued part of the membership, but he or she might never have joined if there had not been the promise of aggressive lobbying in Washington. In the real world, the benefits blend in a member's mind, and it is difficult for entrepreneurs to determine which parts of their package are critical to making the sum so attractive. Only in recent years have political professionals

---

[22]William P. Browne, "Organized Interests and Their Issue Niches," *Journal of Politics* 52 (May 1990): 477–509. For a discussion of a rich ecology of related interest groups, see Christopher J. Bosso, *Environment, Inc.: From Grassroots to Beltway* (Lawrence: University of Kansas Press, 2005).

[23]For a more general account of the multidimensionality of interest group niches, see Michael T. Heaney, "Outside the Issue Niche: The Multidimensionality of Interest Group Identity," *American Politics Research* 32 (2004): 1–41.

[24]Groups that use direct mail do pretest their appeals to see what kind of material inducements produce the largest return. See Paul E. Johnson, "Interest Group Recruiting: Finding Members and Keeping Them," in *Interest Group Politics,* 5th ed., ed. Allan J. Cigler and Burdett Loomis (Washington, DC: CQ Press, 1998).

begun to consider efforts to learn how to target different sets of potential group members with distinct benefit packages. Some professionals are experimenting with ways to identify those who might be enticed to join a group through a purposive appeal, as well as those who might also require a material incentive.

The Internet has made it easier for groups to offer a mixture of benefits. In the past only well-established groups could provide material benefits through magazines, but now any group with a summer intern can create a web page that provides information. Many groups provide purposive benefits through e-mails and special sections of their web sites—including video and audio files. Organizations can even create a sense of community online through meet ups, blogs, and other activities, thereby dispensing solidary benefits.

Marketing Interest Groups: Direct Mail and Internet Fundraising

If an organization operates in a competitive environment and offers benefits similar to those of other groups, how aggressively it markets itself may make the critical difference in its ultimate success. The segment of the interest group community in which competition is probably fiercest is that of citizen groups. For almost every conceivable constituency, there are overlapping groups. Conservatives have a choice between dozens of national citizen groups that promise to lobby vigorously for conservative policies. The same is true for liberals, who face a seemingly endless variety of groups asking for their support. Even on relatively narrow issues, such as opposition to same-sex marriage, a concerned citizen might be asked to join or contribute to several organizations every month.

Citizen groups have traditionally relied on direct mail to solicit members or donations from people around the country. Direct-mail campaigns often involve mailings of hundreds of thousands of letters to prospective members, bringing to their attention the good work of the organization and asking them to join or contribute. Most people who receive a direct-mail solicitation toss it into the wastebasket unopened, considering it junk mail. Studies show that 75 percent of direct mail is tossed in the trash can unopened, and up to 98 percent of solicitations do not result in a contribution.[25] However, if only a small number of donors open the letter, read it, and contribute, direct mail can raise enough money to transform an organization.

Most interest groups hire consultants to run their direct-mail campaigns. These consultants help the groups create mailing lists to prospect for new donors. These may consist of existing lists of donors to political candidates, other interest groups that share an agenda, or of people who subscribe to certain magazines. For a price, however, consultants can also customize lists, looking for people who fit several criteria such as reading

---

[25]Todd Meredith, "Open the Envelope: Getting People to Look at the Direct Mail They Receive," *Campaigns & Elections*, December 2004; and Encyclopedia of American Industries, "Direct Mail Advertising Services," http://www.referenceforbusiness.com/industries/Service/Direct-Mail-Advertising-Services .html (accessed January 21, 2006).

certain magazines, belonging to certain groups, *and* driving certain types of cars, for example. The selection or creation of the list is critical because the profitability of direct mail depends critically on how many people respond to the mailing.

Most direct-mail solicitations have three important parts. The first is the envelope. What is on the outside is significant because it may determine whether or not the individual will open it and read what is inside. In 2005, Concerned Women for America (CWA) sent out an envelope with a picture of a Christian Bible on the right, covered with the word "CENSORED" in bold red letters, and "CONTAINS HATE SPEECH" below. On the top left, bold black letters read "The Holy Bible declared 'Hate Speech'?" Below, in smaller red letters was "It could happen if Ted Kennedy and Hillary Clinton get their way!" Other groups try to get recipients to open and read their letter by declaring that a poll is enclosed. Some groups use reverse psychology, printing nothing on the envelope but an unidentified return address in Washington or New York, forcing the recipient to open the letter to find out what it contains and who sent it.

Inside is the most important ingredient, the appeal letter. The best letters contain a good amount of detail, along with passages that provoke the reader's emotions. Most letters are about four pages long: One study of NOW fundraising letters found that more than 90 percent were either two or four pages long.[26] The Concerned Women for America envelope previously described contained two sheets of paper, covered on both sides with single-spaced text. The letter was formatted to catch the eye, with underlining and indented bullet points with different symbols. The key to direct-mail letters is to provoke anger and fear, usually by dwelling on a villain—someone the reader hates. The first paragraph of the letter warned "Your right to think and live as a Christian is in grave danger because of Ted Kennedy, Hillary Rodham Clinton, and their liberal friends' latest 'hate crimes' bill. You and I must do all we can to stop this evil bill TODAY."

Liberal groups use identical tactics; indeed, fundraising letters by People for the American Way and the American Civil Liberties Union use CWA president Beverly LaHaye in the same way that the CWA letter uses Kennedy and Clinton. One NOW letter warned of new Supreme Court limitations on abortion rights, warning at the end "This means women will die again!"

Letters do not simply request money; they demand action by the severity of the situation they describe. The CWA package included a donor card, with petition signature cards addressed to the president and the donor's representative in the U.S. House. The letter referred to the petition cards in a call for action: *"This vicious attack on Christians' freedom's of speech and religion must be stopped!* The only way we can do this is by working together, so please sign and return the enclosed petitions with your generous gift right away." Others urge members to fill out surveys, to call their representative, or to take other action.

A common third part of the direct-mail package is one or more pieces of literature not written in letter format. The CWA envelope contained a smaller sheet, which listed twelve Bible verses with a bold blue warning in a handwritten font at the top, warning

---

[26]Shauna L. Shames and Greg Weiner, "Raising Money, Raising Hackles: Analyzing Interest Group Responses to Supreme Court Decisions Through Direct Mail Solicitations." Paper presented at the annual meeting of the Southern Political Science Association, Atlanta, 2006.

that these verses in particular might be banned as hate speech. Other letters include brochures or reproductions of stories in national newspapers or magazines.

For all the success many groups have had with direct mail, it is still a risky enterprise because of its substantial costs. When a group prospects with a rented list, it is likely to get a response rate of between 1 and 2 percent, usually not enough to cover the costs of the mailing. A group is willing to risk losing money on such prospecting because those who do contribute can be put on the "house list." This list of those who have already contributed to the organization usually generates a response rate of over 10 percent.[27] For that reason, a group's members are continually solicited for special contributions. Environmental organizations, for example, send each member an average of nine mailings a year, asking for money.[28]

Direct mail works best among older populations, for several reasons. Many elderly citizens report that reading their mail is the most exciting event in their day. Older Americans grew up in a time when people wrote each other letters, rather than e-mail or instant messages. Older citizens may be more likely to be confused by the technology of direct mail, which uses various techniques to make the letter appear to be a personal communication with handwritten sections. Some elderly citizens have sent hundreds of thousands of dollars to groups in response to direct-mail solicitations.[29]

There are some groups that are best described as direct-mail mills, accomplishing little more than providing income to the direct-mail consultants and a few entrepreneurs who started the organizations. Senior citizen groups have been able to form by sending direct mail to older Americans, warning of catastrophic consequences of changes in Social Security or Medicare being considered by Congress. One group, 60/Plus, raised $1.3 million through direct mail in one year, but the whole organization consists of just two staff members. In the 1990s, the United Seniors Association raised $5 million annually, but only a small portion of that was spent on its modest lobbying office of eight employees.[30] When it comes to direct mail from interest groups, let the consumer beware.

Younger donors are less likely to respond to direct-mail solicitations. In the late 1990s, groups hired telemarketers to call prospective and current members to ask for contributions, and this appeared to work better than mail among donors who were under fifty. The national "Do Not Call" register exempted nonprofits but changed citizens' expectations about intrusive fundraising calls and hurt the yields from telemarketing efforts. The increased use of cell phones has also made telemarketing less productive for interest groups.

Many groups are rapidly moving to Internet fundraising as a way to attract younger members, to raise money quickly, and to involve members more broadly. Most interest group web sites have the capacity to receive secure contributions, but some groups use the Internet far more extensively. Interest groups can e-mail solicitations to members and can easily determine which issues inspire different donors to give—and thus customize

---

[27] R. Kenneth Godwin, *One Billion Dollars of Influence* (Chatham, NJ: Chatham House, 1988), 12.

[28] Johnson, "How Environmental Groups Recruit Members," 15.

[29] Thomas B. Edsall, "College Republicans' Fundraising Criticized; Front Organizations Were Used in Direct-Mail Campaign That Collected Millions," *Washington Post* December 26, 2004.

[30] Marilyn Webber Sarafini, "Senior Schism," *National Journal* (May 6, 1995): 1093.

their appeal. Some groups offer online solidary benefits through chat rooms, meet-ups, and other events, where there may be only a brief request for additional contributions. Some have sought to draw visitors to the web site through video and competitions: MoveOn.Org, a liberal group, and Let Freedom Ring, a conservative group, both invited members to submit videos for a political advertising contest, and the winners were posted on the web page. Thus, younger members and prospective donors are invited to become involved in an interactive experience, which might culminate in an impulsive decision to make a small contribution.

It is too early to know just how the Internet will change the dynamics of group formation and fundraising, but MoveOn.Org provides an exemplar in the possibilities.[31] In 1998, the two founders of the group set up an Internet petition to urge Congress to stop trying to impeach President Bill Clinton and to move on to more pressing matters. Within a few days, they had accumulated hundreds of thousands of signatures and had amassed a list of e-mail addresses of interested supporters. Soon the organization formed a PAC, which quickly grew to one of the biggest PACs in the country. The Internet seems especially suited to reaching large numbers of younger activists who give small amounts for ideological reasons. In this way, it is similar to direct mail, with one important difference: Internet fundraising is far cheaper; thus, most money raised can be spent on political work, not on fundraising. In many ways, the members of MoveOn.Org are hard to organize—they are spread across the country, young, and less affluent than members of other groups. However the Internet has made it easier to locate such people, and offer them the right mix of incentives to join.

The Internet is also useful for mobilizing small and dispersed constituencies, such as communities affected by rare diseases. Instead of identifying individuals from existing lists, such groups can rely on those affected by the disease surfing the Internet and finding their organization. Studies suggest that such groups can help build efficacy among participants, as well as social capital.[32]

Maintaining the Organization

Direct-mail and Internet fundraising are only two of the tools by which interest groups market their "product" and retain their members once they enlist them. Whatever the means, all organizations must maintain themselves by raising money on an ongoing basis, so that they can continue to operate. It is not simply a matter of raise money or die. Although organizations can go under if fundraising drops dramatically, the more common problem is keeping funding up to avert project or staff cutbacks. Ideally, of course, interest groups expand their base of support, so that they can take on more advocacy, research, membership outreach, and other activities. Fundraising is difficult and competitive, though, and most groups usually do well to keep up with the annual rate of inflation.

---

[31]For an early account, see Rebecca Fairley Raney, "Cheap Online Fundraising Is a Boon to Political Groups," *New York Times* November 23, 1999.

[32]Lori Brainard, "Citizen Organizing in Cyberspace: Illustrations from Health Care and Implications for Public Administration," *American Review of Public Administration* 33, no. 4 (2003): 384–406.

Corporations have a significant advantage over citizen groups because they can use corporate profits to fund much (but not all) of their political activity. Such decisions are made with an eye toward the bottom line—will establishing a public affairs office or hiring a lobbying firm help the company escape regulation or win a tax break? Will the time spent organizing a political action committee be as profitable as the same time spent on a new strategy to market a product?[33]

Remember that the number of interest groups has grown significantly, and many interest groups that have been in business for many years have expanded their operations. New fundraising techniques, such as direct mail and the Internet, indicate a larger trend: Interest groups have been able to market themselves better. There are two parts to this advance. First, entrepreneurs have successfully identified new or undersubscribed markets where members could be found for their organizations. Second, interest group leaders have been able to expand their funding beyond membership dues.

Interest group funds come from a variety of sources. Research by Mark Peterson and Jack Walker demonstrates that different types of groups vary substantially in their dependence on dues. Groups in the "profit-sector" category (mostly trade associations) draw almost two-thirds (63 percent) of their funds from membership dues. Other types of organizations in their survey sample (citizen groups, nonprofits, and profit and non-profit mixed memberships) receive only about one-third to one-half of their funds from membership dues.[34]

Some organizations have sliding scales of membership dues, so that some types of members pay more. Many trade associations and business groups receive most of their funding from the largest companies. In a sense, these larger companies subsidize smaller ones, and both benefit. Larger companies are willing to pay more because they have more business in the sector, but their voice is amplified if they speak for an entire community of companies, not just for themselves.[35]

Moreover, members can give more often than once a year, when they renew their membership. The same direct-mail and Internet techniques that help groups land new members can also help them induce those members to give repeatedly, and in larger amounts. Most large groups have fundraising professionals who seek to persuade small donors to give larger amounts, and more often. The Sierra Club offers lifetime memberships at $1,000 apiece and generally calls upon those lifetime members for large contributions several times a year. Typically, these solicitations are more personal, involving a phone call from a leading figure in the organization or an invitation to an event.

In addition, groups raise money from the following sources.

Wealthy Patrons

Leaders of organizations know that they can substantially increase their group's activities if they can add large individual donations to the sum raised through regular

[33]Stephen Ansolbehere, John de Figueiredo, and James Snyder, "Why Is There So Little Money in Politics?" *Journal of Economic Perspectives* 17 (2003): 105–30.

[34]Mark A. Peterson and Jack L. Walker, "Interest Group Responses to Partisan Change," in Allan J. Cigler Burdett & A. Loomis eds, zded., 162–82. Cash DC: CQ Press, 1986. *Interest Group Politics,* 174.

[35]Moe, *The Organization of Interests*, 193–94.

membership fees. Furthermore, for groups with little or no membership support, large donations from wealthy patrons may be their lifeblood. The National Welfare Rights Organization could not hope to sustain itself by membership dues, because it sought to represent those poor citizens who received welfare benefits. Instead, its dynamic leader, George Wiley, was effective in face-to-face meetings with wealthy liberals. Some of these, such as Anne Farnsworth Peretz (heiress to the Singer Sewing Machine fortune) and Audrey Stern Hess (granddaughter of the founder of Sears, Roebuck), contributed large sums to keep the militant civil rights organization going for a while.[36]

A group representing people on welfare certainly needs large donations, yet many other kinds of interest groups rely in part on such gifts. Most membership groups have programs to raise not only small contributions through direct mail and the Internet but also larger gifts from wealthy patrons. In recent years, patrons have been especially willing to give money for electoral projects mounted by groups or to help form new groups that will try to influence elections. In the 2000 presidential campaign, large mobilization efforts by Planned Parenthood and the NAACP were funded primarily by large contributions by single patrons.[37] Businessman George Soros and a close associate contributed nearly $40 million to America Coming Together and The Media Fund, two 527 groups active in the 2004 campaign.[38] During the 2006 campaign, three donors combined to contribute $20 million to 527 committees.

Patrons need not be individuals, they can be corporations or other organizations. Paramount Classics, distributors of the film "An Inconvenient Truth" pledged 5% of its domestic box office gross to the Alliance for Climate Control, a group dedicated to informing the public about the dangers of global warming.

Foundations

Many organizations have benefited from foundations' sizable contributions, especially when the group was first starting up. Citizen groups, which receive the smallest part of their money from members, are the biggest beneficiaries of foundation grants among all types of lobbies.[39] Liberal public interest groups received extraordinary support from foundations during the 1970s. Between 1970 and 1980, the Ford Foundation contributed roughly $21 million to liberal groups under its public interest law program.[40] In recent

---

[36]Nick Kotz and Mary Lynn Kotz, *A Passion for Equality* (New York: Norton, 1977), 241–42. See also Anthony J. Nownes and Allan J. Cigler, "Public Interest Groups and the Road to Survival," *Polity* 27 (Spring 1995): 379–404.
[37]Michael Malbin, Robert Boatright, Mark J. Rozell, Richard Skinner, and Clyde Wilcox, "BCRA's Impact on Interest Groups and Advocacy Organization," in *Life After Reform: When the Bipartisan Campaign Reform Act Meets Politics*, ed. Michael N. Malbin (Lanham, MD: Rowman & Littlefield, 2003).
[38]Thomas B. Edsall, "Soros-Backed Activist Group Disbands as Interest Fades," *Washington Post* August 3, 2005, p. A3.
[39]Peterson and Walker, "Interest Group Responses to Partisan Change," 174.
[40]*The Public Interest Law Firm* (New York: Ford Foundation, 1973); *Public Interest Law: Five Years Later* (New York: Ford Foundation, 1976); and "Ford Ends Public Interest Law Program," *Citizen Participation* 1 (January/February 1980): 9. See also Debora Clovis and Nan Aron, "Survey of Public Interest Law Centers," (Alliance for Justice, Washington, DC: Alliance for Justice, n.d.); and Michael Greve and James Keller, *Funding the Left: The Sources of Financial Support for "Public Interest" Law Firms* (Washington, DC: Washington Legal Foundation, 1987).

years, foundations with a conservative outlook have played a key role in funding advocacy organizations on the right. The Smith Richardson, Bradley, and Carthage foundations provided much of the support to get the Center for Individual Rights off the ground. The center is a public interest law firm that specializes in defending college professors and students who see themselves as the victims of "political correctness" on campus.[41] The DeMoss Foundation has made large contributions to a number of conservative groups, including Concerned Women for America.

Fees, Publications, and Products

Publications, conferences, and training institutes are common sources of interest group income. With their unusually good command of the issues, interest group employees are able to produce handbooks, booklets, and even full-size books that can be marketed to the general public. Staffers for the Health Research Group produced a bestseller, *Pills That Don't Work,* which brought roughly $1 million to the organization.[42] Sales of that magnitude are uncommon, but it is not at all unusual for a group to count on publications for a modest segment of its income. The National Audubon Society receives income from the sale of a series of field guides to birds, animals, and plants that bears its name. Audubon, Sierra Club, and several other groups produce and sell annual calendars with pictures of wildlife and nature scenes. Interest groups can also use specialists on their staffs to attract individuals for conferences, including training institutes that teach participants various business, communications, or political skills.

Groups can market other types of products as well. Alliance for Marriage, a group that advocates amending the national Constitution to ban same-sex marriage, has launched AFMstore.com, where the committed can buy a "Protect Marriage" T-shirt or coffee mug with the AFM ring logo or a yard sign.[43] The NRA sells products to its members, including T-shirts in toddler sizes that show a puppy embracing an NRA waterdish. The Internet advertisement for the shirt states that "It is never too soon to start our kids off on the track to protecting America's Freedom."[44] Other groups sell products created by others and keep a portion of the profits. Several conservative groups sold decks of "America's Most Dangerous Liberals" playing cards in 2004. Still other groups have licensed special Visa cards or Mastercards with host banks, in which a portion of all purchases are given to the sponsoring group. The Sierra Club and Concerned Women for America both have profited from these products.

---

[41]Davidson Goldin, "A Law Center Wages Fight Against Political Correctness," *New York Times* August 13, 1995.

[42]Michael deCourcy Hinds, "Advocacy Units Seek New Funds," *New York Times* January 9, 1982.

[43]Judy Sarasohn, "A Marriage Group's 'Interesting' Union," *Washington Post* June 2, 2005, p. A23.

[44]http://www.nrastore.com/nra/Product.aspx?productid=SS%20526%20BW, (accessed September 13, 2007).

Government Grants

A main factor in interest groups' growth during the 1960s and 1970s was the parallel growth in domestic spending by the federal government. The categorical grant programs of this era increased the funds available to citizen groups, nonprofit professional organizations, and trade associations. These groups aggressively sought federal grant money for training, planning, economic development, and other activities and projects.

In 2006, the AARP Foundation received more than $80 million in federal grants to provide job training for low-income seniors, to help them file their taxes, and to help them recognize fraudulent solicitations, among others, and these grants represented approximately 8 percent of the group's revenue. In some cases, critics have charged that these government grants create a conflict of interest. Conservatives were angry when the AARP campaigned against George W. Bush's proposal to create private Social Security accounts and urged the government to withdraw grants from the groups.[45] Liberals worried that some environmental watchdog groups might be co-opted by grants from the Environmental Protection Agency (EPA), although these grants were generally a small portion of the group's revenues.[46]

In the past few years, conservative groups have received substantial government grants as well. For example, several small pro-life organizations have received funds to administer Community-Based Abstinence Education grants. In many cases these grants have exceeded the operating budget of the group in prior years.

Other Sources

Many interest groups explore myriad sources of revenue. Christopher Bosso compares the sources of revenue for a variety of environmental interest groups. Some, such as Earthshare, have only a few funding sources—contributions by supporters, workplace giving plans, and securities owned by the group. The Audubon Society draws money from each of the following sources: membership dues, other contributions by supporters, workplace giving plans, grants from charitable foundations, government grants and contracts, major corporate grants, investments such as securities (often contributed by wealthy patrons), the sale of magazines and books, rental fees for its membership list, royalties on publications, the sale of merchandise, fees for participating in group vacation trips, fees for services, payments from a bank that sponsors a credit card linked to the society, licensing of the Audubon name, and rent from lands owned.[47]

Groups can be affected by changes in the political environment as well as by the economic environment. The environmental movement enjoyed spectacular expansion from the 1960s through the 1980s and was especially successful during the

---

[45]The AARP Foundation does not lobby, and is organized as a 501(c)3. The membership organization does lobby extensively, however.

[46]Rita Beamish, "Environmental Critics Got EPA Grants," *AP Breaking News* December 29, 2005.

[47]Christopher J. Bosso, *Environment, Inc.: From Grassroots to Beltway* (Lawrence: University of Kansas Press, 2005), 107.

early years of the Reagan administration, when Interior Secretary James Watt was a popular fundraising foil. However, the softening economy in the early 1990s appeared to have curtailed growth.[48] NRA Director of Federal Affairs Chuck Cunningham notes, "Fundraising and activism are very cyclical and closely related to the ability to have a 'dragon to slay.'" He noted that conservative groups found it difficult to raise funds in the 1980s, when the GOP controlled the presidency. "During his first two years in office, Clinton policies and proposals—gays in the military, record tax hike, national gun ban, and federal government control of health care—created a political atmosphere that helped conservative groups be founded or explode with tremendous levels of contributions and grassroots activism. . . ." Since the 2000 election, many of those conservative groups are again struggling because of the overall satisfaction of their constituency with those currently running the federal government. But with Democratic victories in the 2006 elections, conservative groups are again seeking to raise money from those who fear the policies that the new majority might enact.

With all the vagaries of fundraising, interest groups must work continually to identify new sources of income. Otherwise, they risk organizational decline. If a group can weather a difficult storm, it may come out stronger in the end. During the heyday of the civil rights movement in the early 1960s, the NAACP, the Student Nonviolent Coordinating Committee (SNCC), the Congress of Racial Equality (CORE), and the Southern Christian Leadership Conference (SCLC) all enjoyed growing support among liberals. As the mood of the country changed and financial support began to diminish, SNCC, CORE, and SCLC did not adapt or devise new ways to appeal to donors or expand their base of funding. Increasingly, they were seen as militant, and the more moderate NAACP prospered in the long run. The other three never regained their support, and all eventually lost their standing in the civil rights movement.[49] Similarly, the Christian Coalition lost its donor base in the late 1990s as negative attention focused on statements by its leader, Pat Robertson, but other Christian conservative groups, such as Focus on the Family and Concerned Women for America, continued to grow.[50]

Who Governs?

Membership dues and other funds raised by interest groups must be converted into actions representing the donors' interests. This work is critical to any lobby's overall effectiveness. Interest groups are organizations, and the way in which each organization makes decisions about its resources directly affects how well members' interests are represented before government.

---

[48]Ibid.

[49]Doug McAdam, *Political Process and the Development of Black Insurgency, 1930–1970* (Chicago: University of Chicago Press, 1982), 208–13.

[50]Clyde Wilcox and Carin Larson, *Onward Christian Soldiers: The Christian Right in American Politics* (Boulder: Westview, 2006).

Authority and Leadership

Like any other type of organization, interest groups must have a means for governing themselves. Even the smallest group with no more than a handful of staff members creates roles giving some workers more authority than others. The leadership structure of an interest group generally provides a framework for decision making on allocation of resources, selection of issues, personnel, change in leadership, lobbying tactics, bylaws, and accountability of staff.

Some organizations have simple authority structures. In many private companies, the CEO or founder makes decisions on lobbying and electoral activities. In some other small groups, the entrepreneur or primary financier of the organization may have ultimate control of decisions.

Many other organizations have some sort of elections to choose their leaders. In some cases, these elections are important opportunities to chart the future of the interest group. The National Rifle Association and the National Organization for Women have both had contested elections that have changed the course of the group.[51] Labor unions also frequently have contested elections, in which candidates take differing positions on the strategies and even the ranking of various goals. Other groups have elections that are mostly empty exercises because (1) there are no policy differences between the candidates, (2) there is a slate of candidates endorsed by current leadership that always wins, or (3) there are no opposition candidates. Also, many organizations do not directly elect their leaders, although they may be replaced by a board of directors.

The founding bylaws of an interest group almost always prescribe a procedure whereby a body representing the membership, such as a board of directors or an annual convention, has final authority over all major decisions. Even if, like some public interest groups, a lobby has no real membership, it is still likely to have an independent governing board with formal (if rarely exercised) authority over staff operations.[52] Even if the board of directors is a passive body willing to let the professional staff run the organization as they please, it is an important safety valve when trouble strikes. When it was revealed that the executive director of the NAACP, Reverend Benjamin Chavis, spent organizational funds to settle a personal lawsuit against him, the board stepped in and fired Chavis for this impropriety and for general financial mismanagement.[53]

Just as it is true that interest groups almost always appear on the outside to be democratic, it also seems that they are almost always oligarchic on the inside.[54] This contradiction will not surprise anyone who has belonged to a voluntary organization. A small cadre of workers invariably dominates such organizations. Relatively few of the rank-and-file members feel they have much time to devote to the organizations they belong to. The full-time staff or officers, with their greater command over information and organizational resources, easily gain preeminent influence within the organization.

---

[51]For a discussion of NOW leadership, see Maryann Barasko, *Governing NOW: Grassroots Activism in the National Organization for Women* (Ithaca: Cornell University Press, 2004).

[52]Jeffrey M. Berry, *Lobbying for the People* (Princeton: Princeton University Press, 1977), 195–99.

[53]John H. Cushman, Jr., "Short of Cash, N.A.A.C.P. Stops Paying Its Employees," *New York Times* November 2, 1994.

[54]Truman, *The Governmental Process*, 139–55.

This natural tendency, which sociologist Robert Michels described as the "iron law of oligarchy," is pervasive among interest groups.[55]

Although interest groups are generally oligarchic, groups differ in the amount of influence the rank and file have within the organization. In some lobbies, members actually exert some significant and direct influence on organizational decisions, yet these differences are not easily explained by the way lobbying organizations are designed. Compare the American Hospital Association (AHA) and the U.S. Conference of Mayors. Both have conventions twice yearly, at which the memberships have an opportunity to formulate policy. Both also have boards that meet periodically during the year to make timely decisions about questions of policy.

The similarity in the formal governing structures of these organizations tells little about the way they are actually run. Mayors have a much larger part in their organization than hospital administrators. An AHA spokesperson said that issues are not brought "raw" to the House of Delegates' conferences. Rather, the staff "massages the issues through the system," so that, by the time they hit the agenda of the House of Delegates, the positions are fairly clear. A spokesperson for the Conference of Mayors paints a different picture. The large conventions and board meetings give the mayors an opportunity to set priorities. "Lobbying is completely determined by the policies passed by the mayors," said one staffer.

Why such differences between the organizations? To the AHA lobbyist, the marginal role played by rank-and-file members makes perfect sense. "Statutory and regulatory problems are the business of AHA. The hospital administrators are too busy running their hospitals." Mayors, on the other hand, see statutory and regulatory problems as very much their business. As elected officials, they feel more comfortable and confident dealing in the political world. Also, the partisan differences between Republican and Democratic mayors place an unusual constraint on the organization. Mayors of the party controlling the White House do not want the organization staff working against the president's domestic policies unless they give them specific permission to do so. The mayors are an exceptional case—city mayors have many political skills and are used to making their own decisions based on staff input.

Some organizations make a concerted effort to elicit the members' views before setting policies. Many citizen groups poll their members; then their boards use the responses in setting priorities. However, the vast majority of interest groups use a governing structure like that of the AHA and the Conference of Mayors, whose boards and possibly national conferences are the means by which members theoretically control the staff. In most of these groups, the staff runs the organization with modest guidance and little direct interference.

In sum, then, we have two conclusions. First, the governing structures of lobbies, as laid out in their written charters, usually do little to stop the iron law of oligarchy from taking hold. Only if a group takes exceptional steps to build in polling or another device for direct control by the members does the formal structure of a lobbying organization affect the way the group is governed. Second, if rank-and-file members of an organization want more than a passive role in making decisions, they must prove to the lobbying

---

[55]Robert Michels, *Political Parties* (New York: Free Press, 1958). Originally published in 1915.

staff that they will be highly active and will not acquiesce to faits accomplis. Few organizations have this type of membership.

This does not mean that interest groups ignore the wishes of their members, however. In most interest groups, members can "vote with their feet" by leaving the group if they don't like what the organization is doing.[56] If members are unhappy with the policy actions of an interest group, they can refuse to renew their membership. If an interest group does not pursue the issues that its members care about, it is possible that other competing groups will use these issues to win away contributions and members.

That membership is generally voluntary is fundamental to the relationship between leaders and followers in these organizations. Members join groups because they agree strongly with their goals. As noted earlier, even if some service is an attractive inducement to join, political goals can remain an instrumental part of the decision. Consequently, rank-and-file members usually do not worry about how important organizational decisions are made because they observe the lobbying group pursuing the issues they feel strongly about. A trade association lobbyist said of his membership: "They care about the results, not how we get them." Environmental groups do not have to stop to think about whether their members are in favor of strengthening the Clean Air Act when it comes before Congress.

Interest groups often face more complicated decisions about priorities. Union members may differ in their preferences for higher wages, better benefits, or more job security. Environmental group members may disagree on whether protecting a particular wildlife area from oil drilling is more important than pushing for stronger enforcement of air pollution laws. Christian conservative group members may not all agree on the relative importance of a national amendment to bar same-sex marriage, as opposed to efforts to end abortions. And even in groups where general goals are shared, specific actions may be controversial. Many members of the American Civil Liberties Union resigned or refused to renew their membership when the organization defended the rights of a neo-Nazi group to rally in front of the town hall of Skokie, Illinois, a suburban community that was home to many survivors of the Nazi holocaust.

A difficult problem arises when an issue affects some members of a group differently than others; an example is the American Petroleum Institute (API). Many proposals pertaining to the oil industry affect companies quite differently because they vary in size, ranging from giants, such as Exxon-Mobil, to small, independent wildcatters. Smaller companies often want to be treated separately by Congress when it is writing tax laws for the industry, knowing that there is more sympathy for the "little guy" than for huge corporations. As a result, says one API lobbyist, consensus on many issues is a "long time coming." On broad issues cutting across the membership, API's stand is sometimes "no stand" due to lack of consensus.

Occasionally, interest groups are subjected to outright rebellion by dissidents in the organization. Labor unions seem most susceptible to open conflict within the ranks. A primary reason is that labor union members cannot really vote with their feet and leave

---

[56]Albert O. Hirschman, *Exit, Voice, and Loyalty* (Cambridge: Harvard University Press, 1970); Lawrence S. Rothenberg, *Linking Citizens to Government* (New York: Cambridge University Press, 1992), 100–24; and Mark E. Warren, *Democracy and Association* (Princeton: Princeton University Press, 2001).

the organization if they are dissatisfied. Workers who begin employment at a plant or an office where union membership is required are not given a choice as to which union to join. Thus, it is not rare for a union presidency to be contested by differing factions. The whole AFL-CIO was divided in 1995, when seventy-three-year-old President Lane Kirkland sought reelection. Under pressure, Kirkland finally bowed out, and an open election between two candidates led to John Sweeney's selection as head of the labor federation later in the year.[57] A decade later, with the political and economic clout of unions still declining, the AFL-CIO formally split in June of 2005, when the Teamsters and the Service Employees International Union (SEIU) left the organization. Other unions followed suit, with still others debating about leaving the union.[58]

For every lobby that has an open fight for control of the organization, however, hundreds of interest groups hear nary a discouraging word from their members. Harmony continues in most groups because of congruence between members' opinions and the avowed purposes of the organization. Also, in voluntary organizations, most internal protest consists of the relatively passive act of failing to renew one's membership. Many interest groups devote considerable energy to promoting their policy agenda and issues to the members, sometimes persuading them of the importance of new issues or new approaches. Finally, peace usually reigns within interest groups because staff members are careful not to move the organization toward policy positions that are likely to alienate a significant portion of the membership. For almost all interest group staffers, maintenance of the organization is more important than ideological purity.

Making Decisions

We have dwelt on how organizations are designed to carry out their tasks and who has the authority to decide what those tasks will be. We can now study the actual dynamics of how decisions are made.

In the minority of organizations whose members are heavily involved, the decision-making structure becomes complex because of the broader participation. Such organizations must develop a practical means of selecting issues to lobby upon. No matter how democratic an organization sincerely wants to be, it is unwieldy to involve large numbers of people in making decisions. One means of getting periodic membership input into decision making is to have an executive council of members, which meets every few months. As noted earlier, when members are given this type of formal opportunity to participate, they must be aggressive in staking out their role; if not, they can quickly come to play a minor part in the organization. Another method is the task force, on which the Business Roundtable relies to draw upon the prestige and influence of chief executive

---

[57]Louis Uchitelle, "Battle for Presidency of A.F.L.-C.I.O. Emerges After Kirkland Withdraws from Race," *New York Times* June 11, 1995; and Peter T. Kilborn, "Militant Is Elected Head of A.F.L.-C.I.O., Signaling Sharp Turn for Labor Movement," *New York Times* October 26, 1995.

[58]Thomas B. Edsall, "Two Top Unions Split from AFL-CIO: Others Are Expected to Follow Teamsters," *Washington Post* July 26, 2005, p. A1.

officers of member firms. To involve these CEOs successfully and to get them to commit time to the organization, they must be given a real say in deciding its direction.

The Business Roundtable has task forces in international trade, regulatory reform, antitrust, taxation, energy, and many other areas, all chaired by a CEO of a member firm. By the staff's account, the chairpersons of these task forces are quite active in developing the policy recommendations to be made. However, in the Roundtable, as in so many other lobbies, deciding on issue positions is not the dilemma they face. Rather, says a top official of the group, the question the CEOs find themselves asking is "Why do *we* have to get in on this issue?"

Even this relatively wealthy organization, with its budget in the low millions and with access to the resources of member firms, is limited in the number of issues it can work on. For interest groups, the law of resources is that, *on any given day, any given group will have more relevant issues before it than it can possibly handle.* Whether a group is staff dominated or has some direct membership influence, allocating resources between issues is the most troublesome part of making decisions.

How do organizations deal with this problem of setting priorities? There are no clear-cut decision rules, but this description by a lobbyist for the National Council of Senior Citizens (NCSC) is instructive:

> We try to [make decisions] on as rational a basis as possible. We first judge the potential impact on older people. Generally speaking, we represent all elderly people, but primarily due to our own lack of resources, we concern ourselves with the low-income elderly. We are more likely, therefore, to be more involved with an issue like a reduction in the cost of living adjustment rather than the reauthorization of the FTC—although there are issues there of concern to all elderly. We try to quantify things. We make judgments based on the [interests of the] needier. We also have to make judgments on the basis of timeliness. Things change. It's an evolving sort of process here in Washington. We have to govern our flow of work on the basis of how things come up on Capitol Hill. This tends to create some confusion. Sometimes it's not easy to decide what to let go of.

A number of important points about decision making by interest groups appear in this account. First, leaders of interest groups do try to think systematically about how to budget their resources. The National Council of Senior Citizens tries to be "rational" and to "quantify things," yet the lobbyist also acknowledges that much of its decision making comes down to "judgment." This is the contradiction that all interest group officials must live with. They do try to think rationally about resource allocations by weighing the merits of each issue in relation to the interests of their constituency. Relative merits, though, can never be calculated by a formula or strict decision rule. Rather, human judgment must be relied upon.

Second, some issues matter so deeply to the organization that, without question, they must receive high priority for lobbying resources. When President George W. Bush nominated Samuel A. Alito, Jr., to fill a Supreme Court vacancy, his record of opposition to legal abortion automatically made his confirmation or defeat a top issue for pro-life and pro-choice groups. Some issues command a large commitment of an organization's resources; other decisions must be made around those issues. As the lobbyist for another group put it, "On the hot issues, we know what they are and there's little debating."

Third, the timeliness of issues makes planning extremely hard. Interest groups do not control their own destiny because they cannot control the political agenda. Social Security has always been of the utmost concern to the elderly, but it has waxed and waned as a major political issue. In some cases, groups have substantial warning that issues will be on the political agenda. Senior citizen groups had plenty of time to anticipate that President George W. Bush would suggest changes to Social Security that would create private accounts and thus were ready with their arguments in opposition. However, just how and when issues begin to take center stage can catch even the most experienced lobbyists off guard. No matter how carefully an interest group plans allocation of its resources over the next year, it is always going to be it-all-depends planning. A lobbyist for a farm group noted, "In this town, you're dead if you're not able to react quickly."

Fourth, and finally, it is much easier for an interest group to take on a new issue than to drop a current one. Just because a new issue vital to the group arises, other issues do not become unimportant. Consequently, it is not easy to decide what to let go of. Issues can become less pressing in a relative sense as the lobbyists rush to an emergency that needs their immediate attention. Nevertheless, interest group staffers do not operate on a zero-sum principle; for every new allocation of their time, they do not consciously eliminate an equally time-consuming activity. In practice, of course, the zero-sum principle must hold because the day has only so many hours. Issues get crowded out by the demands of more urgent issues without some official articulation of a new ordering of priorities.

These generalizations describe the dynamics of resource allocation. There are, of course, variations. Some years can be stable for an interest group, with few surprise issues or relevant changes in the political environment. Eventually, though, the problems outlined here plague all types of interest groups. They have trouble planning, and their allocation of resources evolves out of incremental decisions, many of which are automatic because they involve issues at the core of the group's purpose.

Conclusion

The rapid expansion of interest group advocacy in recent years has focused attention on the sophisticated theorizing on origins and maintenance of lobbying organizations. The work of Truman, Olson, and Salisbury, in particular, provides insight into the ways in which interest groups form and attract support from constituents. Further research is needed, however, to improve our understanding of the relationship between incentives and the success of groups in attracting members. A next step for researchers is to explore fully how interest groups distinguish themselves in competitive markets and how they try to find niches that can be exploited.

Although a good deal of work has been done on how interest groups originate and how they raise their money, relatively little scholarly work has been done on how lobbies govern themselves. Like most voluntary organizations, lobbies with memberships reflect the iron law of oligarchy. Only in theory are most interest groups democratically governed. They are staff-dominated organizations not simply because rank-and-file members do not have the time to participate at a level that would allow them to be influential but also because the governmental process is highly complex. Members have every reason to defer to the expertise and experience of those on the job in Washington.

An interest group's ability to accomplish its goals is affected by its organizational strengths and weaknesses. Lobbies have trouble establishing firm priorities and they often find themselves reacting rather than planning. Selecting issues often results from emergencies crowding out older policy concerns. However, interest groups are not organized in an irrational or even anomalous manner. Whatever their organizational structure or planning process, they have the flexibility to devote the greatest portion of their resources to the policy problems that most affect their members.

Chapter 4

The Party Connection

Interest groups and political parties often forge close ties. Many business groups contribute heavily to Republican candidates and party committees and, in some cases, even run advertising campaigns independently to help party candidates. Labor unions routinely mobilize voters to support Democratic candidates, using volunteers who operate phone banks. However parties and interest groups have different goals and incentives, and they sometimes find themselves on opposite sides of issues. In late 2005, the Republican leadership pushed a bill that would require businesses to verify that all of their workers are in the United States legally and would increase the penalties for hiring illegal employees. The bill was popular with groups within the Republican coalition that opposed immigration, however, business groups argued that the bill imposed an unreasonable cost on companies. The U.S. Chamber of Commerce and other business groups mounted a major effort to kill the bill, working against the same party leaders with whom they usually cooperate.[1] The conflict exemplifies the complicated relationship between interest groups and political parties: one of frequent cooperation but occasional conflict.

Within the groves of academe, American interest groups and American political parties are separate subfields. Distinct groups of scholars study each, and only a few hardy souls cross the boundaries to try to link these two subjects. One reason for this is that the subfields share little in terms of their theoretical perspectives. Another reason is surely the traditional incentive for scholars to specialize, so that they can become a leading expert on a subject.

It is important to examine the relationship between interest groups and political parties because they do many of the same things, albeit in different ways. Both interest groups and parties represent citizens, facilitate their participation in the political process, educate the public, put issues on the agendas of Congress and varied agencies, and monitor program performance. Yet parties and groups are linked together in our system not simply because their functions overlap but also because they need each other to accomplish their most important goals. Groups cannot enact policies or formulate regulations on their own. Parties need the political support of interest groups, which can provide campaign donations, mobilize voters on election day, activate their membership on behalf of a bill, and influence the general public's attitudes.

---

[1] Jeffrey H. Birnbaum, "Immigration Pushes Apart GOP, Chamber," *Washington Post* December 14, 2005, p. A1.

In this chapter, we will look at the interrelationship between interest groups and political parties, focusing on both the ties that bind and the sources of conflict between groups and parties. A beginning point is to examine the advocacy explosion in the context of recent party history. Did interest groups prosper because parties declined?

The Advantages of Interest Groups

If interest groups and political parties are interrelated in many crucial ways, it stands to reason that broad-scale changes among one set of political organizations will affect the other. No one would argue that groups and parties stand in perfect balance—as one goes up the other must go down. However, because they compete for many of the same resources—money, identity, allegiance among political activists, and so on—it may be that the health of parties and that of interest groups are, to some degree, inversely related.

In this context, the decline of American political parties during the 1960s and 1970s may help explain the rise of the interest group society. As people became disillusioned with parties, the number of new lobbies dramatically increased. For political scientists, the principal indicators of party decline were the decreasing proportion of Americans who voted on the basis of party, the drop in the number of people who voted at all, the increasing cynicism toward parties and the political system, and a decline in partisan identification.[2]

Although scholars agree that parties declined during this period, they disagree as to whether the parties have regained strength since. Many believe that the political parties have been reinvigorated, as evidenced by their increased fundraising, the increased party loyalty of members in Congress, and their efforts to develop a coherent policy agenda. During the 1994 election campaign, the Republicans highlighted the "Contract with America." In the early elections of the new century, the GOP developed an impressive in-house voter mobilization effort. In the mid-2000s, Democrats responded with an impressive new fundraising operation that identified millions of new donors, and with increased efforts at party unity.

However, there are more fundamental, more enduring reasons that American interest groups have prospered at the expense of political parties. The nature of our electoral and party system facilitates interest group politics independent of the health of the parties at any one time. Individuals who care about policy issues have limited resources, which they can direct toward interest groups or political parties. In many cases, interest groups are the logical choice because they are committed to a narrower range of issues.

---

[2]The literature on party decline is voluminous. See, for example, David S. Broder, *The Party's Over* (New York: Harper & Row, 1972); Everett Carll Ladd, Jr., with Charles D. Hadley, *Transformations of the American Party System*, 2nd ed. (New York: Norton, 1978); and Norman H. Nie, Sidney Verba, and John R. Petrocik, *The Changing American Voter* (Cambridge: Harvard University Press, 1976). For more recent scholarship, see Martin Wattenberg, "The Decline of American Political Parties, 1952–1996," in *American Political Parties: Decline or Resurgence?* ed. Jeffrey E. Cohen, Richard Fleisher, and Paul Kantor (Washington, DC: CQ Press, 2001).

Policy Maximizers

A central advantage of interest groups over political parties is that they offer individuals a direct, focused, and undiluted way of supporting advocacy on their issue of greatest concern. Assume that you are politically active and are willing to spend $100 to pursue your political goals during a single year. What is the best way to spend that money so that your chances of achieving those goals are maximized? If you care about a particular policy—saving the wilderness, protecting farm subsidies, promoting workplace safety, and so forth—you may easily conclude that an interest group is the better "investment" for that $100 than a political party or one of its congressional campaign committees. Even though one cannot confidently predict the real chances that either a party or an interest group will succeed in accomplishing that one specific goal, it is clear to you as donor of the money that the interest group will work more intensively and single-mindedly toward it. A political party, on the other hand, has a constituency so broad that it will be pushed to move on hundreds of issues. In any year, however, relatively few issues will be assigned priority by party leaders, and, if an issue is highly controversial, the best political course for the congressional party or the president may be to act in a superficial, symbolic manner or to abstain altogether from acting on the issue.

The advantages of interest groups in the United States are accentuated by our two-party system. With plurality elections in single-member districts (and thus no proportional representation), the likelihood is that both political parties will cover a great deal of ideological ground.[3] To win an election, the parties must build a coalition of some breadth, attracting large numbers of those in the center (moderates) to go along with those who form the ideological core of the party. By their very nature, then, American political parties are *vote maximizers*. To win elections, they must dilute some policy stands, take purposely ambiguous positions on others, and generally ignore still others so as not to offend segments of the population that they need in their coalition. For example, the Republican party must balance the votes it can win from those who support tougher immigration policy against its decreased support in the business community as a result of pushing for that policy.

Interest groups are just the opposite. They are *policy maximizers,* meaning that they do better in attracting members if their outlook is narrowly focused.[4] Although a few interest groups work on a broad range of policies, the typical group cares only about a few closely related issues. The Chamber of Commerce is focused narrowly on policies that create a climate where business can prosper. A dollar donated to the Chamber is a dollar spent on its narrow set of issues, not on a broader agenda that might hurt some businesses but attract votes to the GOP.

If the United States had a multiparty system, some political support that now goes to interest groups would likely be channeled to some of the additional parties that would compete with the Democrats and Republicans. For example, in a number of European countries, environmental, or Green, parties have arisen. In 2005, the Greens won 8.1 percent of

---

[3]Maurice Duverger, *Political Parties* (New York: John Wiley, 1963); and Anthony Downs, *An Economic Theory of Democracy* (New York: Harper & Row, 1957).

[4]Jeffrey M. Berry, "Public Interest vs. Party System," *Society* 17 (May/June 1980): 47.

the popular vote in German national elections. The proportional representation system in Germany translated this into fifty-one seats in the Bundestag.[5] In the United States, a party averaging 8 percent in every congressional election would win no seats in Congress because our elections are "winner take all," where only one candidate wins in each district.

The Greens in Germany and elsewhere in Europe are not vote-maximizer parties. Instead, they champion a particular interest with great intensity, much the way environmental interest groups in this country push their agenda. The European Green parties do not realistically hope to win control of the government. Rather, they want to attract the votes of those who care passionately about the environment and related issues, so that they can capture enough seats to be an influential force within the legislature and perhaps become partners in a coalition government. If the United States had a proportional representation system, a viable Green party would likely prosper. Instead, the winner-take-all system means that the Green party primarily wins votes that would have gone to Democrats and sometimes helps elect Republicans in the process. In the 2000 presidential election, for example, Green party candidate Ralph Nader received 2.8 million votes, including more than 20,000 votes in Florida, a state that Bush won by approximately 500 votes. A multiparty proportional system would have resulted in a Democratic–Green coalition government, instead of a victory for Republican candidate George Bush.

Political parties and interest groups understand the role of minor parties on elections. In both the 2000 and 2004 presidential elections, environmental groups ran independent advertising urging environmentalists to *not* vote for the Green party.[6] Meanwhile, Republican party operatives helped finance a petition drive to put Nader on the ballot in more states in 2004 and ran ads supporting the candidate.[7]

If the United States had a system of proportional representation and the American Green party grew, environmentalists would likely give less money and time to interest groups. The Natural Resources Defense Council, the National Audubon Society, the National Wildlife Federation, the Izaak Walton League, Friends of the Earth, the Environmental Defense Fund, Environmental Action, Greenpeace, the Sierra Club, and countless other local, state, and national environmental lobbies would likely suffer, because it is doubtful that there would be enough financial support and activism to maintain such a vast array of environmental advocacy groups as well as a Green party.

Party Systems

Clearly, the opportunity for interest groups to form and prosper is affected by the number of viable political parties in an electoral system. The relationship between the type of party system and the type of interest group system may also be influenced by the internal cohesiveness of the parties in the legislature. In the language of political science, does the absence of a *responsible* party system lead to more interest group politics?

---

[5]Ferdinand Müller-Rommel, "New Political Movements and 'New Politics' Parties in Western Europe," in Russell Jo Dalton and Manfred Kuechler, *Challenging the Political Order* (New York: Oxford University Press, 1990), 216.

[6]In a proportional system, the total vote for Nader and for Gore would have been a clear majority, and a Democratic–Green coalition would likely have formed a government.

[7]Laura Meckle, "GOP Group to Air Pro-Nader TV Ads," *Washington Post* October 27, 2000.

A responsible or strong party system is one that promotes majoritarian policymaking. During the campaign, the parties issue platforms detailing their promises on major policy issues. The party that wins the election is committed to following through on those promises.[8] Parties control the nomination of candidates and thus can punish party members who do not support the promises by keeping them off the ballot in the next election.

In the United States, the Democrats and Republicans fall far short of the responsible party model. Individual legislators often assemble their own coalitions across party lines, collect their own campaign contributions, and choose their own issue positions. This means that members are free to vote against the proposals of party leaders on any issue they choose. Indeed, even members of the party leadership can sometimes oppose proposals backed by the heads of the party. When the Clinton administration and House Democratic Speaker Tom Foley announced their support for the North American Free Trade Agreement in the 1990s, Democratic House Whip David Bonior from Michigan (who had strong ties to organized labor, which opposed the measure) announced that he opposed the bill.

The contrast with British political parties is instructive. Those who wish to run for Parliament on the Conservative or Labour ticket must subject themselves to a gauntlet of interviews at different levels of the party before the party organization chooses who will be its nominee for available seats.[9] Once they get to Parliament, Conservative and Labour members need to vote with their party on major issues; otherwise, the government could fall and new elections would have to be scheduled.

In the United States, a responsible party system is inhibited not only by the way the party system has evolved but also by the divided powers of our government. A responsible party system is compatible with a parliamentary form of government, in which the legislative and executive branches are intertwined and the prime minister is the legislative leader of the party in the majority. In the United States, the president can be of one party while the other party controls one or both houses of Congress. Divided control is common in the postwar era.[10] In such cases, regardless of what one party pledges to do if elected, substantial compromise is usually required before legislation promised in the campaign can be enacted by Congress into law, if it can be passed at all. Even when the same party controls Congress and the White House, there is no guarantee that partisans will agree on legislation.

When political parties are weak and divided, interest groups have greater access. Instead of bargaining centrally with party leaders, interest groups can approach individual legislators, and often they induce members to vote against the wishes of party leaders. Interest groups can offer campaign contributions and other electoral support and can present information that shows that the party position is not advantageous for a particular state or district. During the 1970s and 1980s, it was not uncommon for interest groups to work around Democratic party leaders by lobbying party moderates (especially from the South) on issues such as gun control, defense spending, and crime.

---

[8]See the report by the American Political Science Association's Committee on Political Parties, *Toward a More Responsible Two-Party System* (New York: Rinehart, 1950).

[9]Pippa Norris and Joni Lovenduski, *Political Recruitment: Gender, Race, and Class in the British Parliament* (Cambridge, UK: Cambridge University Press, 1995).

[10]David Mayhew, *Divided We Govern* (New Haven: Yale University Press, 1991), 4–5.

Although it seems evident that a weak party system works to strengthen the role of interest groups in a political system, we cannot assume the opposite, that a strong party system works to weaken interest groups. In the British system, labor unions have great influence over the Labour party. In the 1980s, British unions provided 90 percent of the Labour party's funds and cast 80 percent of the votes at the Labour Party Conference, and, even in the early 2000s, unions provide more than 60 percent of Labour party funding.[11] Although not as formally tied to the Conservatives, business trade associations are highly influential as well. Interest group influence can take many forms, and lobbying organizations are highly adaptable to the requirements of any democratic political system.

In parliamentary systems, there is a tendency for more centralization of interest group advocacy than in the United States. In the United States, a small number of influential groups ostensibly speak for large sectors of society (such as the Business Roundtable and the AFL-CIO), but no lobbying groups enjoy a dominant position in government policymaking. In some parliamentary democracies, however, large, powerful groups are the unquestioned representative of a broad sector of society and enjoy access to government that other interest groups in that country can only dream about. Where governments recognize such groups as the formal representatives of some sector of the economy, and consult with the leadership of those organizations as a matter of course before making policy decisions, such relationships are described as *corporatist* or *neocorporatist*. In Austria, for example, the government recognizes the Federation of Industrialists and the Federation of Business as the representatives of business interests, and the organizations play an integral, formalized role in the policymaking process.[12]

The variety in electoral and party systems among the Western democracies makes it difficult to determine how those structures influence the exact nature of interest group systems. Clearly, multiparty systems provide competition to interest groups, because some of the narrower, more ideological parties (such as the Greens) will attract financial support and activism from people who might otherwise be more supportive of lobbies with similar policy goals. Beyond this, however, considerable uncertainty exists about how the differences in parliamentary party systems and other institutional factors affect the number, size, and role of interest groups.[13] In the United States, however, with its federal structure, separation of powers, and an electoral system that lends itself to two broad, centrist parties, there is every reason to expect that interest groups are going to flourish.

Important changes have occurred in the U.S. party system in the past thirty years. Parties have become more unified, with their members more often voting together on key measures. In the 1970s, House Democrats and Republicans voted with their party on average around 70 percent of the time. In 2005, House Republicans supported their party 90 percent of the time, and the Democrats were only slightly less loyal. In early 2007,

---

[11]Graham K. Wilson, *Interest Groups* (Oxford, UK: Basil Blackwell, 1990), 87; and Graham K. Wilson, personal communication, January 23, 2006.

[12]Graham K. Wilson, *Business and Politics* (Chatham, NJ: Chatham House, 1985), 106. See also Robert H. Salisbury, "Why No Corporatism in America?," in *Trends Toward Corporatist Intermediation,* ed. Philippe C. Schmitter and Gerhard Lehmbruch (Beverly Hills: Sage, 1979), 219–36.

[13]See Robert A. Dahl, *Dilemmas of Pluralist Democracy* (New Haven: Yale University Press, 1982), 55–80.

the new Democratic majority remained generally cohesive, although Republicans were more likely to defect from their party's position on bills. Moreover, the average ideological gap between the parties has increased over time, so that the average Republican is now more conservative than in the 1970s, and the average Democrat more liberal.

Parties have become more unified in part because moderates of both parties have been defeated in primary and general elections. In addition, the narrow margins enjoyed by the GOP in both chambers of Congress have led members, at least temporarily, to allow their party leaders greater powers in order to help their party stay unified.[14] The United States still does not have a responsible party system, but party leaders have more clout than in the past, and party members are increasingly likely to support their party on major issues.

Interest groups have played a role in this polarization. Many interest groups have become involved in party primaries and have helped more ideological candidates win elections. Over the past several years, ideological groups have even helped support challengers in party primaries against popular incumbents, intending to warn them to toe the party line more often. This has been especially true in the Republican party, in which pro-life, Christian Right, and other groups have worked actively in party primaries to influence nominations and to alert GOP incumbents to the dangers of a liberal voting record.

Working Together

Most American interest groups are torn between partisanship and nonpartisanship. For some interest groups, there is little chance that their policy agenda can advance unless one party controls government. The most obvious example is organized labor. The Democratic party has championed the right of unions to organize, has worked for health and safety standards at the workplace, and consistently has advocated raises in the minimum wage. The Republicans have been just as steadfast in their opposition to labor issues. Consequently, the AFL-CIO and its member unions have no reason to pretend they are not politically affiliated with the Democratic party.

Other groups try to maintain ties with both political parties, because control of the government is often divided between the two parties and because having supporters in both parties helps even when one party controls both branches. Agricultural groups, for example, seek subsidies from whichever party has the majority in Congress, and frequently work with legislators from farm states, regardless of party. Lobbyists need access to both parties, and historically this has meant that many large interest groups will hire some lobbyists who have worked for Republicans on the Hill or in an agency and some who have worked for Democrats.

Although access to both parties is paramount, the leaders of interest groups usually have a preference between the parties. Most business leaders prefer the Republican party

---

[14]This is especially true in the U.S. House. See John H. Aldrich and David W. Rhode, "The Consequences of Party Organization in the House: The Role of the Majority and Minority Parties in Conditional Party Government," in *Polarized Politics: Congress and the President in a Partisan Era*, ed. Jon R. Bond and Richard Fleisher (Washington, DC: CQ Press, 2000).

because of its greater sympathy for low taxes, smaller government, and antipathy to organized labor. Business groups have historically walked a delicate line, trying to help the Republicans win control of Congress and the White House while being friendly enough with Democrats through their campaign donations and hiring enough Democratic lobbyists so as not to alienate the party. Even in 2001, with the GOP firmly in control of government, business groups knew that the Democrats would likely one day win back control of one or more chambers of Congress or the presidency and thus wished to maintain good relations.

Over time, however, it has become more difficult for interest groups to maintain a bipartisan approach. As the parties have grown further apart and party loyalty has increased in roll-call voting, interest groups have found it harder to justify supporting candidates of both parties. Party leaders have pushed groups to move toward a more partisan stance. The Republican K Street Project pressured business groups to give money only to Republicans, and even to hire only Republicans as lobbyists.[15] In one instance in 1998, the House Ethics Committee privately warned a party leader after he had threatened to retaliate against the Electronics Industry Alliance for hiring a Democrat.[16] This meant that, over time, more and more lobbyists for corporations and trade associations were Republicans with ties to the GOP House leadership.

When Democrats captured control of the House and Senate in 2006, business groups were quick to adapt. Many put out the word quickly that they wanted to hire Democratic lobbyists, and a bidding war ensued for those best connected to Democratic leaders in both chambers. Business groups also routed PAC contributions to Democratic candidates in 2007. Whether the GOP will be able to entice business groups to help them try to regain control of Congress in 2008 is not yet evident, but early polling suggests that the Democratic majority is likely to continue after the election, and this gives businesses a big incentive to give to candidates of both parties.

It is not only business interests that have become more partisan in the past decade. Citizen groups have also become more closely aligned with one or the other party. Democrats began to pressure environmental and feminist groups to support only Democratic candidates, and Republicans did the same for conservative citizen groups. Over time, groups such as the Sierra Club, National Right to Life Committee, National Organization for Women, and National Rifle Association all became more partisan in their campaign activity, and in their lobbying. In some cases, they even abandoned incumbents with whom they had long-term relationships when the opportunity arose to win the seat for their preferred party. The NRA, however, has continued to back friendly Democratic incumbents.

When party leaders pressure interest groups to become more partisan, many feel they must comply. Party leaders have become more important to the legislative process. Often, party leaders can insert language in bills a few minutes before a vote, or during a

---

[15]Jim VandeHei, "GOP Monitoring Lobbyists' Politics; White House, Hill Access May Be Affected," *Washington Post* June 10, 2002, p. A1.
[16]Jeffrey Birnbaum, "GOP Freezes Jobs List, a Vestige of the K Street Project," *Washington Post* January 26, 2006, p. A2.

conference committee. Having access to party leaders has become more important.[17] In December of 2005, for example, health insurance lobbyists worked closely with the Republican congressional leadership to alter language in a Medicare bill that ultimately saved the industry some $22 billion. Democrats were not invited to the meeting, which changed language in a conference committee report without a formal vote by the committee.[18] In other words, having access to the Republican party leadership was very financially valuable to health insurance lobbyists, and having access to Democrats would have had no positive impact, at best, and, at worst, would have angered GOP leaders who might then have been less generous. After 2006, health insurance lobbyists needed access to Democratic lawmakers, and this underscores the dangers of a partisan approach for business groups that want to make their case to whichever party controls Congress.

Party leaders often work closely with interest groups to draft legislation, and then to push it through Congress. When House Republicans drafted the bills that would implement the 1994 Contract with America, they consulted closely with interests. Party leaders then asked those interests in return to work hard to lobby on behalf of the entire package. In this way, lobbyists were essentially representing their own groups, as well as the larger agenda of the party.[19] The new Democratic majority in 2007 held hearings on a proposed Employment Non-discrimination Act (ENDA) that would ban discrimination against gays and lesbians in hiring and firing, something that Democratic constituencies favored but that GOP-leaning groups opposed.

Although interest groups and parties have worked more closely together in the past decade, there remains tension. Parties represent broad coalitions of interests, many of which do not agree on some issues. As noted at the start of the chapter, the Republican party includes groups that advocate for restrictions on immigration, and business groups resist some of those policies. Christian conservative groups push for sanctions on China for human rights abuses, but business groups want to develop ties to the huge Chinese market. Within the Democratic coalition, environmental groups push for tighter clean air statutes, while labor unions fight them because they might cost jobs. Gay and lesbian rights groups support same-sex marriage, which many African American leaders oppose.

Parties find it frustrating to deal with citizen groups because these organizations work against the parties' vote-maximization strategy. Rational parties want to place themselves squarely in the center of the American electorate, maximizing their appeal to those with moderate political outlooks. Since most Americans are not highly ideological, most of the votes in elections come from those who are moderates, rather than from

---

[17]John H. Aldrich and David W. Rhode, "The Consequences of Party Organization in the House: The Role of the Majority and Minority Parties in Conditional Party Government," in *Polarized Politics: Congress and the President in a Partisan Era*, ed. Jon R. Bond and Richard Fleisher (Washington, DC: CQ Press, 2000); and Barbara Sinclair, *Unorthodox Lawmaking: New Legislative Processes in the U.S. Congress* (Washington, DC: CQ Press, 2000).

[18]Jonathan Weisman, "Closed-Door Deal Makes $22 Billion Difference: GOP Negotiators Criticized for Change in Measure on HMOs," *Washington Post* January 24, 2006, p. A1.

[19]Stephen Engelberg, "GOP and Lobbies Passed Contract; Success Marks a New Partnership, Era," *Houston Chronicle* April 17, 1995, p. A6.

hardened liberals or conservatives. Citizen groups, on the other hand, want the parties to emphasize their issues, even though those issue stances may be highly controversial and push moderates away from the party. Citizen groups assume that, even if a majority of Americans do not currently share their views, an election campaign that enlightens them about the organization's issues will eventually produce a majority backing those positions.

In recent years, Republicans have increasingly tried to contact interest group members directly, rather have groups do the communications themselves. In 1992, the Christian Coalition mobilized voters on behalf of George H. W. Bush, and its leader Ralph Reed expected to be consulted on policymaking by the new administration. In 2004, George W. Bush's re-election campaign contacted conservative Christian voters directly through mailings and phone calls, bypassing Christian Right groups.

In contrast, interest groups remain vitally important in the Democrats efforts to mobilize voters. Labor unions, environmental groups, feminist organizations, and various liberal 527 committees contact their members and other potential voters, urging them to vote and to support Democratic candidates.

Keeping Parties Straight and True

One of the most interesting developments in contemporary party politics is the increasingly important role of citizen groups in campaigns and elections. Citizen groups differ from vocationally related interest groups in that they are organized around members' ideological beliefs about the political system. They tend to be more passionate, more self-righteous, more abrasive, and more partisan than other interest groups. They speak for broad sectors of the American population. When party margins in Congress are tight and presidential races close, the parties depend on these groups to mobilize their members to vote.

The Republicans' primary citizen group constituencies are the Christian Right and "pro-family" groups, antiabortion groups, and gun owners groups such as the National Rifle Association. The Democrats embrace women's groups, black and Hispanic civil rights organizations, environmentalists, gay and lesbian organizations, and the senior citizens' lobby. These citizen groups are involved in different ways in the two parties, but all aggressively push their issues, which are often the most controversial and emotional issues before the country.

One way to influence the policies that parties support is to change the politicians who represent the parties in Washington. Many citizen groups (and, to a lesser extent, unions and even corporations) try to influence the outcome of party primaries, so that policymakers more sympathetic to their cause become the party nominees. Some groups encourage their own members to run for office; others recruit nonmembers who support their agenda to run for public office. Still others ask primary-election candidates to answer questions or fill out surveys in order to determine which would be best for the group's agenda. Candidates seek out the interest groups they have sympathized with over the years and ask for the votes of those who identify with those organizations.

Citizen groups can help supportive candidates win their party's nomination, thereby moving the center of the party toward their preferred policies. There are many ways that interest groups can help primary-election candidates, including endorsements, voter guides, volunteers, and monetary contributions. We will discuss these in more detail in Chapter 5. If groups are persistent, they can have a significant effect on who represents the party in government.

In the 1970s, Republican and Democratic politicians did not differ in their positions on abortion. Over time, however, Republican legislators became more pro-life because, when a member retired, pro-life groups worked especially hard to help select the next party nominee; a similar process took place with pro-choice groups in the Democratic party. As a result, by the late 1990s, the party delegations in Congress had taken consistently different positions on abortion.[20] Of course, to influence policy, the candidate must also win the general election. In some cases, citizen groups have helped candidates win primary elections, but those candidates have taken issue positions that were too extreme to win in the general election.

As elections near, candidates often sharpen and emphasize a particular issue stance so as to attract an interest group's followers or at least neutralize their potential opposition. As the 2004 election neared, George W. Bush endorsed a national constitutional amendment that created a national definition of marriage that would apply to all states. This would prevent states, such as Massachusetts, from allowing same-sex marriages. Although Bush did not mention the issue in his public speeches, the campaign sent many targeted mailings on the issue to members of Christian Right and pro-family groups, as well as to those who attended evangelical churches.[21] Candidates who do not reach out to citizen groups during the campaign may find those groups unwilling to mobilize voters on their behalf.[22]

Citizen groups lobby the candidates as well. In 2007, gay and lesbian rights groups have pushed Democratic candidates to promise to try to enact a series of bills. Candidates frequently try to avoid promises to groups, because they can become liabilities when in office. During the 1992 presidential campaign, gay and lesbian groups pushed Bill Clinton to take an unequivocal stand on lifting the ban on gays in the military. Clinton told the groups that, if elected, he would instruct the Pentagon to allow homosexuals to serve openly in the armed services. No sooner had Clinton taken office than the press and his opponents began to ask when he was going to lift the ban. Public opinion was not supportive, and Clinton quickly beat a retreat with a hastily cobbled compromise of "don't ask, don't tell." (The military would not ask, and gay soldiers would not voluntarily tell people that they were homosexual.) The consequence was that this handful of citizen lobbies caused Clinton to lose valuable momentum at the beginning of his term and shortened his honeymoon with the Congress.

---

[20]Greg D. Adams, "Abortion: Evidence of Issue Evolution." *American Journal of Political Science* 41, no. 3 (July 1997): 718–37.

[21]David E. Campbell and J. Quinn Monson, "The Religion Card: Gay Marriage and the 2004 Presidential Election." Presented at conference on the 2004 election, Ohio State University, January 2006.

[22]Carin Larson, "An Uphill Climb: The Christian Right and the 2004 Election in Colorado," in *The Values Campaign? The Christian Right in the 2004 Elections,* ed. John C. Green, Mark J. Rozell, and Clyde Wilcox (Washington, DC: Georgetown University Press, 2006).

Business groups and labor unions also push the parties to back their issues. What is significant about the efforts of citizen groups is that the impact of their lobbying may push their targeted party away from the center of the electorate. A business group pushing the Republican party to adopt a plank in its platform calling for a lower depreciation allowance in the tax code is not going to drive moderates from the party, but emotional issues, such as same-sex marriage, can both attract and repel voters. Although a majority of Americans opposed same-sex marriage, the George W. Bush campaign decided to endorse a moderate version of a national constitutional amendment and then to avoid the issue during the campaign. The campaign leadership worried that taking an extreme position on the issue would cost them votes, but many Christian Right groups sought to pressure the campaign to focus on the issue because, to them, principle was more important than victory in November.

Citizen groups have also worked hard to influence the platforms of the political parties at the national and state levels. This kind of behavior by citizen groups is hardly uncommon. In recent years, citizen groups have provoked most of the platform fights at national conventions.[23] Usually, these are hot-button, "wedge" issues that are highly controversial, such as affirmative action, abortion, gay rights, and the Equal Rights Amendment. The motivation of the groups is to draw out the differences between the two parties on the issue. One study of platform fights between 1980 and 1992 showed that, in twenty-three of twenty-four cases, the parties ended up on opposite sides of the issue. In short, citizen groups appear to be quite successful at using conventions to pull the party they are lobbying away from the center of the electorate on at least a few key issues. If pressuring the party they favor to move further to the left or the right costs its candidate votes in November, so be it.

In recent years, national conventions have been stage-managed affairs, with few visible platform fights, but there have been contentious battles behind the scenes. In 1996, Republican nominee Bob Dole tried to insert a supplemental minority plank into the GOP platform that stated that the party respected the rights of party members to hold different views on abortion. Dole's proposal would have left in place a strong antiabortion plank in the platform but added "We also recognize that members of our party have deeply held and sometimes differing views on issues like abortion, capital punishment, term limits and trade." Although only 25 percent of members on the platform committee needed to approve the measure, pro-life and Christian Right forces defeated him in a hotly fought but private battle.

In 2004, the Family Research Council, a pro-family group that opposes same-sex marriage, successfully pushed to strengthen language in the GOP platform after Vice President Dick Cheney stated that the issue should be left to the states.[24] Although citizen groups get most of the attention in platform debates, it is noteworthy that many corporate

---

[23]Jeffrey M. Berry and Deborah Schildkraut, "Citizen Groups, Political Parties, and the Decline of the Democrats." Paper delivered at the annual meeting of the American Political Science Association, Chicago, September 1995.

[24]Mark J. Rozell, Clyde Wilcox, and David Madland, *Interest Groups in American Campaigns: The New Face of Electioneering* (Washington, DC: CQ Press, 2006).

lobbyists served as senior staffers for the GOP platform committee in 2004, which was chaired by a lobbyist.[25]

Christian Right and pro-life forces have gone further than other groups in seeking to influence state political parties. Christian conservative groups, such as the Christian Coalition, sought to "take over" state and local party committees in the 1990s by electing their members to party committees. In 2000, the Christian Right was a dominant force in the Republican party in eighteen states and had moderate influence in another twenty-six.[26] The state party platform in Texas had long passages that were designed to appeal to Christian Right activists but that would be less popular among moderates, something that was clearly not true of the party platform in Massachusetts.

Historically, though, Democrats face a broader and more diverse set of interest group constituencies, citizen and otherwise. There is tension within the party between labor and environmentalists, as well as between white conservatives and the many citizen groups working to expand the rights of blacks, Hispanics, women, and gays and lesbians. The success of citizen groups in focusing the party's agenda toward their issues may have worked against the Democrats by making the party appear to be more concerned with the issues of the poor, minorities, and wealthy liberals than with the issue of how middle-class people make ends meet.[27]

Financial Support

Interest groups provide substantial amounts of funding and volunteer support for political parties to help with their campaigns. In Chapter 5, we will consider the ways that interest groups help candidates; here, we focus briefly on direct support for political parties. Political parties raise money from individuals and interest groups, and they spend it to help elect their candidates. Parties approach interest groups for contributions for obvious reasons. As Larry Sabato puts it, "Like Willie Sutton who robbed banks 'because that's where they keep the money,'" parties look to interest groups because they hold vast sums of money to contribute.[28] Unlike robbing banks, soliciting interest groups happens to be legal.

For more than twenty years, interest groups supported the parties by contributing *soft money.* "A term of epic imprecision," soft money is contributions that interest groups can make for party-building efforts.[29] This includes voter registration drives, voter education, get-out-the-vote efforts, and generic party advertising. The amount of soft money that groups could give was not limited, and it could come directly from group treasuries—from corporate profits, union dues, and other sources. Corporations were the dominant

[25]Jeffrey Birnbaum and Thomas Edsall, "For Lobbyists, Big Spending Means Big Presence," *Washington Post* July 28, p. A1.

[26]Kimberly H. Conger and John C. Green, "Spreading Out and Digging In: Christian Conservatives and State Republican Parties," *Campaigns & Elections* 23, no. 1 (2002): 59–61.

[27]Berry and Schildkraut, "Citizen Groups, Political Parties, and the Decline of the Democrats."

[28]Larry J. Sabato, *The Rise of Political Consultants* (New York: Basic Books, 1981), 273.

[29]Sorauf, *Inside Campaign Finance,* 147.

source of soft money, but labor unions and even citizen organizations contributed. Over time, party leaders increasingly pressured groups to give larger sums.

As the aggregate sums of soft money rose and as individual contributions by corporations and other groups increased, political scientists, journalists, and even lawmakers began to worry that these contributions had an undue influence on policymaking. Agribusiness giant Archer-Daniels-Midland (ADM), for example, relied on soft money to buy itself goodwill with both political parties. ADM has a strong interest in policies promoting the use of ethanol, a corn-based fuel that can be mixed with regular gasoline. ADM produces 70 percent of the nation's ethanol, and its chairman, Dwayne Andreas, donated vast sums to the parties to promote the fuel and other ADM interests. During the 1992 campaign, ADM donated $1.1 million in soft money to the Republican party. Undaunted by the GOP's loss of the White House, Andreas began to channel more money to the Democrats and gave $200,000 to the party in the first fifteen months of the Clinton administration. When the Democratic National Committee held a fundraising dinner, Andreas served as cochair of the event and kicked in another $100,000. When the EPA subsequently issued a regulation mandating that, by 1996, 10 percent of gasoline sold contain ethanol, was it mere coincidence that ADM had been such a good friend of the party? It is hard to argue that the EPA adopted the rule strictly on environmental grounds, since most environmental groups view ethanol as having little benefit to the environment.[30]

In 2002, Congress passed the Bipartisan Campaign Reform Act, which eliminated most forms of soft money. Although some soft money donors shifted their contributions to 527 committees and other types of campaigns that could help the parties, it appears that the new law did eliminate most of the contributions from corporate treasuries.[31] Because these contributions totaled more than $400 million in 2000 and 2002, the elimination of soft money made a difference in the way that groups sought access to parties.[32]

Interest groups have other ways to give to parties. The two major parties each have several committees that receive contributions from PACs and from individuals who are associated with interest groups, and interest groups can give to state and local party committees as well. Figure 4.1 shows the amount given to national party committees by interest group PACs from 1980 through 2006. The data show that PAC contributions to party committees increased sharply after soft money was eliminated, but the increase was only a tiny fraction of the amount of soft money that Bipartisan Campaign Reform Act eliminated. Not included in this figure is the money that interest groups give to personal PACs sponsored by party leaders, but this also has increased sharply in recent years.

---

[30]Peter H. Stone, "The Big Harvest," *National Journal* July 30, 1994, pp. 1790–93; and Michael Parrish, "EPA Rule on Ethanol Overturned," *Boston Globe* April 29, 1995.

[31]Robert G. Boatright, Michael J. Malbin, Mark J. Rozell, and Clyde Wilcox, "Interest Groups and Advocacy Organizations After BCRA," in *The Election After Reform: Money, Politics, and the Bipartisan Campaign Reform Act,* ed. Michael J. Malbin (Lanham, MD: Rowman & Littlefield, 2006).

[32]Studies show that groups with the most money made the largest soft money donations when this was legal, but that it was primarily the lack of alternative resources to use in elections that led many groups to soft money giving. See D. E. Appollonio and Raymond J. La Raja, "Who Gave Soft Money? The Effect of Interest Group Resources on Political Contributions," *Journal of Politics* 66, no. 4 (2004): 1134–54.

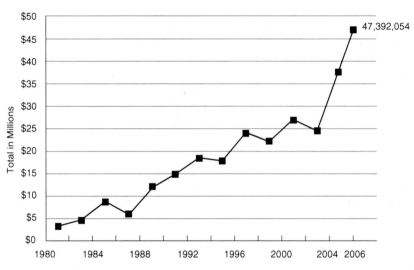

FIGURE 4.1
PAC Contributions to Party Committees over Time.
Source: Federal Election Commission.

Interest groups also make connections to parties at party conventions. Many corporations provide substantial in-kind services to conventions. In 2004, General Motors provided 300 vehicles to both conventions, and Panasonic donated video equipment. Many companies threw lavish meals or parties in honor of various politicians. At the 2004 Democratic convention, for example, the Chicago Board of Trade threw a $19,000 luncheon to honor Illinois senator Richard Durbin. Texas Republican Joe Barton, chair of the House Energy and Commerce Committee, was honored at a party sponsored by energy interests. At the GOP convention in 2004 the list of these types of events is long and varied. Interest group contributions to party conventions are often portrayed as civic-minded support of American democracy, but they also provide an opportunity for informal lobbying. Already in 2007, groups are lining up to host similar events at the party nominating conventions in 2008.

Conclusion

Parties and interest groups are involved in a complicated dance of cooperation and conflict. Parties need interest groups to help finance their activities, to provide access to distinctive constituencies of voters, and to help them keep in touch with the needs of party constituents. Interest groups need parties to help pass and implement public policy. This mutual need frequently creates close cooperation between parties and interest groups, and this cooperation has increased as the parties have become more united and increasingly have taken different positions on policy issues.

Parties and interest groups also have different interests. Parties need to win elections, which means appealing to majorities of voters. If a party is seen as too closely tied to a particular interest, or endorses an extreme interest group agenda, it might cost the party votes in the general election, so parties frequently try to win interest group support without alienating moderate voters. Interest groups in contrast may care more about particular issues—such as regulations on businesses, abortion, or AIDS in Africa—and therefore try to push parties to adopt specific proposals, regardless of their popularity with voters.

What is probably most disturbing about the relationship between interest groups and parties is the importance of interest group money in the electoral process. Although campaign finance reform bans soft money contributions by interest groups, the parties still depend upon groups for funding, and party leaders enjoy lavish fetes at party conventions. In Chapter 5, we will explore the role of interest groups in financing the candidates who run under the party label.

In the 1970s and 1980s, many interest groups sought to maintain ties to both political parties. They contributed money to candidates of both parties, hired lobbyists from both parties, and tried to assure that they had access to the leaders of both parties. In the past decade, this has changed, and interest groups have increasingly supported a single party, often under pressure from party leaders. Political scientists do not know if this is a permanent change. With the Democrats in control of Congress, many business groups have sought to gain access to the new leadership. Other GOP-leaning groups may become even more committed to electing Republicans in 2008, if the Democratic Congress enacts policies that they oppose. It might be that, if either party were to gain a larger majority in Congress, party loyalty would decline and interest groups would find it easier to work with policymakers of each party.

What is generally worrisome about the increasing involvement of interest groups in party politics is that one of the great values of parties is that they can serve as a counterweight to the narrowly focused demands of lobbying organizations. Parties can try to balance the efforts that interest groups make by articulating broader, national interests. Walter Dean Burnham writes,

> To state the matter with utmost simplicity: political parties, with all their well-known human and structural shortcomings, are the only devices thus far invented by the wit of Western man which with some effectiveness can generate counter-vailing collective power on behalf of the many individually powerless against the relatively few who are individually—or organizationally—powerful.[33]

As parties become closer to groups, their majoritarian instincts can be constrained as they must search for ways to reward the groups that are providing their funding or volunteers. Parties, of course, cannot be insensitive to groups' demands—they cannot win elections unless they build coalitions of many parts. More than anything else, though, parties should speak for the broad classes of people whose interests are not well represented by lobbying groups.

---

[33]Walter Dean Burnham, *Critical Elections and the Mainsprings of American Politics* (New York: Norton 1970), 133.

Chapter 5

Interest Groups in Campaigns

From grade school on, Americans are encouraged to participate in political life lest government become unresponsive to the will of the people. Such activities as writing one's member of Congress, joining an interest group, and signing a petition are presented as virtues, and citizens are encouraged to participate in elections as a vital source of democracy. However, when interest groups become involved in elections, it raises a larger worry. When groups help mobilize their volunteers and money, it is seen as good—up to a point—but, when groups provide a lot of support to candidates, and especially when they give a lot of money, it is widely seen as a danger. The concern, of course, is that those who give a lot may get back a lot. Maintaining the integrity of government means that we must somehow balance the need to staff and fund campaigns, the desire to have people actively involved in elections, and the obligation to keep government from being unduly influenced by those with the most money to contribute.

In practical terms, the question of balancing these needs is one of determining limits on how much individuals and interest groups can support candidates for office. Although these questions were directly addressed by campaign finance legislation in the 1970s and by reforms in 2002, the role of interest groups in supporting campaigns continues to spark controversy. Their importance in the electoral process forces us to confront again the classic dilemma of interest groups in a democratic society: How can the freedom of people to pursue their own interests be preserved while prohibiting any faction from abusing that freedom? The difficulty of choosing an appropriate policy involves not only the abstract question of conflicting rights but also the problem of assessing the effect of campaign contributions. What exactly are the effects of interest group money on both election results and legislative decisions? Would-be reformers must not only try to determine the answers to these questions but also try to assess the future consequences of their actions—consequences that are not always easy to foresee.

In Chapter 4, we explored the relationship between interest groups and political parties. Here we focus on the relationship between groups and candidates. These are related questions because party leaders frequently ask interest groups to give money to candidates from their party, and candidates sometimes contribute money that they receive from interest groups to their political parties. But most of the time interest groups support candidates for their own reasons. Group involvement in elections serves two purposes. By helping particular candidates win, groups can create a government that is more favorable to their issues. And, by supporting candidates, groups can build comfortable relationships that enhance lobbying. The largest part of group activity in elections involves financing campaigns—direct contributions through PACs or bundled contributions of executives, and spending on advertising and voter mobilization. However, groups can support candidates in other ways as well.

Nonfinancial Support

The simplest way for a group to support a candidate is to endorse him or her for office. Most labor unions endorse candidates, as do many citizen groups. An endorsement provides a clear signal to group members that the candidate supports the group's agenda. It provides useful information to citizens who are not members of the group but who support the group's goals as well. An endorsement by the NRA signals to gun enthusiasts that the candidate opposes gun control policies, while an endorsement by the Sierra Club signals a pro-environmental candidate. Since endorsements are free, why do most groups not endorse candidates?

First, corporations do not endorse candidates because they fear it would be bad for their business. Corporations wish to sell products to everyone, regardless of their partisanship. If a company endorsed George W. Bush for president, Democrats might well be less likely to buy its products. When corporations engage in openly partisan activity, they often do so through "shadow PACs," such as Citizens for Better Medicare, a group that was heavily funded by drug companies but whose political activity had no negative impact on the business of any corporation because consumers did not connect the group to any particular company.

Many citizen groups do not endorse candidates because they are organized under tax law as charities and are barred from engaging in electoral politics. Groups that are 501(c)(3) organizations, for example, can educate the public on issues but not endorse candidates. 501(c)(4) organizations are allowed to engage in some electoral activity, as long as it is not their primary function. Organizations that violate these restrictions can lose their tax exempt status, and this may cost them some large contributions from donors who expect a tax deduction for their gift, as well as contributions from foundations that are bound by their rules to give only to charities.[1] Some groups are structured so that there are multiple related organizations, each filling a different need. The Sierra Club, for example has a 501(c)(3) and a 501(c)(4), along with a 527 committee which can run issue ads, and a PAC which can contribute to candidates.

The difference between electoral activities and educating the public is often a fine line. The Christian Coalition organized itself as a 501(c)(4) committee and distributed voter guides in conservative evangelical churches in the 1990s on the Sunday before the election. These guides did not endorse a candidate but, instead, showed pictures of both candidates and positions attributed to the candidates on a range of issues. Although the guides were "nonpartisan" and did not show the position of the Christian Coalition on the issues, they made it quite evident which candidate was favored.[2] Moreover, public

---

[1]For a discussion of 501(c)3 nonprofits, see Jeffrey M. Berry and David F. Arons, *A Voice for Nonprofits* (Washington, DC: Brookings Institution, 2003).
[2]Clyde Wilcox and Carin Larson, *Onward Christian Soldiers: The Christian Right in American Politics,* 3rd ed. (Boulder: Westview, 2006).

statements by the organization's leaders made it clear that the organization's goal was to help Republicans win control of Congress. The Internal Revenue Service (IRS) eventually ruled that the Coalition's guides were electoral activity and that they constituted the major activity of the organization and stripped it of its tax exempt status. Other citizen groups continue to distribute voter guides that are less overtly electoral but that do help communicate subtly the group's support for a candidate.

More recently, the IRS launched an investigation into the tax exempt status of the NAACP, based on statements made by the organization's board chairman Julian Bond at its annual meeting on July 11, 2004, after two members of Congress requested an investigation. Bond's speech made clear his lack of support for Bush, although he did not call for the use of NAACP resources in anything other than a voter registration drive, which is allowed under the tax code. Two years later, after the NAACP had spent considerable sums in preparing a defense, the IRS ruled that after reviewing a video of the Bond speech, they deemed the speech to be not a violation, but the mere investigation worried many nonprofits on both sides of the political aisle.[3]

Churches also engage in political advocacy and even partisan politics, and often bump up against the legal limits of nonprofit politics. Churches that endorse candidates could lose their tax exempt status, although this has happened very rarely. Republicans in Congress have sought to promote a "Houses of Worship Freedom of Speech Act," which would allow churches to engage in partisan activity without losing their tax exempt status. Many conservative religious leaders have opposed the act, however, anticipating that its passage would lead to pressure by Republicans to endorse candidates and become more partisan.

Another tool that tax exempt groups can use is scorecards, which rate the votes of incumbents on issues of concern to the organization. Scorecards provide a way to show which policymakers support the organization without explicit endorsements. In 2006, the Human Rights Campaign, a gay rights group, listed the positions of senators on seven key issues, ranging from the Federal Marriage Amendment to hate crimes laws to HIV. The scorecard showed that even senators from the same state and party voted differently: Democrat Russ Feingold of Wisconsin voted consistently with the group's goals on six of seven measures, while Herb Kohl voted "correctly" only four times. Republican Senator Arlen Specter voted with the group on four bills, while his colleague, Rick Santorum, was "wrong" on all seven measures. Scorecards can be useful lobbying tools as well. Interest groups frequently tell lawmakers that an upcoming vote is so important that it will be included in their scorecards. This may help persuade wavering lawmakers to vote according to the group's wishes.[4]

Interest groups can also provide volunteers for campaigns. Christian Right and pro-life groups have historically provided many volunteers for Republican candidates. In the 2004 presidential campaign, Planned Parenthood coordinated hundreds of volunteers from California who traveled to Oregon to work door-to-door to convince unmarried women to vote for John Kerry.[5] Environmental groups often train workers who help

[3]Jeffrey M. Berry, "Who Will Get Caught in the IRS's Sights?," *Washington Post* November 21, 2004, p. B03.
[4]John Cochran, "Interest Groups Make Sure Lawmakers Know the 'Score,'" *CQ Weekly Report* April 19, 2003.
[5]Marjie Lundstrom, "Planned Parenthood Volunteers Seek to Be Election Force," *Sacramento Bee* July 17, 2004, p. A3.

coordinate group support for candidates. These workers help assure that volunteer efforts are especially effective. Christian Right groups have provided scores of volunteers to candidates who backed their policies.

Interest Group Money in Campaigns

A persistent worry about the role of groups in elections is that their campaign contributions might influence the decisions of government, and give them great advantages over groups that lack the funds to give. Much of this attention is focused on the role of business groups in financing campaigns because business profits constitute a potentially huge pool for possible contributions. Others worry that labor unions might use their many members and labor union dues as a powerful electoral resource. Since 1907, direct contributions from corporate treasuries to candidates for federal office have been banned. Subsequent reforms banned labor unions from giving to federal candidates and sought to limit the amount that wealthy individuals could give. These laws had significant loopholes and were poorly enforced.

In the early 1970s, Congress created a comprehensive series of regulations for the financing of federal campaigns. The 1974 comprehensive amendments to the Federal Election Campaign Act (FECA) provided partial public funding of presidential campaigns, required disclosure of all contributions of more than $200, and imposed a complicated array of limits on contributions and campaign spending. The Supreme Court subsequently struck down spending limits but upheld the power of the government to limit the size of contributions.

For interest groups, the most important parts of the law regarded political action committees (PACs). Labor unions pressured Democratic lawmakers to allow PACs in the FECA. For many years, the AFL-CIO Committee on Political Education (COPE) was the best-known PAC for its widespread contributions to supporters of labor. However, union leaders were afraid that litigation in the courts would put an end to labor PACs, because unions were forbidden to make direct contributions to federal candidates. In going to Congress, the AFL-CIO knew it was taking a risk because the legislation would have to treat business and labor equally if it was to stand a chance of passage. Labor leaders believed, however, that businesses would not form large numbers of PACs.[6] They were wrong. As Figure 5.1 demonstrates, the most significant growth in the number of PACs came from individual corporations. One observer notes that, "if the labor movement has suffered a worse self-inflicted political wound, it does not come readily to mind."[7]

After the FECA amendments of 1974 were passed, the Sun Oil Company went to the Federal Election Commission, which administers the FECA, and asked for a ruling concerning the administration of its PAC. The Federal Election Commission further

---

[6]Edward M. Epstein, "Business and Labor Under the Federal Election Campaign Act of 1971," in *Parties, Interest Groups, and Campaign Finance,* ed. Michael J. Malbin (Washington, DC: American Enterprise Institute, 1980), 112–13.
[7]Mark Green, "Political PAC-Man," *New Republic* December 13, 1982, p. 24.

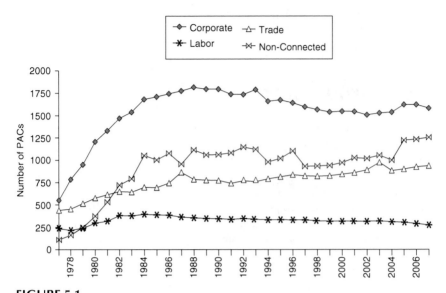

FIGURE 5.1
Number of PACS by Type.
Source: "FEC Releases Semi-Annual Federal PAC Count," Federal Election Commission, July 10, 2007, p. 2.

broadened the opportunity for active corporate participation in the electoral process by declaring that corporate PACs could solicit money from both stockholders and employees and that general corporate funds could be used to administer and solicit donations.[8] With the amended act and the commission's broad interpretation, the floodgates were opened.

The law allowed groups to form PACs and to raise up to $5,000 from group members and, in the case of unions and corporations, from employees and shareholders. PACs could give up to $5,000 to any candidate for federal office in any election (where primary, general, and runoff elections count separately), up to $5,000 to other PACs, and up to $15,000 to political parties. The individual members of PACs (along with all other citizens) could give up to $1,000 to federal candidates in each election, up to $20,000 to political parties, and $25,000 combined to all committees in any year. These latter limits have been increased by BCRA, as discussed below.

Because members of PACs can give to candidates along with PACs, a handful of PACs "bundle" contributions to a specific candidate and then send them on to him or her. A spokesman for the Council for a Livable World, which uses this tactic extensively, explains, "We'll send a letter to contributors, saying please send [us] a check to 'Joe

---

[8]Epstein, "Business and Labor Under the FECA," 113. Amendments to the FECA in 1976 restricted solicitations to stockholders and corporate management. Also included in the 1976 law was a nonproliferation clause. Its purpose is to prevent an organization from getting around the contribution limit by utilizing multiple committees.

Smith's' campaign for Congress. One hundred percent of that money goes directly to the candidate." The advantage to PACs is that, since the checks are made out to the candidate and never pass through a PAC's account, the total is not subject to the $5,000 gift limit. Thus, a PAC can send on a bundle of checks that total a considerable amount and earn the deep gratitude of the candidate. EMILY's List, a nonconnected PAC that supports pro-choice Democratic women candidates, has been particularly successful in bundling contributions. The group claims that it channeled more than $10 million in contributions in the 2004 campaign. Members must send $100 to the organization itself and pledge to contribute a minimum of $100 to at least two Democratic women backed by EMILY's List.[9]

Groups can also make noncash, in-kind contributions. For example, the National Committee for an Effective Congress (NCEC) puts the bulk of its money available to candidates into its Campaign Services Program.[10] Using its expertise and taking advantage of economies of scale, it provides liberal congressional candidates with services that would be more difficult or more expensive for the campaigns to purchase on their own. One such form of assistance is NCEC's precinct-targeting effort, which uses sophisticated computer technology and know-how to isolate precincts that, for example, contain high percentages of split-ticket voters. "We have a greater impact on a campaign by doing this [kind of thing]," says one NCEC staffer. In the 1980s the American Medical Association (AMA) conducted a number of polls for candidates early in the campaign, and other groups provided services instead of cash. In many cases, in-kind contributions are far more valuable to a campaign than cash.

In addition to contributions, PACs can also devise their own independent advertising campaigns for or against candidates. The allows PACs (and individuals) to spend unlimited amounts of money to advocate the election or defeat of a candidate, as long as they did not coordinate this with the campaign. In this case, the PAC would create and run an ad on radio, television, or the Internet. The Supreme Court ruled that independent expenditures are free speech and do not count as contributions if they are not coordinated with the campaign. Most PACs do not engage in independent expenditures, but some groups, such as the National Rifle Association and the American Medical Association, have mounted large, independent expenditure campaigns. In 2006, the League of Conservation Voters made more than $1 million in independent expenditures, mostly in races against candidates that the group had tagged the "Dirty Dozen" for their past votes on environmental legislation.

In the 1990s, federal courts ruled that advertisements that did not use a set of specific words (such as "vote for" or "defeat") were not campaign spending and, therefore, were not regulated under the FECA. Quickly, many groups moved to form 527 committees to run "issue advocacy" campaigns that were transparently aimed at influencing elections but that did not use the words listed by the courts. These committees are named after a section of the tax code that regulated the behavior of nonprofit corporations. 527 committees had several advantages over PACs. They did not have to disclose the identity of their donors, and they could raise their money in very large contributions from a few

---

[9]Chris Cillizza, "Emily's List Celebrates Clout As It Turns 20," *Washington Post* October 18, 2005, p. A13.
[10]See Paul S. Herrnson, "The National Committee for an Effective Congress: Liberalism, Partisanship, and Electoral Innovation," in *Risky Business?*, 39–55.

donors. In some cases, groups have mounted multimillion-dollar issue advocacy campaigns funded by a single donor through 527 committees. Existing interest groups could create special 527 committees that could spend treasury funds on these "issue advocacy" campaigns. The only disadvantage was that the advertisements could not officially call for the election or defeat of a candidate. In practice, however, this was not a major barrier. The "Swift Boat Veterans for Truth" aired issue ads against John Kerry, and one ended with the following: "He dishonored his country and, more importantly, the veterans he served with. He sold them out." Although the ad did not urge a vote against Kerry, its purpose was clear.

In 2002, Congress passed the Bipartisan Campaign Reform Act (BCRA), which banned soft-money contributions and regulated issue advocacy campaigns. The law defined electioneering as any advertisement on television or radio within sixty days of the general election or thirty days of a primary, and it required that such ads be paid for by "hard money"—that is, by small contributions like those raised by PACs. This means that 527 committees can spend unlimited amounts in issue advocacy before the "window" of the campaign on mass communications advertising. They can spend unlimited amounts during the campaign on direct mail, telephone mobilization, Internet, and door-to-door solicitations as well, throughout the campaign.[11] For some groups, this means spending large sums on television advertising early in the campaign, then mounting voter mobilization efforts after the election window.

In 2007, the U.S. Supreme Court ruled that BCRA's restriction on issue ads in the campaign window was too restrictive, but did not explicitly overturn the BCRA provision. The precise limits on issue advocacy for the 2008 campaign are thus ambiguous, but it is clear that 527 groups (among others) will air many issue ads during the campaign.

BCRA also increased the individual contribution limits to candidates from $1,000 to $2,000 and increased this limit to inflation, but did not increase the amount that individuals can give to PACs or that PACs can give to candidates. Thus in 2008, individuals can give $2,300 to a candidate, and still only $5,000 to a PAC. In a different law passed the same year, Congress required that the donors to 527 committees be disclosed, but this requirement did not apply to committees organized under other sections of the tax code, and some interest groups began to solicit large donations from patrons who preferred to be anonymous for other types of committees.

PAC Contributions

The major way that many political groups are active in campaigns is through PAC contributions to candidates. PACs today are a major, but not dominant, source of campaign funds in federal elections. In 2004, PACs provided 24 percent of all money raised by House and Senate candidates, a figure that has been largely unchanged for more than a decade.[12] PAC contributions represent a much higher portion of receipts for House

---

[11]Michael M. Franz, Joel Rivlin, and Kenneth Goldstein, "Much More of the Same: Television Advertising Pre- and Post-BCRA," in *The Election After Reform: Money, Politics, and the Bipartisan Campaign Reform Act*, ed. Michael J. Malbin (Lanham, MD: Rowman & Littlefield, 2006).

[12]http://www.fec.gov/press/press2005/20050609candidate/20050609candidate.html (accessed January 27, 2005).

candidates (32 percent) than for the U.S. Senate (13 percent) because Senate candidates have higher name recognition and run statewide and even national fundraising efforts, attracting large sums of individual contributions.

Although Figure 5.1 showed that the number of PACs has remained steady for some time, Figure 5.2 shows that the total contributed by PACs to federal candidates has risen steadily. In 1984, PACs gave $105 million to federal candidates; in 1994, they gave $189.6 million; and, in 2004, they gave $310.5 million. In 2006 the total increased to nearly $350 million. The fact that the total amount of PAC contributions has risen sharply, but the percentage of money that candidates raise from PACs has remained steady, showed that campaigns now raise more money from all sources than previously. Most PACs are small and give only modest amounts to political candidates, but some are very large and give to candidates in almost all states and districts. Indeed, of all the PACs registered with the Federal Election Commission during the 2004 election cycle, a majority (51 percent) of PACs contributed a total of $5,000 or less to candidates, while forty-eight separate PACs gave more than $1 million each.[13] Table 5.1 shows the largest PACs in the 2006 election cycle.

Aggregate funding levels vary considerably among the different categories of PACs. During 2005 and 2006, corporations gave $136.0 million to all federal candidates running for office; labor unions, $55.8 million; the "nonconnected" category (which includes ideological citizen groups), $70.2 million; and trade, membership, and health

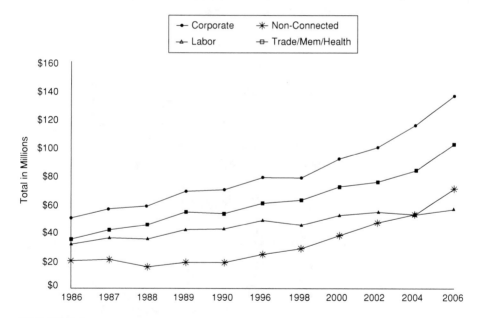

FIGURE 5.2
PAC Contributions to Candidates by PAC Type.
Source: Federal Election Commission.

---

[13]Mark J. Rozell, Clyde Wilcox, and David Madland, *Interest Groups in American Campaigns. The New Face of Electioneering*, 2nd ed. (Washington, DC: CQ Press, 2006), 141.

organizations, $101.8 million. This latter category includes many business trade association PACs, such as the National Association of Home Builders, as well as numerous professional association PACs, such as the American Optometric Association.[14] In the past decade, corporate PAC contributions have increased by 73 percent; labor PACs by 16 percent; nonconnected PACs by 192 percent; and trade, membership, and health PACs by 69 percent. Figure 5.2 shows the total contributions by PACs from 1980 through 2006.

These figures understate the impact of interest group contributions in two important ways. First, many interest groups not only contribute money from their PAC but also through individual contributions from their members. Coordinated giving need not be done through bundling. A corporate PAC can give a $5,000 contribution and present it at a campaign dinner where many company executives and their spouses have each contributed $2,300 apiece. In this way, the PAC contribution might show up as $5,000 but the total given by the company might be far higher. Corporate lobbyists also frequently host fundraising events, inviting their associates, contractors, and others to contribute to the candidate. These events might raise $100,000 or more and, although the money comes from many sources, the lobbyist who set up the event will claim credit for the funds.

Second, candidates do not only take PAC contributions for their campaigns. Many current and potential party leaders also form their own leadership PACs, which can receive $5,000 from other PACs and then give it to candidates to help further their political goals. In 2006, the *Washington Post* reported that officials and lobbyists for one

TABLE 5.1
Top Ten PACs, 2005–2006.

Contributions to Candidates for Federal Office	
National Association of Relators PAC	$3,756,005
National Beer Wholesalers Association PAC	$2,946,500
Build PAC of the National Association of Home Builders	$2,896,500
Dealers Election Action Committee of the National Association of Automotive Dealers	$2,821,600
International Brotherhood of Electrical Workers Committee on Political Education	$2,784,625
American Bankers Association PAC (BankPAC)	$2,642,564
American Association for Justice PAC	$2,558,000
Credit Union Legislative Action Council of Credit Union National Association	$2,391,318
Laborers' Political League-Labourers' International Union of North America	$2,317,500
Engineers Political Education Committee (EPEC)/International Union of Operating Engineers	$2,271,980

Source: http://www.fec.gove/press/press2007/20071009pac/top50paccontrib2006.pdf (accessed July 3, 2007).

---

[14]The Federal Election Commission's six categories are hardly a model of clarity, and the trade, membership, and health grouping is especially troublesome. It throws together such organizations as the American Bankers Association, the National Rifle Association, and the National Association of Retired Federal Employees.

California company helped raise at least $85,000 for Representative John Doolittle (R-CA) for his campaign and leadership PAC over a four-year period.[15]

At the simplest level, the huge sums of money that PACs contribute reflect the desire of interest groups to gain access to policymakers. As one corporate PAC director put it, "My job is to get access so I can get my information in there." Groups also participate because they see themselves as competing with other interest groups. They are afraid of being at a disadvantage if they do not give. This striving to be heard extends beyond the natural antagonism between business and labor and between ideological groups of the left and the right. Interest groups fear being lost in the shuffle among all the thousands of groups. Contributing money is seen as an important advantage in getting policymakers to pay attention to *their* problems rather than someone else's. One businessman defended his company's PAC with this simple logic: "Talking to politicians is fine, but with a little money they hear you better."[16]

One reason that PACs give so much is that candidates ask them to. As campaign costs have risen, candidates have become increasingly focused on fundraising, and they frequently imply to PACs that, if they want to have access to government, they must make contributions. Incumbent lawmakers of both parties hold fundraising events prior to "markup" sessions, when they will make decisions on the content of bills. Many companies and other groups feel that they have no choice but to give, if they later wish to be able to talk to policymakers. A survey of PAC managers more than a decade ago revealed that 84 percent said that incumbents pressured them for a contribution at least occasionally.[17] It is likely that this perception has grown since.

Members of the House and Senate constantly troll for contributions—they are like fishermen who never leave the lake. It is not surprising that incumbents place a premium on raising campaign money from all sources. "Their lives and jobs depend on it," said one PAC official. In the past decade, however, two changes have made this pressure by incumbents more troubling. First, Congress has increasingly targeted benefits to particular companies—changes in the tax code that can have a major effect on a company's profits, earmarked contracts to particular companies to provide services to the government, or special relief from costly regulations.

Earmarks are congressional directives to the bureaucracy to spend money on particular programs and products. The number of earmarks in the federal budget went from slightly more than 4,000 in 1994 to more than 14,000 a decade later, and jumped from $29 billion to more than $53 billion. Although some earmarks are for small, nonprofit groups who provide social services to disadvantaged groups, most are to significant interests in home states and districts. In many cases, these earmarks fund most or all of small companies' operations. Representative Jeff Flake (R-AZ) has referred to these earmarks as "the currency of corruption."[18]

---

[15]Jonathan Weisman and Charles Babcock, "K Street's New Ways Spawn More Pork," *Washington Post* January 27, 2006, p. A1.

[16]Green, "Political PAC-Man," 20.

[17]Dan Clawson, Alan Neustadtl, and Denise Scott, *Money Talks* (New York: Basic Books, 1992), 61.

[18]Jonathan Weisman and Charles R. Babcock, "K Street's New Ways Spawn More Pork: As Barriers with Lawmakers Fall, 'Earmarks' Grow," *Washington Post* January 27, 2006, p. A1.

In 2007, Congress adopted rules that were designed to make all earmarks transparent and allow Congress to strip them from bills, but in the early going the new rules appear to have had less effect than reformers had hoped.[19]

Second, members of Congress have increasingly pressured interest groups to contribute and to help them raise money if they want to be consulted as part of the policy process. Thus, corporate donors, in particular, feel an increasing pressure to give and see an increased opportunity to benefit directly from contributions. If a group is seeking an earmark that will provide a contract to its company or funding for its organization in some other way, it is difficult for it to refuse an invitation to contribute to those who help it.

PAC Decision Making

For all the millions of dollars that are collectively given by the PACs, donations are still doled out in small increments, from a few hundred dollars to $5,000. For each PAC, large or small, decisions must be reached on whom to give to and how much they should receive. Nearly all PACs are asked to give more money than they have available. The decisions that groups make reflect their own needs and judgments, as well as the judgments of the broader political community in Washington.

PAC contribution strategies are often described as access-oriented or ideological, although many PACs pursue a mix of both strategies. Access strategies are pursued by many corporations and trade associations; they are aimed at ensuring that the lobbyist can meet with policymakers when key decisions are made. This means giving to key party leaders or committee chairs, to representatives from the district where a business might be located, and to others who might advocate for the company. Often access-oriented PACs give to incumbents who are running unopposed and who have substantial campaign funds sitting in bank accounts because their contribution is basically a lobbying strategy, not an attempt to influence an election. In 2004, more than 800 PACs gave only to incumbent candidates.

Committee chairs and party leaders are in an especially good position to receive campaign donations from access-oriented PACs because of their crucial role in the legislative process. They can often determine whether a bill or an amendment will even be considered. Members on committees with well-endowed interest group constituencies are similarly blessed. The House Ways and Means Committee, for example, is a magnet for PAC money because it has jurisdiction over tax legislation. In 2004, Representative Bill Thomas (R-CA), chair of the House Ways and Means Committee, received more than $1 million in contributions from business PACs and more than $400,000 from individuals who were mostly business executives. Thomas ran unopposed for reelection.[20] After the Democrats recaptured control of Congress, PAC money flowed to Representative Charles Rangel (D-NY) who became the new committee chair, and who also faced no real reelection pressure in 2008. Other committees enable members to solicit more

---

[19]Robert Pear, "Select Hospitals Reap a Windfall Under Child Bill," *New York Times,* August 12, 2007; http://www.nytimes.com/2007/08/12/washington/12health.html?er=1190174400&en=5163ec5dc5f447c5 &ei=5070. (accessed September 17, 2007).

[20]Data from the Center for Responsive Politics, query of online database.

specialized constituencies. Those who serve on the Senate Defense Committee, for example, raise substantial sums from defense contractors, while those who serve on the Agriculture Committee raise large sums from agribusiness.

Ideological PACs, in contrast, try to influence the composition of Congress. These PACs try to concentrate their contributions to candidates who are in close races, where the contribution might help tip the balance. Labor unions and citizen groups frequently pursue ideological strategies. EMILY's List, for example, gives to candidates who meet four criteria: they are female, Democratic, pro-choice, and able to run a competitive election. Many candidates who meet the first three criteria have sought an endorsement from EMILY's List, only to leave disappointed. Labor unions channel more funds to close elections, and in years when Democrats are likely to gain seats they support more challengers, and in years when the Republicans are likely to pick up seats unions give more to vulnerable Democratic incumbents. Citizen groups frequently give to challengers and open-seat candidates. In 2004, approximately one in five PACs gave at least half of their contributions to nonincumbents. Candidates who take strong ideological stands on issues are in the best position to raise money from ideological PACs.

Sometimes the needs for access clash with the basic ideology of the organization. In the 1980s and early 1990s, business PACs that preferred Republican economic policies faced a Congress in which key decisions were made by Democrats. Democratic party leaders made it clear to business leaders that they expected them to contribute to candidates if they wished access to policymakers. As a consequence, corporate PACs divided their contributions evenly between Republicans and Democrats in 1992. Their preference for Republicans was evident in their giving to nonincumbents—more than two-thirds of all corporate PAC contributions to nonincumbents in 1992 went to Republicans, and a majority of their contributions to Democrats went to those who did not face serious challenges.

Early in the 1993–1994 election cycle, Republican leaders began to tell corporate leaders that they had a chance to win control of Congress. However, corporate and trade PACs did not increase their giving to Republican candidates, preferring to play it safe and give to incumbents of both parties. After the election, access-oriented PACs quickly reallocated their contributions to favor the new majority party. This change was facilitated by Republican leaders. New House Majority Whip Tom DeLay wrote to PACs that had supported losing incumbent Democrats, citing the specific amount given and noting his "surprise" at the contributions. He then noted that the PAC had "the opportunity to work toward a positive future relationship" with the GOP.[21] With Republicans constituting a majority of incumbents, corporate and trade PAC ideology meshed with their strategy of supporting incumbents to gain access.

Corporate PACs increased their contributions to Republicans from 50 percent of their total in 1992 to 73 percent in 1996. Trade, membership, and health PACs increased their GOP contributions from 42 percent of all contributions in 1992 to 65 percent in 1996. After the Democrats regained control of Congress in 2006, business and trade

---

[21]Richard Berke, "GOP Seeks Foe's Donors, and Baldly," *New York Times* June 17, 1995.

PACs gave more to Democrats in 2007 than to the GOP. It is uncertain whether this pattern will continue through the 2008 elections, but unless Republicans appear to have a real chance to regain control of the legislature, it is likely that business will continue to play it safe by giving to senior Democrats.

Because most PACs have neither the resources nor the incentives to assess new candidates thoroughly or closely analyze the competitiveness of all the House and Senate contests, they must rely on other organizations when they need additional information. The two most important channels through which PACs acquire campaign and candidate information are the congressional committees of the two national parties and a small group of large and well-respected PACs. The Republican National Committee and the Democratic National Committee have PAC liaison staffers who work with the congressional campaign committees to help sympathetic PACs direct their money where the party most needs it. These staff help nonincumbent candidates prepare to meet the Washington PAC community. Party leaders sometimes host PAC fundraisers for challengers and open-seat candidates, so that even access-oriented PACs attend in order to gain more favor with the party leader.

The second source of information and direction for PAC managers are "lead PACs." The Business-Industry Political Action Committee (BIPAC) is highly respected among Washington lobbyists for trade groups and corporations, and a contribution from BIPAC signals to other business leaders that the candidate is pro-business. The AFL-CIO's Committee on Political Education works to guide the donations of labor PACs. The organization prepares a "marginal list" to identify labor sympathizers who are in relatively close races. This, in turn, generates substantial sums in donations by PACs who follow COPE's advice.[22] A contribution from EMILY's List helps signal that a candidate is running a good campaign. PAC directors and political activists exchange information in formal and informal meetings, so information from EMILY's List might guide decisions by the Sierra Club, even though abortion rights is not part of the latter's agenda. Sometimes a PAC director or lobbyist will help raise money for challengers, introducing them to the Washington PAC community. One bank lobbyist said it was common for him to get calls from trade associations and PACs saying, "We have a candidate. Come meet him."

Many smaller PACs have a single director who makes most allocation decisions, sometimes with advice from a board of directors. These PACs may have a list of candidates to whom they routinely give and, in some elections, have money for one or two discretionary contributions that are made by the director. Other PACs make many contributions and have adopted formal rules for the decision to contribute, as well as a separate set of rules for the decision of how much to give. The National Rifle Association rates incumbent votes on gun issues and assesses the closeness of the race.[23] The National Association of Realtors has changed its rules over time, allowing for input from local realtors,

---

[22]Clyde Wilcox, "Coping with Increasing Business Influence: The AFL-CIO's Committee on Political Education," in *Risky Business?*, 24–25.

[23]Kelly D. Patterson, "Political Firepower: The National Rifle Association," in *After the Revolution: PACs, Lobbies, and the Republican Congress*, ed. Robert Biersack, Paul S. Herrnson, and Clyde Wilcox (Boston: Allyn & Bacon, 1999).

as well as the national lobbying staff.[24] The Sierra Club allows local chapters to take the lead in asking for contributions to support candidates.[25]

Issue Advocacy and 527 Committees

Although PAC contributions remain the primary way that interest groups are active in campaigns, over the past decade issue advocacy has become an increasingly important avenue for interest group involvement in elections. Issue advocacy campaigns by 527 committees are driven in part by a combination of two factors. First, as the political parties have taken increasingly divergent positions on abortion, the environment, taxes, and other issues, groups and some wealthy patrons have become convinced that the party that controls government matters enormously. They are, therefore, willing to invest substantial sums of money and great political energy in affecting election outcomes.

Second, control of Congress has increasingly hinged on the outcome of a relatively narrow set of races. In January 2006, both political parties believed that the Democrats could become the majority party in November, and that the outcome of thirty-five House races and fewer than ten Senate contests would be decisive. However, large PACs cannot simply give all of their money to candidates in these races because of contribution limits. Similarly, control of the presidency has, in the past two elections, hinged on the outcome of a handful of battleground states, and in both 2000 and 2004 George W. Bush won by carrying a single state by a narrow margin.

With a lot at stake, interest groups have a strong incentive to channel their resources into the limited number of states and districts that are "in play" in any given election. Issue advocacy campaigns allow them to harness the financial resources of a few enthusiastic patrons and to concentrate their efforts where they might influence electoral outcomes. In the process, issue advocacy allows some groups to help define the debate and focus the campaign around their own issues. When unions engage in issue advocacy in a congressional election, it is likely that the public will be more aware of labor issues and that the candidates will be forced to address them.

Over the past several election cycles, the amount of spending by 527 committees has exploded. Groups such as "Swift Boat Veterans for Truth" were formed to help George W. Bush win the presidential election, but most of the 527 committees in 2004 sought to help Democrat John Kerry. Some of the 527 committees that were formed in 2004 were affiliated with existing PACs, but many were separate organizations formed by existing networks of political activists to perform specific functions. In all, eight 527 committees in 2004 spent more than $10 million apiece. Some of this went to issue advertisements in competitive states, some went to direct mail and telephone campaigns, and some was spent on door-to-door mobilization efforts to register voters and get them to the polls.

---

[24]Anne H. Bedlington, "The Realtors Political Action Committee: Covering All Contingencies," in *After the Revolution: PACs, Lobbies, and the Republican Congress,* ed. Robert Biersack, Paul S. Herrnson, and Clyde Wilcox (Boston: Allyn & Bacon, 1999).

[25]David Cantor, "The Sierra Club Political Committee," in *After the Revolution: PACs, Lobbies, and the Republican Congress,* ed. S. Robert Biersack, Paul S. Herrnson, and Clyde Wilcox (Boston: Allyn & Bacon, 1999).

Among the top 527 committees in 2004 was Americans Coming Together (ACT), which was financed primarily by businessman George Soros. ACT focused on identifying and mobilizing Democratic voters in key states. The group built lists of potential voters and contacted them through the mail, over the phone, and in person with volunteers and paid workers going door to door. The Media Fund, another 527 group, primarily developed and aired television and radio advertising in swing states. America Votes was an umbrella of various labor, environmental, and feminist groups that help coordinate liberal group activity. Voices for Working Families was formed by labor union activists.

The heavy Democratic advantage in 527 committees in 2004 may have been the result of several factors. First, George W. Bush raised record sums of contributions, primarily from business officials and professionals, so Republican activists may have believed that he had enough money to win, while Democrats felt motivated to help their candidate match Bush's spending. Second, Democrats benefited from a few big donors who pledged to help unseat the president: More than $40 million came from just two businessmen. Finally, however, the Republican party has sought in recent years to manage many campaign functions within the party, while the Democrats have allowed interest groups to perform those functions. Thus, the Republican party made voter mobilization phone calls and mounted significant mail campaigns, a service that labor unions and 527 committees performed for Democrats.

In 2006, with no presidential election to invigorate ideological donors and the FEC more aggressively enforcing BCRA's limits on 527s, these committees still spent nearly 120 million on congressional races. Fully 19 committees spent at least $1 million, although none matched the large efforts of the 2004 campaign. Meanwhile, political activity was being channeled into other organizational forms, including 501(c) groups and new taxable non-profit groups.[26]

Do Contributions Matter?

It is much easier to document the amount of money being contributed than to account for its influence. We have no way of knowing for sure whether any group's contribution made a difference in an election. Likewise, interpreting the influence of money on votes in Congress is always a matter of inference.

Elections

Although no one doubts that money matters in elections, political scientists disagree about how much it matters, when it matters, and how it matters. The question is more complex than it initially seems, because good candidates both attract contributions and win votes. Also, many contributions come to candidates *because* they are going to win, not to help them win.

---

[26]For an excellent overview, see Stephen R. Weissman and Kara D. Ryan, "Soft Money in the 2006 Election and the Outlook for 2008: The Changing Nonprofits Landscape." Report prepared for the Campaign Finance Institute. (accessed September 13, 2007)

It is widely accepted that money is especially important at the start of the campaign for challengers and open-seat candidates, who must spend large sums to introduce themselves to the voters. Challengers who raise only limited funds are unknown to the voters on election day and have no chance of winning. For this reason, some citizen groups focus especially on giving money early in the election cycle to challengers because this "seed money" helped with later fundraising. Indeed, EMILY's List is an acronym for "early money is like yeast," suggesting that early money helps candidates raise even more "dough" later.[27]

Studies differ in how much money helps candidates in the heat of the general election campaign. Some studies suggest that contributions to challengers matter more than how much the incumbent raises, but other studies suggest that, in competitive elections, spending helps both challengers and incumbents equally.[28] At a minimum, challengers and open-seat candidates benefit greatly from additional fundraising, and incumbents benefit some and perhaps greatly if they are involved in close elections. Thus, PAC contributions do influence the outcome of elections, and the impact of interest group contributions is even greater when the total amounts given by members of the group are added in.

Although money given to challengers probably has a greater effect on their chance of winning an election, the largest share of PAC money goes to incumbents. Among all candidates seeking a House or Senate seat during the 2005–2006 period, PACs gave $279.3 million to congressional incumbents, $36.3 million to challengers of incumbents, and $32.3 million to those fighting for an open seat. Some of the incumbency advantage in PAC fundraising is because access to incumbents helps lobbyists make their case, but access to challengers does not. In addition, most incumbents win reelection, and, in fact, most do not face a serious challenge. Thus, there are few challengers who stand a chance of winning, and to whom it would make sense for a PAC to contribute. House incumbents who run for reelection win more than 90 percent of the time, and Senate incumbents win between 60 percent and 90 percent of the time. As previously noted, in most elections, there are at most thirty-five competitive House races, usually far fewer. In the Senate, there are often a handful of competitive races, and seldom more than ten.

The propensity of PACs to back incumbents has increased over time. Figure 5.3 shows the percentage of contributions to incumbents by corporate; labor; and trade, membership, and health PACs from 1978 to 2006. Over this period, incumbents' share of PAC contributions increased from less than 60 percent to 80 percent, while the share going to challengers dropped from over 20 percent to just 7 percent in 2004. In 2006,

---

[27]For evidence that this works, see Robert Biersack, Paul S. Herrnson, and Clyde Wilcox, "Seeds for Success: Early Money in Congressional Elections," *Legislative Studies Quarterly* 18 (1993): 535–52.

[28]Jacobson, *Money in Congressional Elections*, 53. On incumbent spending, see, *contra*, Donald P. Green and Jonathan S. Krasno, "Salvation for the Spendthrift Incumbent: Reestimating the Effects of Campaign Spending in House Elections," *American Journal of Political Science* 32 (November 1988): 884–907; and the rejoinder, Gary C. Jacobson, "The Effects of Campaign Spending in House Elections: New Evidence for Old Arguments," *American Journal of Political Science* 34 (May 1990): 334–62. For a recent argument that money helps incumbents and challengers equally in close races, see Robert S. Erikson and Thomas R. Palfrey, "Equilibria in Campaign Spending Games: Theory and Data," *American Political Science Review* 94 (September 2000): 595–609.

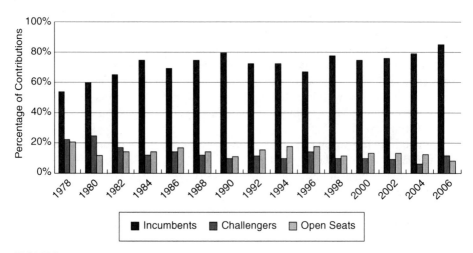

FIGURE 5.3
PAC Contributions by Type of Candidate.
Source: Federal Election Commission.

because many Democratic challengers ran competitive elections, PACs gave them more money, but even in 2006 challengers received only 10 percent of all PAC money. That is, the ratio of total contributions to incumbents and challengers changed from less than 3 to 1 in 1978 to 8 to 1 in 2006.

But the behavior of PACs can make the incumbent's victory a self-fulfilling prophecy. By contributing to incumbents and not challengers, PACs help increase the advantages that incumbents have in elections and deny challengers the means to get their message out. Potential challengers see how hard it is to raise money and take this into account when they decide whether or not to run for office. Moreover, as PACs direct money to incumbents, they help them amass formidable war chests, which incumbents hope will discourage active challengers from appearing in the first place.[29] Thus, most challengers face a double disadvantage—they find it hard to raise money from PACs, and they face incumbents who start the campaign with bank accounts bulging from PAC contributions.

Some nonincumbent candidates do raise substantial sums from PACs. Because there are limited numbers of competitive races in the House and Senate in any given year, those challengers and open-seat candidates who mount strong campaigns often can raise substantial sums. Seventy-one House nonincumbent candidates received more than $300,000 in PAC contributions in the 2006 election cycle, and eleven Senate non-incumbent candidates received more than $1 million apiece in PAC contributions in the

---

[29]Research has produced mixed results on whether incumbent war chests deter quality challengers. See Jay Goodliffe, "The Effect of War Chests on Challenger Entry in U.S. House Elections," *American Journal of Political Science*, 45, no. 4 (2001): 830–44; Johnathan S. Krasno and Donald Philip Green, "Preempting Quality Challengers in House Elections," *Journal of Politics*, 50, no. 4 (1998): 920–36; Johnathan S. Krasno, Donald Philip Green, and Johnathan A. Cowden, "The Dynamics of Campaign Fundraising in House Elections," *Journal of Politics* 56, no. 2 (1994): 459–74; and Janet Box-Steffensmeir, "A Dynamic Analysis of the Role of War Chests in Campaign Strategy," *American Journal of Political Science* 40 (1996): 352–71.

same period. Thus, most nonincumbent candidates raise little in the way of PAC contributions, but experienced candidates who are running in districts where their party has a chance of winning, perhaps against an incumbent tainted by scandal or other weakness or running in a year when their party is expected to make gains, often find that PACs seek them out to support their campaign.

In recent years, Republican lawmakers have redistributed some of these contributions, with safe incumbents contributing from their campaign committees to challengers and candidates in close races. GOP incumbents raise far more than they need for their campaigns, but then share the wealth with other candidates in the party.[30] Incumbents also contribute to political party organizations, which then spend money to help challengers and open-seat candidates. Democrats have followed suit, and asked their safest incumbents to contribute to the party committees from their personal PACs or campaign committees.

Because issue advocacy spending has only recently exploded onto the political scene, we know less about its impact on elections. In 2004, Democratic-leaning 527 committees claimed credit for a large increase in the total number of votes cast for the Democratic presidential candidate, but George W. Bush increased his vote totals even more. Today interest groups are doing systematic analyses of the impact of their spending, even conducting experiments in the best ways to mobilize and persuade voters.

Public Policy

The problem of interest groups and campaign finance is not new. Some PACs were active, of course, prior to the FECA amendments. More important, corporations and their broader industries were represented outside the PAC system by large, individual contributions from executives in various businesses. The oil industry did not have to wait for the FECA amendments to have a say on Capitol Hill. One turning point was the 1940 elections, when a young Texas congressman, Lyndon Johnson, aggressively sought out wealthy oilmen and channeled their money into the hands of his Democratic colleagues across the country.[31]

Nevertheless, PACs are now the instrument through which interest groups get their money to candidates. Does all the money they contribute influence public policy? There has been an enormous body of research on whether PAC contributions influence roll-call voting in legislation. There is a high correlation between which PACs contribute to a member and how that member votes on key legislation, and many journalists and citizen groups point to this correlation as proof that money buys votes.

The relationship between money and policy is more complicated than simple correlations can reveal. Consider the correlation between accepting contributions from tobacco companies and voting for legislation favorable to tobacco interests. It is possible that this correlation is because PAC money buys votes. It is also possible that tobacco company PACs give to members who have historically supported their cause and thus are rewarding them for past behavior, not seeking to bribe them for future behavior.

---

[30]Michael J. Malbin and Anne H. Bedlington, "Members of Congress Contributors." Presented at the annual meeting of the American Political Science Association, 2002.

[31]Robert Caro, *The Path to Power* (New York: Random House, 1982), especially 606–64.

And it is also likely that members of Congress who represent districts that grow tobacco will vote for these bills, regardless of PAC contributions. Thus, the correlation between contributions and roll-call voting does not prove that the contribution *causes* the vote.

Careful statistical analysis is needed to see if PAC contributions matter when other factors are held constant. After reviewing the available research, one scholar concluded, "Empirical evidence about the influence of PAC contributions on congressional voting is filled with ambiguity and apparent contradiction."[32] A number of studies show that PAC contributions do not seem to influence congressional voting decisions or influence them only in rather marginal ways.[33] Other studies suggest that PACs influence some votes on some bills.[34] In one recent study, Thomas Stratmann concluded that an extra $10,000 in contributions from banking PACs increased the chances that a member of the U.S. House would shift her vote on a piece of financial services legislation by 8 percent.[35] It is worth noting that most studies to date have focused only on PAC contributions and have not considered contributions by group members. Total contributions from individuals associated with an industry may well exceed those of PACs. In 2004, for example, the Center for Responsive Politics showed that the accounting industry contributed more than $5 million to federal candidates through PACs, and more than $9 million through contributions by accounting executives and employees. Thus, any study of the impact of PAC contributions on policy understates the importance of the interest group more broadly.

The most important impact of campaign money may not be on final votes on legislation. For many groups, what is important is what ends up in legislation that is likely to pass. Votes on defense appropriations may be influenced by party and constituency and presidential persuasion, but what special earmarks are actually *in* that legislation may be influenced by contributions. One study, for example, found that contributions had an effect on mobilizing sympathetic legislators to actively push the group's position in committee.[36] Another study of committee voting found that, by themselves, PAC contributions did little to influence policy decisions. However, PAC contributions facilitated access by lobbyists, and contact with lobbyists was linked to the way members of the committee acted on the legislation.[37] A more recent study showed that contributions helped interest groups gain access to Senators during the deliberations over the Medicare Modernization Act of 2003.[38] In all three of these carefully nuanced studies suggest that

---

[32]John R. Wright, "PACs, Contributions, and Roll Calls: An Organizational Perspective," *American Political Science Review* 79 (June 1985): 401.

[33]See, for example, Janet M. Grenzke, "PACs in the Congressional Supermarket: The Currency Is Complex," *American Journal of Political Science* 33 (February 1989): 1–24.

[34]Thomas Stratmann, "What Do Campaign Contributions Buy? Deciphering the Causal Effects of Money and Votes," *Southern Economics Journal* 57 (1991): 606–20.

[35]Stratmann, "Can Special Interests Buy Congressional Votes? Evidence from Financial Services Legislation" *Journal of Law and Economics* 45 (2002): 345–74.

[36]Richard L. Hall, "Buying Time: Moneyed Interests and the Mobilization of Bias in Congressional Committees," *American Political Science Review* 84 (September 1990): 797–820.

[37]John R. Wright, "Contributions, Lobbying, and Committee Voting in the U.S. House of Representatives," *American Political Science Review* 84 (June 1990): 417–38.

[38]Robert Hall and Robert Van Houweling, "Campaign Contributions and Lobbying on the Medicare Modernization Act of 2003." Presented at the annual meeting of the American Political Science Association, Philadelphia, September, 2006.

the real impact of PACs in terms of access and policy decisions comes at the committee level, rather than on the floor.

Campaign money may be especially important in relatively obscure provisions in bills that have a major impact for particular companies. In recent years, a number of companies have benefited from the rewriting of tax laws and regulations. Generally, there are no significant organized interests fighting *against* such changes, so a few or even a single legislator can sometimes succeed in changing the language. One survey of corporate lobbyists found that 90 percent described a tax loophole benefiting their company or industry as an example of an issue they had won.[39] Campaign contributions may also be especially useful in helping companies secure earmarked contracts—that is, appropriations by Congress that an agency can spend on a contract only with a particular company. Recall that lobbyists for a single company helped John Doolittle raise more than $85,000 over a four-year period. Doolittle inserted earmarked contracts to the same company in defense appropriations bills over the same period. It is unlikely that Doolittle's efforts were unrelated to these contributions.

Campaign contributions may also have a powerful negative effect by blocking consideration of legislation that might otherwise pass. It is far easier to block legislation in Congress than to pass it, and interest groups stand to gain much by preventing the passage of certain legislation. Thus, in 2004, the Senate leadership removed from a tax bill a measure that would have allowed the Food and Drug Administration to regulate tobacco. There was no roll-call vote on this decision; instead, senators voted on a broad tax bill without the provision. But the Republican leadership was very aware of the $2.7 million given to Republicans in the 2004 campaign by tobacco interests and made sure that senators in the party knew it as well.

Many constituency groups that do not make campaign contributions enjoy good access to their legislators, and a number of groups win earmarks that do not contribute to campaigns. Still, legislators do not have the time to work strenuously on behalf of all constituency groups that approach them (and with whom they agree). It seems inevitable that their choice of how to spend their time will be affected by PAC contributions. Legislators compound this problem not only by pressuring PACs to give a donation but also by asking lobbyists to raise funds for them. Members of Congress who ask lobbyists and PACs to help them are surely prepared to reciprocate. Senator Richard J. Durbin (IL-D) voiced concerns of senators in both parties during a debate on lobby reform in 2006: "Why is it that we warm up to all these lobbyists? It isn't for a meal. . . . We know when it comes time to finance our campaigns, we're going to be knocking on those same doors."[40]

The role of PACs in the campaign finance system is routinely defended by lobbyists as a means of providing them with access to those who make policy decisions. "The whole system is built on access," says one lobbyist. Some may argue that access cannot be divorced from influence because the policymaking process is not neatly divided into an access stage and a hermetically sealed policy formulation stage that excludes group

---

[39]Clawson et al., *Money Talks*, 95.
[40]Dana Milbank, "For Would-Be Lobbying Reformers, Money Habit Is Hard to Kick," *Washington Post* January 26, 2006, p. A6.

participation. If access had no value in influencing policy, why would it be so important for lobbies to possess it? When lobbyists were pressed and asked if access was really a form of influence, they were divided in their responses. Some rejected the idea that access was anything more than an opportunity to talk to legislators. The PAC director of a professional association said, "We just want our day in court. . . . Access is just a chance to say our piece." An official of a drug company PAC took offense at any notion that access is influence: "[Contributions] help your ability to have a dialogue with people but that does not mean that you are buying a vote."

Influence does not have to be thought of as crude vote buying, and some PAC officials have acknowledged that influence was, in fact, what they were after in making donations to members of Congress. The spokesperson for a health association PAC said bluntly, "Influence is an extension of access. Influence gives you a leg up on people who don't have it." An insurance company's PAC director defined his job as using contributions to gain influence: "The more influence that I have, the better the job I'm doing for my employers and customers."

In early 2006, a series of scandals led to guilty pleas by a member of Congress and a prominent lobbyist, and this led journalists and politicians to focus attention on the web of connections between lobbyists, PACs, and politicians. Among Democratic and Republican politicians alike, there was a sense that the system needed reform. In the summer of 2007 the Democratic Congress had passed some reforms of lobbying and earmarks, but it will take time to see what kind of impact these reforms have. Among the reforms include the requirement that lobbyists that bundle contributions to candidates disclose that activity, and that legislators make clear which earmarks they have sponsored.

Conclusion

Change in campaign finance law that came with the Federal Election Campaign Act Amendments of 1974 led to sharp growth in participation by interest groups in the electoral process. Since 1974, interest groups have formed PACs that raise money from individuals and contribute to candidates. PAC contributions are a mixed blessing at best. PACs give people a way to participate in the electoral system, and many provide their donors with information about issues and elections. They give people a tangible means of trying to influence the issues they care about most. PACs also put badly needed funds into the electoral system.

Unfortunately, PACs and interest groups more broadly have become caught up in a growing web of fundraising and policymaking. Groups believe that, without campaign contributions, their interests will not be heard as well in Congress. Policymakers solicit contributions with the implied threat that those who do not give will not be granted access. Lobbyists have become increasingly involved in helping coordinate fundraising for candidates, then approach those candidates for favors. Indeed, incumbent politicians have increasingly hired lobbyists to chair their personal PACs. Moreover, PACs give their money to incumbents in overwhelming margins, probably helping to make U.S. elections less competitive.

In recent years, the rise of 527 committees has changed the possibilities for interest groups in elections. Although most groups have not formed 527 committees, those who do are then able to spend unlimited amounts in a limited number of states or districts to try to mobilize and sway voters. The 527 committees are also a mixed blessing. It is likely that the concerted efforts of these groups helped increase voter turnout in the 2004 election, especially in swing states, but these committees have allowed fat-cat donors to give unlimited sums to politics, providing the possibility that a small number of organized groups can help swing election outcomes.

When some groups in a policy area begin to contribute, other groups may feel they have no choice but to organize a PAC to try to keep their opponents from gaining an advantage in Congress. The price for this "equal representation" of PACs is that, whatever policy actions Congress takes, large segments of the American people will believe that the "other side" bought the decision with their campaign contributions. Overall, the increased involvement of interest groups in elections has heightened concern about the role of interest groups in a democracy.

Chapter 6

Lobbyists

In 2006, in the minds of most Americans, the word *lobbyist* conjured up the image of someone like Jack Abramoff. Stories about the Abramoff scandal were prominent in the media in early 2006; the *Washington Post* mentioned Abramoff in fifty-three stories in February alone. These stories showed a lobbyist who collected huge sums from clients—in one case, perhaps over $1 million to arrange a meeting between the prime minister of Malaysia and President George W. Bush.[1] They depict a lobbyist who cheated his clients, who jetted off with lawmakers to golf excursions in Scotland and the Pacific Islands, and who admitted to conspiring to bribe public officials. The public did not think of Abramoff as unusual in any way; surveys showed that a large majority of Americans believed that lobbyists bribing lawmakers was common on Capitol Hill.[2] In July of 2007, Democratic lawmakers were mounting investigations of Abramoff's ties with GOP policymakers, assuring that he would remain the symbol of corrupt lobbying in the near future.

In fact, Abramoff is not a typical lobbyist. Paul Miller, president of the American League of Lobbyists, testified before a Senate Committee in late February of 2006, that "Mr. Abramoff is not the norm in our profession. He is truly the exception. . . . Effective lobbying is not about access or money, it's about forthright, ethical communications on issues . . . research and analysis of legislation or regulatory proposals, monitoring and reporting on developments, attending congressional or regulatory hearings, working with coalitions interested in the same issues, and educating . . . government officials and also employees and corporate officers on the implications of various changes."[3]

Most lobbyists follow ethical codes of conduct. They work long hours under trying conditions to represent their constituents before government. Some work for professional firms that represent many clients, while others work on the staff of a corporation, a labor union, or citizen groups. Some are deeply involved in fundraising for candidates; others represent small, nonprofit associations that give no more than an honorary wall plaque for their strongest supporters. All are unhappy with the public's disdain for their profession and wish that the public better understood their work.

---

[1]"Ex-Malaysian Leader Says He Paid Abramoff," http://www.washingtonpost.com/wp-dyn/content/article/2006/02/21/AR2006022100259.html. (accessed Feburary 26, 2006).

[2]"Americans Taking Abramoff, Alito, and Domestic Spying in Stride." Pew Research Center for the People & the Press, January 11, 2006.

[3]Testimony of Paul A. Miller, President of the American League of Lobbyists Before the United States Senate Committee on Homeland Security and Governmental Affairs on Lobbying Reform: Proposals and Issues Wednesday, January 25, 2006. http://www.alldc.org/pdf/millertestimony012506.pdf. (accessed February 26, 2006).

A Day in the Life of a Lobbyist

To appreciate and understand what lobbyists do, it is best to begin by simply asking how they spend their time. In interviews, a number of legislative lobbyists were asked to describe their "typical" day. The head lobbyist for a large midwestern corporation described her typical day in the late 1980s:

> We get the *Washington Post, New York Times, Wall Street Journal,* and the Bureau of National Affairs' *Tax Reporter,* so I read the tax-related articles in those papers. Then I go through my in-box. Then I might have meetings on the Hill. I make calls to Capitol Hill or to other lobbyists to obtain information, like current updates on legislation we're following. I might make final preparations on testimony that we're giving. . . . I might attend one or two meetings, either in-house or on the Hill or downtown with other lobbyists. This would be a coalition setup, where we share information, find out the current status of whatever we're interested in, or hand out materials or a document of some sort. . . . Then I might have a luncheon appointment with either another lobbyist or with someone from the Hill, which usually involves talking about jobs. Or someone wants to take me to lunch to give me a resumé. I might then attend a hearing on the Hill. I talk to people from Labor or Treasury on the telephone. Then I might do some correspondence. I might write a follow-up letter to someone I met with the day before or the week before. I talk to my company, which is based in Chicago. I give them updates on legislation or talk about testimony they're going to give here. Then I return phone calls and go back to my in-box. In the evening I attend fundraisers.

Although the essential job has not changed much over the past decades, technology has changed the way that job is done. One younger lobbyist for a firm that handles primarily corporate clients noted recently:

> On the technology front, a lot has changed since the "old days" of lobbying. The competition for getting information and sending information quicker than your opponent has become a huge focus. With the ability to use the Internet and on-line search engines, we spend a lot of time monitoring news coverage of committee priorities, industry websites, and other forms of information that are available on the web—and we even use advanced technology to search by specific policy issues and terms and then immediately (and before the client or staffer gets to work) send that relevant information, electronically.
>
> That said, the best way to really get information has been—and will continue to be—by talking to and visiting with key leadership and committee staff on both sides of the Congress. We work to make sure that our relationships and our policy knowledge is as deep and as wide as possible—so that we can inform our clients and help them make the best strategic decisions. Probably, the biggest advantage—in terms of new technology—has been the ability to use wireless technology during a debate or legislative mark-up—in real time. In other words, if points need to be added to a floor or committee debate as it is

happening, the ability to get those messages in a member or staff person's hands is a huge advantage. Again, however, without those relationships I referenced earlier, there is little chance that the staff or member you are trying to communicate with will even read the email.

What these accounts and others we have collected have in common is the premium that lobbyists place on collecting the latest information. Close attention is paid to all relevant sources of news. Lobbyists constantly check for voice, text, or e-mail messages, scan the Internet, and touch base with office colleagues to see if anything has happened since the last time the lobbyist was in the office. A good deal of the contact they initiate with government officials is of the "what's happening?" kind.

The emphasis on current information comes, in part, from the culture of Washington. One measure of status in Washington is the amount of inside information you have. To do the job well, a lobbyist must know what earmarks are being considered, which amendments are being drafted, if a key senator has met with the opposition, or if the administration is flexible on some provisions of the legislation. She must know whether the party leaders will insert something into legislation that comes out of conference, and how many members are undecided on a provision. Day-old information is as valuable to a lobbyist as day-old bread is to a bakery, and, increasingly, information that is a few hours old is dated. Developments in wireless technology allow lobbyists to update their information continually.

Contrary to the image of lobbyists as back-room operators, much of their time is taken up in trying to be visible. They spend valuable time at congressional hearings even though nothing of great consequence is likely to happen there—it is a chance to touch base with other lobbyists and congressional staffers. They will make repeated visits to different Capitol Hill offices, even if all they are likely to accomplish is leaving a message with a secretary that they had stopped by to see the administrative assistant. They will attend fundraising events in the evening, personally handing over a PAC contribution and using the opportunity to remind members or their aides whom they represent. Much of what a lobbyist does is to remind legislators, staffers, and other lobbyists that they represent a group whose views ought to be considered when policy decisions are being hammered out. This does not mean that lobbyists always claim credit for their victories—indeed one corporate lobbyist notes that "when I do my best for my company, there are no fingerprints on a bill."

Washington representatives also keep in touch with interest group allies of all sizes and types. The constant interaction is a means for exchanging information, but it also affords an opportunity to develop strategy, offer and receive moral support, and politely push the other group to do more. In recent years, coalitions have become more important in legislative action, and lobbyists have increasingly coordinated their efforts with others from other groups or firms.

Lobbyists differ, of course, in the way they carry out their job. In part, this may depend on the resources of the groups they represent. Public interest lobbyists are not as likely as their counterparts from large corporations to show up at congressional fundraisers, because they represent groups that may not have PACs. Some lobbyists are able to rely on letters written by their constituents to aid their efforts; others do not have large memberships on which to draw. Some lobbyists seek to attract media attention to their efforts; others work on issues far from the public eye.

These descriptions have dealt only with legislative lobbying. Trying to influence the content of a regulation involves considerably less time prowling the corridors than lobbying on Capitol Hill. There are various reasons for this: To begin with, an agency usually has fewer relevant offices to visit on forthcoming regulations. More important, though, the civil servants who do the lion's share of the work in drafting regulations can feel constricted in their relations with lobbyists. They may take the attitude that frequent meetings with industry representatives can compromise their neutrality. Ex parte rules prohibit private communications between group representatives and agency officials when a case involving the group is underway. At the same time, bureaucrats recognize that meetings with interest group representatives can help them learn what all the facts are. At some agencies, officials cannot do their jobs without data supplied to them by industry representatives.

For all lobbyists, the daily work is being the eyes and ears of their organizations. They must keep the members of their group abreast of policy developments and they must stand ready to provide information for the organization's newsletter, answer phone calls from members, and keep their superiors supplied with a steady stream of information. Lobbyists are the nerve endings of an interest group; they spend most of each day carrying messages back and forth between the political system and their organization.

Effective Lobbying

Lobbying is a difficult and sometimes frustrating occupation. The hours are long and the prestige rather low in a town of senators, ambassadors, and cabinet secretaries. The pressures can be great when a critical vote in Congress or an administrative decision approaches. Regardless of how hard lobbyists work, policy outcomes are often determined by factors out of their control.

The job is not without its satisfactions, however. It can be heady, exciting work. As with any other job, accomplishing what one sets out to do has its own inner rewards. Like any other job, lobbying has its own valued skills and professional norms. Lobbyists are convinced that effective lobbying is maximized by close adherence to following the "rules."

These unwritten rules of effective lobbying are, of course, general. Because they are so widely accepted and quickly grasped by any aspiring Washington representative, simply following them does not ensure success. Wide differences in the skill and perseverance of lobbyists remain as they try to become issue experts or facilitators of compromise. Furthermore, no matter how skilled lobbyists are, they are severely restricted in accomplishing their goals by the political popularity of their group's stand on issues and the strength of the group's constituency. As far as any one lobbyist can make a difference, adhering to these norms will help maximize his or her influence.

Credibility Comes First

When lobbyists are interviewed about a variety of subjects, no theme is repeated more frequently than their need to protect their credibility. "Washington is a village," said one labor lobbyist. "You are known by your good name and integrity." A lobbyist for a large corporation said that "my reputation is my most valuable asset. Members know they can trust what I tell them. If I ever misled a member, they would never trust me again. And the word would spread, so that no one else would trust me either."

Of course, lobbyists are expected to have a position and to argue one side of an issue. But no single issue is so important that a lobbyist is willing to destroy his or her reputation in order to win. One lobbyist for a trade association noted, "Sometimes I will even tell a member that I would love for him to support our position, but that the bill might have a negative impact on his district. Next time I meet with him, he will remember that I dealt with him honestly, and he will trust me when I say that this new bill will be a winner for him."

Only the Facts Count

Credibility is a precondition for getting a message heard, but it is not sufficient to exert influence. What makes a lobbyist's communications persuasive? Lobbyists are unequivocal about what makes an effective message—the more factual, the better. In memos, handouts, reports, formal comments on regulations, and conversations, the only content that counts is the specific fact. "You have to know how to separate the wheat from the chaff, facts from rhetoric," said a trade association lobbyist. When lobbyists have facts that are specific and useful to a policymaker, they are especially likely to gain that policymaker's ear.

It is of little value to a policymaker to hear platitudes about what is in the "public interest." They are already aware of the general pro-and-con arguments on an issue. If lobbyists are to do anything to influence members of Congress or administrators beyond the opinions they already hold, they must have something new to bring to their attention. One environmental lobbyist put it this way: "When I talk to members about clean air and water, they get impatient. Some of them, or their aides who deal with the environment, want to know specifically what the position of my group is on thresholds for particular pollutants, or how a particular standard might affect a factory in their district."

Lobbyists increase their effectiveness as they increase their knowledge of their policy area. Amid the deepening complexity of public policy problems, the lobbyist must become a determined and continuing student of these issues. Although the increasing technical complexity of issues makes lobbying a more difficult challenge, therein lies the opportunity. Lobbyists who have mastered the complexities of their policy area enter a select group of experts who speak the same language. Washington representatives with a high level of policy expertise are more valuable to those in government because policymakers can draw upon their knowledge in efforts to solve difficult issues.[4]

Try Not to Burn Your Bridges

Alliances can shift rapidly, or, as one trade association lobbyist put it, "You may be friends on one issue and enemies on the next." Lobbyists cannot afford the luxury of venting their anger toward policymakers who act contrary to their wishes. This is especially true of those who work for large lobby firms, which may have many clients

---

[4]Jeffrey Berry, *The New Liberalism* (Washington, DC: Brookings Institution Press, 1999), 119–52.

who would benefit from access to a lawmaker or regulator. Lobbyists may have reason to approach a senator or House member dozens of times over the course of a year, and an angry response to a particular vote might endanger their ability to have those later conversations.

In the past decade, however, some lobbyists who work exclusively for single interest groups have been more willing to try to punish lawmakers who do not support them on key issues. Labor unions have traditionally forgiven Democrats who voted against union positions on issues such as the North American Free Trade Agreement (NAFTA), but there is evidence that labor PACs punished Democrats who voted in 2000 in favor of the Permanent Normal Trade Relations (PNTR) that made permanent more liberalized trade relations with China.[5] Citizen groups, such as the National Rifle Association and National Organization for Women, frequently do not bother to lobby those who oppose their policies, preferring instead to try to replace them in the next election. Instead, they especially focus their lobbying on those who might be uncertain on a particular issue.

When citizen group lobbyists fail to follow the don't-burn-your-bridges rule, it is not always because they place an exalted premium on principle. It is true that some of them approach their work with a degree of moralism that makes it difficult for them to tolerate those who are unfaithful to the cause, yet it is more than a pious attitude that leads some public interest lobbyists to go out of their way to personalize issues. Frequently, they see it as a tactical advantage to identify a villain. The idea is to portray the issue at hand as a fight between good and evil; ridicule and vilification are useful for putting their opponents on the defensive.

Corporations have long tried to maintain access to lawmakers of both political parties, because Democrats frequently support laws that benefit companies in their states and districts, and Democrats sometimes have a majority in Congress and therefore are in charge of the agenda. But in the 1990s and early 2000s, many corporations and trade associations hired strongly Republican lobbyists as part of the K Street Project discussed in an earlier chapter. Many of these lobbyists never had connections to Democrats, and some made little effort to maintain friendly relations with moderate Republicans, either. Instead, they specialized in gaining access to Republican party leaders. When Democrats recaptured control of Congress in 2006, many lobby firms quickly sought out former Democratic staffers to hire to help repair relations with the new majority party, and many corporations shifted their accounts to Democratic-leaning lobby firms.

Although one Republican lobbyist said that the Democratic victories meant that it was time to "buy a fishing pole and take yoga classes," in fact GOP lobbyists still have many clients. Some are especially motivated to resist Democratic policies, but others just want to remain friendly with both parties. With the GOP in control of the White House and able to mount a filibuster in the Senate, it still pays to keep good relations.[6]

---

[5]David J. Jackson and Steven T. Engel, "Friends Don't Let Friends Vote for Free Trade: The Dynamics of the Labor PAC Punishment Strategy over PNTR," *Political Research Quarterly* 56 (2003): 442–48.

[6]Jeffrey Birnbaum, "Don't Cry for Republican Lobbyists," *Washington Post* November 13, 2006, p. D1.

Success = Compromise

It is often said that "politics is the art of compromise." If so, lobbyists must be fine artists. No interest group ever achieves all it wants, so the difference between success and failure is achieving an acceptable compromise. An integral part of a lobbyist's job is to aggressively seek out workable compromises that can satisfy all necessary parties. The task each day, says one business lobbyist, is to "go solution searching." Lobbyists must see themselves as a catalyst for compromise, finding and promoting policy changes that are going to get a bill or regulation through in acceptable form.

Lobbyists attempt to give up that which is least valuable to their group while persuading policymakers and other interest groups to agree to the higher priorities their group is pursuing. The skill that is involved is knowing how much to give up and just when to make those concessions. For Congress, that skill consists of determining which trade-offs or policy changes will attract votes from legislators who have strong reservations about the bill at hand. Lobbyists and their congressional allies look for sweeteners that will make the bill more attractive by adding or subtracting particular provisions. Sometimes compromises cannot be reached because one or more factions must give up too much to keep the result palatable for them, but the good lobbyist keeps searching for the middle ground.

Create a Dependency

The optimal role for a lobbyist to play is that of a trusted source of information whom policymakers can call on when they need hard-to-find data.[7] A reputation for credibility and high-quality factual information is a prerequisite for becoming a lobbyist from whom government officials request help. The final ingredient is developing the relationship gradually, with the lobbyist providing the right kind of information at the right time. "Maintain constant communication," says one public interest representative. "Churn out a lot of material at their request. Create a dependency."

Lobbyists in particular policy areas try to develop working relationships with the agency officials and congressional committee members and staffers who have responsibility for relevant programs. Over time, this familiarity gives lobbyists the advantage of repeated opportunities to interact with policymakers and to display their expertise. The best of all possible worlds for a lobbyist is to be respected by key policymakers who come to value them as a friend. This will maximize access for the lobbyist and, thus, give this person a competitive advantage over other lobbyists who are trying to bring information to the attention of the same official. With thousands of lobbyists in Washington competing for policymakers' attention, however, interest groups can hardly depend on personal relationships as the basis for influence.

Lobbyists have increasingly been able to use other resources to build personal relationships with legislators. The Center for Public Integrity reports that, from 1998 through 2006, lobbyists served as treasurers of seventy-nine lawmakers' campaign committees and leadership PACs. These leadership PACs not only provide lobbyists with a chance to do a favor for members but also allow them to set up fundraising events, such

---

[7]See John Mark Hansen, *Gaining Access* (Chicago: University of Chicago Press, 1991).

as golfing at resorts or fishing tournaments off the Florida Keys, where the lobbyists can mingle with policymakers.

Work with Whoever Will Help

Most lobbyists find that they must work together with other groups to accomplish their goals. Often, groups work together through official coalitions; at other times, they unofficially cooperate on issues. Many groups have logical partners with whom they collaborate regularly, such as pro-choice and feminist groups, or pro-life and Christian conservative groups. Many business interests cooperate on a set of policies. A coalition of the National Federation of Independent Businesses, the Business Roundtable, the U.S. Chambers of Commerce, the American Association of Health Plans, the Health Insurance Association of America, and other groups have regularly worked together to defeat legislation that would increase the government's power to regulate health insurance or consumers' power to sue insurance providers.[8]

Professional lobbyists think of cooperation in rational terms, and are usually willing to work with any group that agrees with them on an issue. Citizen groups sometimes have more difficulty in cooperating because they may see the other group as allied with the enemy and have low levels of trust. Pro-life and environmental groups have worked together to oppose cloning technology, although this has not always been easy. When the National Association of Evangelicals decided to be more active in environmental politics, they used the phrase "Creation care" to separate themselves from the more secular "environmentalist" groups, although they have cooperated in lobbying. However, even citizen groups representing different ideologies do cooperate on occasion, as when the Concerned Women for America (a Christian conservative group) and the National Organization of Women (a feminist group) have worked together to change policy on sexual trafficking.[9]

Lobbying as a Career

Lobbying is an unusual profession, and few of those who end up as professional lobbyists began with that as a career goal. There is no single career path that leads someone to become a professional lobbyist, and most lobbyists do not have specialized educational certificates.

Recruitment

If individuals do not set out to become lobbyists, how do they end up in such jobs? Generally, people become lobbyists because previous jobs lead them to it. Specific

---

[8]Amy Goldstein, "GOP Leaders Embrace Business Campaign to Defeat Health Care Measures," *Washington Post* November 5, 1997, p. A14.
[9]Kevin Hula, "Dolly Goes to Washington: Coalitions, Cloning, and Trust" in *The Interest Group Connection: Electioneering, Lobbying, and Policymaking in Washington*, ed. Paul S. Herrnson, Ronald G. Shaiko, and Clyde Wilcox (Washington, DC: CQ Press, 2004); for a description of evangelical environmental activism see www.creation care.org.

skills or areas of expertise are acquired, and soon opportunities present themselves or may even be pursued. A common route into lobbying is government work. Legislative aides frequently leave their positions to take lobbying jobs at significant increases in salary. In recent years, some have moved back and forth between jobs as lobbyists and as Hill staffers. When Susan Hirschmann, who was Chief of Staff to then House Majority Leader Tom DeLay, decided to leave Congress for lobbying, she actually hired an attorney to field her many job offers.

A similar pattern occurs in the bureaucracy. Richard E. Wiley is a managing partner of a communication law firm, and a former FCC chairman. The current FCC chairman is a former associate of the same firm. Not surprisingly, this firm was hired by Sirius to represent them in a large merger of satellite radio companies in 2007.

Members of Congress who retire or are defeated routinely increase their salaries by working at top lobbying firms as well, or as lobbyists for associations. Legislators can usually greatly increase their salaries by lobbying their former colleagues, with whom they have special access and expertise. Many former members of Congress now represent the pharmaceutical industry, including Billy Tauzin (R-LA), who heads the Pharmaceutical Research and Manufacturers Association, where he receives ten times his congressional salary. The drug industry employs many former House and Senate members and staffers—by one count, more than half of the 625 registered lobbyists for the industry are former government officials.[10] Larry Combest, former chair of the House Agriculture Committee, now heads a lobbying firm that was recently awarded a large contract from the American Sugar Alliance because he had helped engineer current agricultural subsidies legislation. Former Senate majority leader and presidential candidate Bob Dole lobbied unsuccessfully on behalf of a deal that would allow a Dubai-owned company to take over security operations of certain ports. Dole's wife, Elizabeth Dole, serves in the U.S. Senate. Officials in the executive branch also frequently become lobbyists when they leave public service.

There are other routes to lobbying besides government work. Some lobbyists start out doing substantive work for an organization or a firm and then move into lobbying as they acquire more expertise. A lobbyist for a computer manufacturer described his career ladder:

> My background is as a lawyer. I practiced in private firms in Washington for 16 years. Before I came [here] I was a partner in a large Washington firm. I started out as a lawyer [with this company] and I worked on intellectual property, copyright, and trade issues. When the government relations office moved I went with it and last year I became head of government affairs.

Whatever the route taken, the common denominators are *experience* and *expertise*. Experience does not require that someone work for decades before they start a career in lobbying. Generally, once someone reaches a position of responsibility, interest groups and lobbying firms begin to take notice. Expertise is usually acquired through the task specialization that comes from working in any organization, although academic training can provide the necessary background as well.

---

[10]Leslie Wayne and Melody Petersen, "A Muscular Lobby Rolls Up Its Sleeves," *New York Times* November 4, 2001, p. 1.

Some aggressively seek out lobbying positions instead of being recruited or falling into them. Most commonly, those who search for and avidly pursue such jobs are citizen activists. They are looking not so much for a job as a lobbyist as for a job that will allow them to work for a cause. The satisfaction derived by pursuing ideological goals makes jobs with citizen groups highly attractive. As an environmental lobbyist put it, "It doesn't give you a hell of a lot of money and it may not give you much prestige, but when you come home at the end of the day you feel good about your work." For the private sector lobbyist, the issues they will be lobbying on may not be the main attraction to the job.[11] It is not necessary to have a "moral commitment to that which you are lobbying for," said one oil company representative.

Despite the divergent career paths that lead into lobbying positions, the jobs themselves usually are filled by word of mouth. Although some jobs are advertised, organizations looking for an outside candidate rely heavily on personal recommendations from those they consult. "In D.C. in the job market, what's open is really off the record," noted a business lobbyist. In any issue network, most participants are already well known to each other. If a farm group loses one of its lobbyists, the director of the organization will naturally consider respected staffers on the agriculture committees in Congress and officials in the Department of Agriculture, whether those people are looking for new jobs or not. Intermediaries may put the director in touch with others who might fill the group's needs. One lobbyist described his recruitment as "one of those typical Washington stories. You know, where you know someone who knows someone."

Background

Although no precise route opens into the lobbying profession, three spawning grounds nurture most Washington representatives: government, law, and business. Because expertise and experience are the most important qualities in a lobbyist, it is easy to understand why these three backgrounds predominate. Service in government not only gives prospective lobbyists experience in the workings of Congress and agencies but also gives expertise on policy and contacts that may help open doors. Lawyers easily metamorphose into lobbyists because their education and experience make them familiar with the way statutes and regulations are written. A few years of work as an associate in a Washington law firm or in an agency's legal counsel office gives them added preparation. Business is also a common background because the majority of lobbyists represent either trade associations or individual corporations. The technical complexity of most public policy issues makes experience in one's industry a helpful credential.

One of the most serious ethical dilemmas involving interest group politics is circulation of people out of government and into lobbying. The issue is this: You are working for the government at the taxpayer's expense, developing expertise and experience that make you attractive to the private sector. When you leave government and parlay that background into a lobbying job, it is usually at a much higher salary and for a position designed to exploit your contacts in government. Moreover, if you plan on working as a lobbyist in the future, you may be tempted to do favors for your future employer while still in office.

---

[11]Lester Milbrath, *The Washington Lobbyists* (Chicago: Rand McNally, 1963), 109–14.

One top lobbyist first worked for Jerry Lewis (R-CA), who chaired important subcommittees in the House of Representatives. He left there in 1999 to work for a top Washington lobbying firm, where he made more than $1.5 million in 2004. When Lewis won a key committee chairmanship, he returned as a top committee staffer at $160,000, but his firm gave him a severance package of nearly $2 million and hired his wife as a consultant lobbyist. Presumably, he will be even more valuable to lobbying firms when he leaves his current post.[12] In the meantime, he will deal with the same lobbyists who once paid his salary and now pay his wife's salary.

Top officials in the Clinton and George W. Bush administrations have either joined top firms with lucrative salaries or started their own companies. Soon after he left his post as attorney general for President Bush, John Ashcroft opened a firm called the Ashcroft Group, a firm that received more than $260,000 in lobbying contracts in the first quarter of 2005 alone, not including funds received for other services, such as strategic planning. The problem of "in and outers" is especially common and problematic in the Department of Defense, where many officials who work on weapons procurement issues leave to take jobs in companies that sell these products to the government or in consulting firms that help companies win these contracts.

Rules govern lobbying by those who have recently left government. These rules are complicated and generally ineffective. When he took office, President Clinton imposed rules that prohibited former administration appointees from lobbying their former agencies for five years after they left their posts, but he lifted this ban in December of 2000 after George W. Bush won the presidency. Even when the ban was in effect, however, several top Clinton aides became lobbyists soon after leaving the administration. Executive branch personnel generally are banned from lobbying their agency for a year—in some cases, this includes the White House. But this does not prevent them from working with other lobbyists who do contact their former employers or from offering advice to clients. New lobby reforms passed by Congress in 2007 ban top House and Senate staff from lobbying anyone in Congress for one year, put a two-year moratorium for House and Senate members, and required that any member of Congress disclose all job negotiations that take place while they are in office. In 2007, Republican Senator Trent Lott resigned from office so that he could begin his lobby career before these new rules went into effect.

There are frequent calls to establish more restrictive rules on former government employees. The counterweight to such arguments is the freedom of individuals to pursue the kinds of jobs they want and the fear that tightening such restrictions will deter good people from joining government in the first place. Many smart, hardworking citizens may be willing to work for government for relatively low pay for several years, but they might be less likely to do so if they were barred for several years from using their skills to earn more.

Lobbyists are impressive in their educational backgrounds, commonly holding advanced degrees beyond the bachelor's. The most popular advanced degree is in law, but assorted master's degrees in fields such as economics, business, and political science are

---

[12]Timothy J. Burger, "The Lobbying Game: Why the Revolving Door Won't Close," *Time Magazine Online Edition* February 16, 2006. http://www.time.com/time/nation/article/0,8599,1160453,00.html (accessed Feburary 28, 2006).

often found, too. The relatively high educational level that characterizes the lobbying profession has to do with the requirements of the jobs that frequently precede work as an interest group representative. Beyond the earlier need to advance in business, law, government, or other fields, lobbyists find their advanced educations useful, if not essential, to their interest group work.[13] Again, the technical nature of many public policy areas and the need to understand administrative law and other arcane legal matters make academic credentials highly valuable to a lobbyist.[14]

Traditionally, lobbying has been a "man's world." A survey conducted in the early 1980s found that only 22 percent of all lobbyists were women.[15] Today, men dominate the ranks of top lobbyists, although a number of women have established substantial reputations. In April of 2005, *The Hill* newspaper ranked the top lobbyists for citizen groups, associations, and lobbying firms. Women constituted fewer than 10 percent of the lobbying elite.[16] It is likely that these numbers will change as women move into corporate boardrooms in larger numbers and assume positions of power on Capitol Hill.

Although women are not yet heavily represented in the lobbying elite, Jeffrey Birnbaum reported in early 2006 that "women-owned firms are proliferating, and a few are, at least for now, all female."[17] He lists Tarplin, Downs, & Young as an all-female, Republican healthcare lobbying firm, run by Linda E. Tarplin, who is one of Washington's top healthcare lobbyists. Neuva Vista Group is owned by three Democratic women partners who each have young children, and have set their schedules to accommodate childcare issues. Yet Birnbaum notes that women still have a long way to go to achieve equality, and quotes Patricia Griffin (a partner in Neuva Vista), who says, "You're often still the only woman in the room, or one of only two or three. The culture is very aggressive and white-male-oriented."

In the summer of 2007, the *Washingtonian Magazine* published its list of the top fifty Washington lobbyists. Few of those on the list have been lifetime lobbyists. On the list were twelve former members of Congress, and two relatives of longtime members. Nearly all of the rest had served in government in some capacity, usually as aides to members of Congress, but often in the bureaucracy.[18] Of the top fifty, only five were women.

---

[13]John P. Heinz, Edward O. Laumann, Robert L. Nelson, and Robert H. Salisbury, *The Hollow Core* (Cambridge, MA: Harvard University Press, 1993), 147.

[14]The ability and credentials of contemporary lobbyists contrast with the opposite pattern found in one major study of the 1950s. See Raymond A. Bauer, Ithiel de Sola Pool, and Lewis Anthony Dexter, *American Business and Public Policy* (New York: Atherton, 1963), 345.

[15]Kay Lehman Schlozman, "Representing Women in Washington: Sisterhood and Pressure Politics," in *Women, Politics, and Change*, ed. Louise A. Tilly and Patricia Gurin (New York: Russell Sage, 1990), 339–82.

[16]Bob Cusack, Jeff Dufour, Geoff Earle, Josephine Hearn, Jonathan E. Kaplan, Megan Scully, Jim Snyder, and Jeffrey Young, "Top Lobbyists: Hired Guns," *The Hill* April 27, 2005; "K Street Spread," *The Hill* April 20, 2005.

[17]Jeffrey H. Birnbaum, "Women, Minorities Make up New Generations of Lobbyists," *Washington Post* May 1, 2006, p. D1. For an academic discussion of female lobbyists at the state level, see Anthony J. Nownes and Patricia K. Freeman, "Female Lobbyists: Women in the World of 'Good Ol' Boys,'" *Journal of Politics* 60 (2006): 1181–201.

[18]Kim Eisler, "Hired Guns: The City's Top Lobbyists." *The Washingtonian Magazine.* http://www.washingtonian.com/articles/mediapolitics/4264.html, (accessed September 13, 2007).

Lobbyists are usually well paid for their work, and salaries have increased rapidly since the mid-1990s, as corporations have invested increasing sums into lobbying efforts. It is not uncommon for well-connected public officials to win employment packages of more than $1 million per year. Starting salaries for well-connected Hill staff have risen to nearly $300,000 per year, and when lobby firms were frantically searching for Democratic lobbyists in early 2007, they were willing to pay even more. Attorneys in private firms have the highest salaries: Big firm partners net on average more than $800,000 per year.[19] Lobbyists for citizen groups are paid considerably less, but they prefer to work for groups that represent causes that they support.

Lobbyists for Hire

Many lobbyists work full-time for a single interest group. Many companies, unions, and citizen groups have full-time lobbyists; in some cases, they work for the group for many years. However, many lobbyists work for hire for clients who retain them for a single project or long-term representation. Many corporations both use in-house lobbyists and retain companies. When Microsoft Corporation beefed up its lobbying presence in the 1990s, it fielded a staff of sixteen full-time lobbyists and retained more than twenty firms.[20]

Many groups, especially corporations and trade associations, do not need full-time lobbyists and do not have a Washington office. They need lobbyists infrequently and, when they do, they may need specialized expertise or access. Other groups may wish to mount a major campaign on a single issue but lack the resources to do this in-house. In both cases, it is more economical to hire outsiders to do these tasks than to develop and train a full-time staff and carry them on the payroll all year. In Washington, the pool of labor for lobbying work is deep. Lobbyists for hire come from the many lobbying shops, law firms, and public relations firms that eagerly court government relations work.

Lobbying Firms

Most lobbying shops are small to medium-sized firms started by people with some expertise or experience that makes them of value as advocates before government. Many lobby firms are built around a set of former lawmakers or presidential aides whose visibility and experience easily attract clients who need help with the executive branch. Some firms are built around particular individuals, such as former Attorney General John Ashcroft or former Representative Bob Livingstone. Others boast the names of many former policymakers in their partners—such as DLA Piper, which has forty active lobbyists, including former Senate Majority Leader George Mitchell and former House Majority Leaders Dick Armey and Dick Gephardt.

---

[19]Jeffrey Birnbaum, "The Road to Riches Is Called K Street," *Washington Post* June 22, 2005, p. A1.

[20]Ronald G. Shaiko, "Making the Connection: Organized Interests, Political Representation, and the Changing Rules of the Game in Washington Politics," in *The Interest Group Connection: Electioneering, Lobbying, and Policymaking in Washington*, 2nd ed., ed. Paul S. Herrnson, Ronald G. Shaiko, and Clyde Wilcox (Washington, DC: CQ Press).

Although some firms have a general lobbying practice, many others specialize in a particular niche, using their high level of expertise in a policy area as their primary marketing tool to attract clients. Capitol Associates, with eight lobbyists on its payroll, is known for its work on health issues. Mayberry and Associates focuses on regulatory lobbying for trade associations, and Herrin Associates, a relatively new firm, specializes in issues relating to international education and foreign affairs. SmithBucklin specializes in providing a variety of services to small trade associations.

Sometimes the small boutique firms develop such good reputations that they are able to grow into much larger firms with diversified interests. Cassidy & Associates was begun by two former staffers for the Senate Select Committee on Nutrition and Human Needs. They worked initially on nutrition issues and with universities seeking government grants. The firm expanded over the years and became one of the top firms in Washington. In 2006, its fifty-one associates brought in $29 million. In the late 1990s, Cassidy & Associates was bought by a large, multinational advertising firm. This is part of a larger trend in which larger, often multinational companies are buying up smaller lobbying firms. In some cases, competing lobby firms are owned by the same companies.

Many firms have a long list of clients on retainer, who pay a monthly fee for services, but clients typically pay more when they need extensive lobbying campaigns. When the Democrats regained control of Congress in 2006, some firms lost clients, and others gained them, as companies sought continued access to congressional leaders.

Law Firms

Washington law firms are no ordinary law firms. They are largely in the business of representing clients before government. Lawyer-lobbyists in Washington can earn lucrative salaries by developing expertise in an area of regulatory policy. Senior partners in successful firms can easily make $1 million a year or more.

Corporations are by far the largest group of customers for Washington law firms. The complex administrative process is intimidating to corporate executives who have little Washington experience. Even Washington representatives of a corporation can find themselves unable to understand adequately the technical jargon and legalese of administrative regulations. The stakes can be very high, and a company will search for a lawyer who can do the most for it in a particular area. As one corporate lobbyist put it, "We decide who to use based on the issues, the firms' specialty, track records, contacts, and reputation. If you have a brain tumor, you go to a brain surgeon. The issues are very important."

Individuals who join Washington law firms are aware of the special nature of this type of law practice. They know a good part of their time will be spent pleading some corporation's cause before government. They choose Washington law over, say, Wall Street law (arranging stock offerings and mergers) because they find it more challenging or find the politics of lawmaking and rulemaking more intriguing. Frequently, Washington lawyers enter private practice after gaining valuable experience working for a congressional committee or an administrative agency. Thus, they become part of the in-and-out pattern of using a government job to later command handsome fees from those who have a problem with the government.

As pointed out in chapter 2, the number of lawyer-lobbyists has climbed steadily. This growth has made Washington law more competitive, and firms are aggressive in marketing what they offer. Amounts spent on lobbying firms have soared in the past decade, and firms compete with one another to attract clients. The Carmen Group, a mid-sized firm in Washington, has publicized its fees (it collected more than $1 million in 2005) and the returns to its clients (it claims to have won more than $1 billion for its clients during the same period). By publicizing the expected return on an investment with the firm, the company hopes to attract new clients.

The best-known law firm in Washington, renowned for its lobbying prowess, is Patton Boggs. The nearly 400-member law firm with more than 170 registered lobbyists is, in the words of the *National Journal*, "the icon of Washington's mercenary culture."[21] It has thousands of active clients, most of whom hire the firm because they want something from the federal government. Their clients include foreign governments, such as Kuwait and Costa Rica; major companies, such as Wal-Mart and Sony; and many others. In 2005, the firm accepted a large contract from the Office of Hawaiian Affairs to help lobby for legislation that would grant native Hawaiians the same legal status as Native Americans. The firm even does pro-bono lobbying. Its web page boasts that the firm's partners secured more than $800,000 in funding for the Cheyenne River Youth Project of the Cheyenne River Sioux Tribe in Eagle Butte, South Dakota.[22] Its most famous partner is Tommy Boggs. Politics is in Boggs' blood. His father, Hale, was once majority leader in the House, and his mother, Lindy, replaced her husband in Congress when he died in a plane crash. Connections, however, are only a minor part of Boggs' success. He is a brilliant legislative strategist and a dogged advocate for his clients. In the early 2000s with the Republicans firmly in control of Washington, Boggs spoke publicly about retirement, but with the change in party control his long ties to Democratic politicians are especially valuable.

Public Relations Firms

Organizations and industries in need of Washington representation make use of public relations firms when they feel they need to change public opinion. The government of India, for example, hired Barbour, Griffith, and Rogers because it wanted the company to improve India's image and expand relationships between Indian officials and the U.S. Congress and foreign policymaking community. The Indian government paid the firm $700,000 in 2005 for public relations and lobbying work, while India's rival, Pakistan, paid Van Scoyoc Associates $570,000 for similar services, including persuading Congress and the American people not to block the sale of F-16 fighters to Pakistan while providing $3 billion in military aid over the next five years.[23]

The stock-in-trade for Washington-based public relations firms is gaining favorable publicity from the print and television reporters who cover national politics. To that end, they pitch stories to reporters they know, set up interviews for clients, and create events

---

[21]W. John Moore, "The Gravy Train," *National Journal* October 10, 1992, p. 2295.

[22]http://www.pattonboggs.com/probono/RecDevDetail.aspx?publication=68 (accessed March 1, 2006).

[23]Judy Sarasohn, "India, Pakistan Sign with U.S. Lobby Shops," *Washington Post* September 15, 2005, p. A31.

TABLE 6.1

Top Twenty Lobby Firms in 2007

Patton Boggs LLP $41,900,000	Williams & Jensen $16,120,000
Akin, Gump et al $31,420,000	Holland & Knight $15,870,000
Van Scoyoc Associates $25,150,000	Ernst & Young $13,969,480
Cassidy & Associates $24,310,000	K & L Gates $13,780,000
Barbour, Griffith, & Rogers $22,460,000	Brownstein, Hyatt et al $12,980,000
Ogilvy Government Relations $22,200,000	Carmen Group $12,740,000
Dutko Worldwide $22,192,500	DLA Piper $12,600,000
Hogan & Hartson $18,650,000	Covington & Burling $12,489,512
Quinn, Gillespie & Associates $17,980,000	Podesta Group $11,060,000
PMA Group $16,370,132	Ferguson Group $10,981,000

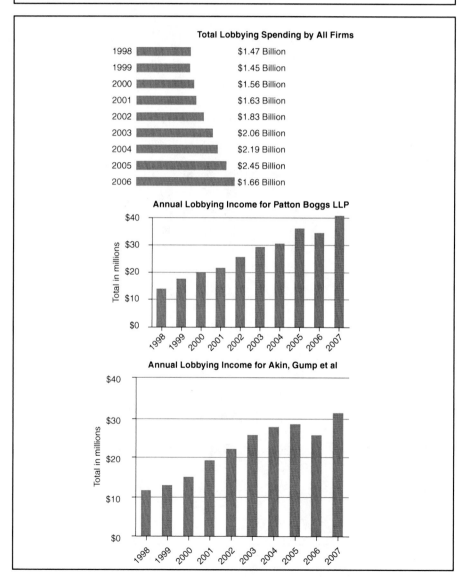

Total Lobbying Spending by All Firms

1998	$1.47 Billion
1999	$1.45 Billion
2000	$1.56 Billion
2001	$1.63 Billion
2002	$1.83 Billion
2003	$2.06 Billion
2004	$2.19 Billion
2005	$2.45 Billion
2006	$1.66 Billion

Annual Lobbying Income for Patton Boggs LLP

Annual Lobbying Income for Akin, Gump et al

TABLE 6.1 (continued)

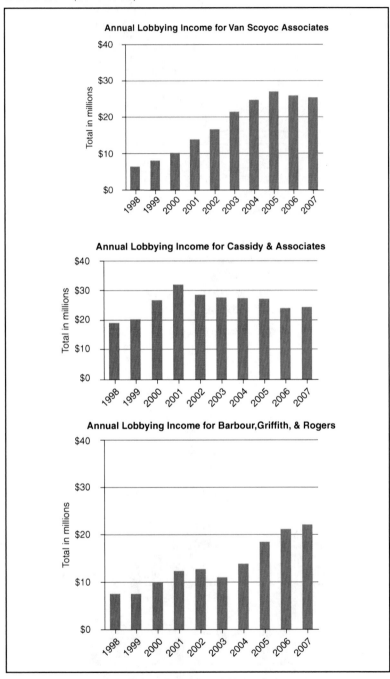

Source: Center for Responsive Politics, Open Secrets lobbying database.
http://www.opensecrets.org (accessed February 22, 2008)

worthy of media coverage. These firms also design campaigns to sway mass opinion, a difficult process at best.

The advantage public relations firms have over law firms is that they offer more services to clients. A large public relations firm will have specialists in lobbying, advertising, and media work. Some firms will even teach a corporate executive how to be effective in a television interview. The largest firms are trying to expand their services to offer "one-stop shopping" to potential clients in need of a wide range of services. Table 6.1 shows the largest lobby firms in 2007, and also trends in lobbying income for some of the largest firms over time.

Conclusion

As scandals over illegal lobbying activities and the bribery of federal officials dominate the news, it is important to remember that most lobbyists do their best to represent their clients without violating the law. Lobbyists have a difficult job. They must negotiate the complexities of legislation and regulation and determine how to best help their clients. Some work for nonprofits or for citizen groups who promote policies they believe in, even though they might be able to earn much more if they joined a for-profit firm. Some specialize in particular issues—health care, foreign aide, international law, or congressional appropriations. Others use their access to former colleagues to help advance their client's interests, and they earn very high salaries working for lobbying firms.

In the late 1990s and early 2000s, the demand for lobbying services exploded, as corporations increasingly saw a large expenditure for lobbying help as a smart investment. Lobby firms were able to tell corporate clients that large retainers were a relative bargain, and many companies agreed. Many professional lobbying firms grew quickly and offered high starting salaries and starting bonuses for those who had good connections. The boundaries between government and lobbying blurred even further. Many former officials now work for a time as lobbyists, then work again for government, then work again as lobbyists. Government officials have sought in some cases to influence the hiring of lobbyists by trade associations and companies, thereby creating closer ties between politics and advocacy.

Although most lobbyists are ethical and hardworking, recent scandals have raised important questions about the ethics of many lobbying practices. In the summer of 2007, Congress enacted lobby reform, but there has not been enough time to tell just how these reforms will influence lobbying practice. Even before the reform package was enacted, some firms had adopted new policies about lobbying practice.

Chapter 7

Public Opinion and Grassroots Lobbying

When Democrats took over the reins of Congress in January of 2007, they began to consider policies that were different from those adopted by the Republican majority. Suddenly a compromise bill on immigration seemed possible. The GOP-controlled House had produced a very conservative bill in 2006, and compromise with the Senate and the president (who preferred more moderate approaches) had failed. Other ideas were suddenly on the agenda. Environmental groups pushed Congress to address greenhouse gases, including increased federal mandates for fuel economy for automobiles and trucks. As Democrats worked to find a way to pay for increased health coverage for children, an increase in the tobacco excise tax emerged as a possible revenue source.

A number of interest groups had positions on these issues, and sought to lobby in a variety of ways. In all three cases, interest groups sent lobbyists for quiet insider lobbying, described in the next chapter, but groups also mobilized their members to directly contact Congress to express their views on these issues. Conservative groups flooded Congress with letters, phone calls, telegrams, and e-mails opposing provisions in the immigration package that would have allowed immigrants who had been working illegally in the United States to earn legal status. Meanwhile, religious groups circulated documents that would express the views of their communities—in some cases in favor of allowing illegal immigrants to earn citizenship, and in other cases in opposition.

The petroleum and auto industries opposed the new fuel efficiency standards because they would decrease industry profits. The Alliance of Automobile Manufacturers spent more than $1 million on a series of TV and newspaper ads that warned truck and SUV drivers new rules that would make these vehicles more expensive, would narrow consumer choices, and would result in less safe vehicles. Auto and oil interests also worked through Washington lobby groups to train advocates to appear on talk radio shows across the country, warning that the new standards would endanger the U.S. auto industry and American jobs.

To fight the proposed 61-cents-per-pack increase in taxes on cigarettes, Phillip Morris USA mobilized tobacco growers, wholesalers, and retailers to contact members of Congress directly. The company also posted signs at stores where tobacco was sold, urging smokers to complain directly to Congress. The company hosted a web page, http://StopTheFETIncrease.com, to make it easier for smokers to send their message, and created a toll-free number to connect those who wanted to complain.

These efforts by interest groups to convince the public on issues central to their agenda are not unique. Many interest groups, especially citizen groups and labor unions, engage in "outside lobbying," or "grassroots lobbying," to influence policymakers.[1] Instead of relying on the access of Washington-based lobbyists, these groups use their members to signal their preferences to Washington officials and to pressure them to support or oppose policies. Sometimes groups seek to expand the scope of conflict and engage the broader public, trying to change the content of public opinion, change the importance of the issue to the broader public, or both. By mobilizing the broader public, groups hope to make various policies more or less likely to be enacted. Conservative groups hoped to kill the immigration bill with their pressure, instead of allowing the policy to be made in a quiet conversation between government and business leaders. Automakers sought to counter the large volume of letters, phone calls, and e-mails from the environmental community with others that opposed new emission standards.

Interest groups also sometimes work to alter the broader framework of the policy debate. Many groups focus on trying to change the importance of various core values for the general public, and in defining various issues as involving these values. In this way, they hope to make possible some kinds of policies that are currently not under consideration or to rule out entire categories of policies that might otherwise be considered. One type of advocacy organization, think tanks, specializes in research and tries to influence policymaking through the new knowledge the think tanks generate. Some offer broad sets of policy proposals supported by research, which they hope may make possible sweeping policy changes.

Outside lobbying has become more common in recent years, for several reasons. First, new technology has helped lower the costs of grassroots mobilization. Where once grassroots mobilization required a large staff to type or mimeograph letters, now desktop printing, cell phones and other handheld devices, and especially the Internet allow groups to contact activists quickly with specially targeted communications. When the Recording Industry Association of America sought to increase royalties for songs played on Internet radio sites, Pandora.com (an Internet radio site) observed a day of silence on July 26th, 2007. Instead of music, their site informed listeners of the "Internet Radio Equality Act"—a bill that would block the royalty increase—and urged them to contact their representatives to support the bill.

Second, as interest groups have become more involved in election campaigns, policymakers have had more reason to listen carefully to the preferences of interest group leaders and members. If group leaders or members care deeply about an issue, that issue is likely to influence their support for the candidate in the next campaign. Finally, grassroots mobilization has become intertwined with fundraising. This means that, even when a grassroots campaign has only a limited chance of succeeding, it might be worthwhile for the group if the issue also helps raise money in the process.

Some types of interest groups use grassroots lobbying more than others. Many citizen groups and labor unions have many members who care deeply about issues and are willing to contact policymakers to express their views. This makes it relatively easy for

---

[1]For a comprehensive study, see Ken Kollman, *Outside Lobbying: Public Opinion & Interest Group Strategies* (Princeton, NJ: Princeton University Press, 1998).

them to mount grassroots campaigns. Environmental groups can often appeal to the public, because the public supports cleaner air and water. In contrast, corporations have no members, and they often find it difficult to mobilize the public behind proposals that might help increase their profits. One study of outside lobbying found that corporations and trade associations were far less likely to use the technique than citizen groups and labor unions.[2] However, corporations and trade associations do use outside lobbying on occasion. As we saw in chapter 6, many firms specialize in mobilizing public opinion on behalf of the business community—in some cases, stimulating a grassroots response and, in other cases, manufacturing it.[3]

Direct Citizen Lobbying

When a bill is being debated in Congress or an agency is about to write a new regulation, interest groups often try to stimulate contact between citizens and policymakers. Washington lobbyists are nearly unanimous on how valuable this kind of support is to their own work. In interviews, they have made these kinds of comments about their members:

> They're essential.
>
> That's where the leverage is.
>
> The strength of our organization is our grassroots.
>
> We depend on our constituents heavily—they are the salvation of our power.

For lobbyists, contacts by members make their other activities more effective. One lobbyist for a business association stated simply, "When a Congressman hears business leaders in the district voice the same concerns that I raise in Washington, I can more easily schedule a longer meeting to lay out our case." Lobbyists understand intuitively what political scientists have demonstrated empirically: Members of Congress are more influenced by their constituents than by Washington lobbies.[4] To maximize their own influence, then, lobbyists try to couple their efforts with those of their rank-and-file members.

Direct citizen lobbying takes many forms. On some occasions, groups have their members go to Washington to meet with legislators in their offices. On critical votes, the business community rallies top corporate officials to visit congressional offices, where they inevitably are able to meet directly with legislators. Other groups can sometimes rally their famous members—especially celebrities, such as movie and television stars, recording artists, and professional sports figures—to visit Congress to lobby on an issue. When Bono (lead singer for the band U2) visits the Capitol, members of both parties

[2]Kollman, op. cit.

[3]Kenneth M. Goldstein, *Interest Groups, Lobbying, and Participation in America* (New York: Cambridge-University Press, 1999).

[4]William P. Browne, "Organized Interests, Grassroots Confidants, and Congress," in *Interest Group Politics,* ed. Burdett A. Loomis and Allan J. Cigler (Washington, DC: CQ Press, 288); and John W. Kingdon, *Congressmen's Voting Decisions,* 2nd ed. (New York: Harper and Row, 1981).

want to meet with him. Actress Meryl Streep has testified about the use of the pesticide alar on apples, and Kermit the Frog lobbied Congress about restricting the breeding and sale of exotic animals as pets. The band Metallica's drummer Lars Ulrich testified before the Senate Judiciary Committee in favor of laws that would limit file sharing of MP3 files, but Napster users besieged Capitol Hill with nearly 70,000 e-mails during the period, opposing the legislation.

Not all citizen lobbying in Washington is done by the famous and powerful. The Sierra Club trains and coordinates the lobbying of activists on Capitol Hill. When crucial environmental legislation is under consideration in the House or Senate, groups of members from various states travel to Washington and meet with legislators to voice their concerns, reminding their representatives that they speak for many more environmentalists who care about the issue. Citizen groups may take advantage of a protest rally to have their members meet with their legislators. It is common after pro-life or pro-choice marches to see delegations of interest group members walking the halls of the House and Senate office buildings.

More commonly, members are encouraged to contact policymakers through letters, phone calls, telegrams, and increasingly through e-mails. Some groups merely provide their members with details of the policy, information on whom to contact, and key points to make in their letter or call. Other groups provide letters or postcards that members can sign and send to key representatives. Policymakers report that these preprinted letters have far less impact than individual communications in the constituents' own words. Many members of Congress do not respond to postcards or, in some cases, even count them.

Of course, policymakers know that these communications are coordinated and that interest groups have spent time and money to encourage their members to be active. But this grassroots contact provides important signals to policymakers. It can demonstrate that a group's leaders care enough about an issue to spend money and time to mobilize the membership. And it can signal the willingness of group members to remember an issue in the voting booth. Some scholars believe that the most important element of grassroots lobbying is the signal that it sends to policymakers about group preferences, resources, and intentions.

The volume of this citizen contacting is substantial. Most congressional offices receive an enormous volume of letters and postcards every day, and e-mail floods into offices as well. According to the Congressional Management Foundation, in 2005 the House received more than 10 million letters and nearly 100 million e-mails. The Senate received nearly 8 million letters and postcards and more than 83 million e-mails. The overall number of these communications increased by more than 400 percent over the past decade, almost all of which was due to e-mail.[5] Nearly all of this contacting is organized by interest groups.

As the volume of e-mail to congressional offices has exploded, legislative offices are increasingly requiring addresses of those who send e-mails to verify that they are indeed constituents of the member. A study by Capitol Advantage showed that six of ten companies that specialize in delivering e-mail on behalf of interest groups had failed to deliver over half of their messages. Earlier studies have shown that congressional aides

---

[5]"Communicating with Congress: How Capitol Hill Is Coping with the Surge in Citizen Advocacy," http://www.cmfweb.org/cwcsummary.asp#ft1 (accessed March 4, 2006).

discount e-mails, believing that they frequently come from outside the district and that constituents frequently were unaware that e-mails had been sent on their behalf.[6]

Interest groups understand that their members will respond only a limited number of times during a year and thus are selective in their efforts to mobilize. Many groups maintain lists of members sorted by congressional district. When there is an important issue under consideration by a committee or subcommittee, most groups contact only those who live in the districts of legislators who might be swayed on the policy. In this way, groups do not waste the energies of their members to contact those who cannot vote in committee or even to contact those who are committed to one side or another. Groups also maintain lists of more active members—those who might do more than write a letter and who might make phone calls, visit a member when he or she returns to his or her district, or communicate with a bureaucrat who is considering language for a new regulation. The National Restaurant Association has a "GO-Network," made up largely of food-service executives who do government relations work in their own firms. The association has a Public Affairs Conference annually, at which approximately 700 restaurateurs get together to discuss industry issues and meet with elected officials.

The critical assumption in activating group members to contact Congress is that legislators can be moved by such efforts. This assumption seems well grounded in fact. Members of Congress do keep a close eye on how the mail and faxes are running. Most legislators are briefed regularly—usually daily—on trends in mail, phone, and e-mail contacts from constituents. Members of Congress watch trends in constituent communications closely and may edit the standard letters that the office sends to constituents who have written on a particular issue. They care about constituent contacts because their responsiveness helps them win reelection and because it is part of their job, and they take their job seriously. Letters do not usually make those with well-established positions switch sides, but they can be helpful in swaying opinion among fence-sitters. Equally important, the mail can help influence members of Congress at an early stage, before an issue has fully crystallized into legislation before a committee.

On rare occasions, the outpouring of constituent opinion that interest groups orchestrate can make Congress overturn laws quickly. One of the most impressive letter-writing campaigns ever conducted was prompted by a law that would have instituted tax withholding on interest and dividend income earned by individuals. The law did not raise anyone's taxes—interest income was already taxed, but an effort against the law was spearheaded by bank lobbies, such as the American Bankers Association and the U.S. League of Savings Institutions.[7] These groups and many banks prompted letters with ads in newspapers, posters in bank windows, and inserts in monthly bank statements. (Putting a flier into bank statements was virtually free, since the postage was already paid.) The outpouring of mail was so great—22 million people wrote—that Congress repealed the withholding law, which it had passed only the year before. One reporter called the letter-writing campaign "the Hydrogen Bomb of modern-day lobbying, an effort whose firepower was awesome, whose carnage was staggering."[8]

---

[6] Jeffrey H. Birnbaum, "Study Finds Missed Messages on Capitol Hill," *Washington Post* October 2, 2006, p. D1.

[7] These groups opposed the law for two reasons. First, it would cost them money to enforce the law. Second, individuals would automatically pay a portion of their taxes from their savings accounts.

[8] Paul Taylor, "The Death of Withholding, or How the Bankers Won a Big One," *Washington Post* July 31, 1983.

Congress passed a catastrophic health insurance plan for seniors in 1988 by an overwhelming majority, but interest groups representing the elderly, including the National Committee to Preserve Social Security and Medicare, mobilized against the plan. The law was repealed the following year, after members of these organizations contacted members of Congress in person and by mail. One staffer reported that mail in his office opposed the new law by a margin of 5,000 to 8. Seniors met with policymakers in their districts and voiced great anger. The chairman of the House Committee that drafted the legislation was chased by an angry mob of seniors.[9] These examples are unusual but demonstrate the capacity of groups to mobilize intense member opinion.[10] What made these two efforts especially successful was that there were no interest group efforts opposing them. Members of Congress receive many letters on other kinds of issues, from same-sex marriage and abortion to environmental bills and gun control, but in each case there are some groups who are mobilizing constituents on each side of the issue.

New technologies have made grassroots lobbying easier and have reduced the amount of time it takes for groups to mobilize their members. During the interest group lobbying over the nomination of Harriet Miers for the U.S. Supreme Court in 2005, conservative groups were able to contact their members as soon as they had decided their position on the issue. When the conservative Concerned Women for America decided to oppose Mier's nomination, they posted the information immediately on their web page and e-mailed their most active members. Senate offices began to hear from the group's members almost immediately. Interest groups' web pages contain action alerts, and they can e-mail URLs to web pages that contain video messages that urge them to contact Congress or the president. Cell phones and instant messaging make it easier to contact the most important members of a group, who in the past might have been unreachable for hours at a time.

Impressive as this is, it is important to remember that such lobbying is a variation on a theme, not a whole new symphony. In the last analysis, faxes and e-mail are simply letters that constituents send to their members of Congress—they just get there faster and are easier to send. However, the explosion of electronic communications with policymakers came at the end of a period of dramatic increase in regular mail, telephone, and telegraph contact. At some point, a difference of degree can become a difference of kind. The Internet has made it much easier for interest groups to mobilize their members and supporters. Groups that lack the technical capacity to develop Internet mobilization tools can often hire such expertise, or even depend on friendly groups to help them. Environmental Defense helps other environmental groups use action alerts to contact their members, allowing smaller groups with fewer resources to use the Internet more effectively to mobilize their members.[11]

High-tech enthusiasts claim that the Internet and other advanced technologies are beneficial to our political system because they empower citizens. Nothing about the Internet

---

[9]Ken Kollman, *Outside Lobbying: Public Opinion & Interest Group Strategies* (Princeton, NJ: Princeton University Press, 1998).

[10]For a discussion of these and other important cases, as well as an excellent theoretical analysis, see Kenneth M. Goldstein, *Interest Groups, Lobbying, and Participation in America* (New York: Cambridge University Press, 1999).

[11]Christopher J. Bosso and Michael Thomas Collins, "Just Another Tool? How Environmental Groups Use the Internet," in *Interest Group Politics*, 6th ed., ed. Allan J. Cigler and Burdett Loomis (Washington, DC: CQ Press, 2002).

makes lawmaking any less arcane and public policy any less complicated. In short, no lobbyist will lose his or her job because of electronic access to government databases. Lobbyists will still be the ones who monitor government, read the documents, and mobilize the troops. High-tech tactics empower the same people who have always been empowered by interest group politics: those who are educated and have the necessary financial resources.

For organizations that do not have members who can be mobilized, there are firms to help them mobilize others. Jack Bonner, a grassroots consultant, helps companies mobilize constituent contacting. When Congress considered high fuel standards for automobiles as part of the Clean Air Act, Bonner mobilized a group of senior citizens, groups representing people with disabilities, and groups that transported children (such as the Boy Scouts) to contact Congress to argue that higher standards would lead automakers to produce less safe cars. His firm and others like it can generate substantial numbers of letters and e-mails to key committee members and can help identify sympathetic citizens who might be aversely affected by the bill. In some cases, other lobby firms have sent computer-generated letters that are allegedly from constituents who had no idea that their names were being attached to the letters. These campaigns are sometimes called "astroturf" campaigns to distinguish them from genuine grassroots efforts.

Lobbying the Public

When interest groups mobilize their own citizens, they try to signal policymakers, to persuade the undecided, and to provide political support to their allies. However, interest groups also attempt to mold the opinion of the general public on issues of the day. Groups attempt to change public opinion on narrow issues that are being decided by policymakers. This can involve disseminating research, working with the media, and mounting public relations campaigns. If public opinion polls show that the public is strongly opposed to a policy, then lawmakers will be less likely to adopt it, even if they are not faced with a large, coordinated campaign of constituent contacting.

Interest groups also try to change the broader contours of the public debate. Groups lobby to change the underlying values of the American public and to "frame" a set of issues as being related to particular values. They try to highlight differences between core values and key policies.

Disseminating Research

Interest groups often try to educate the public on the issues the interest groups care about. They understand that most people care only marginally about most political issues. Moreover, the complexity of public policy problems makes it difficult for nonspecialists to acquire more than a superficial knowledge of issues unless they conscientiously seek information. Interest group officials believe that, if they can bring their facts to people's attention, they will win them over because of the "truth" in their case.

To get their facts out to the public, interest groups frequently engage in research to uncover data on their own or try to make people aware of largely ignored studies by academics and others. An interest group with one or more staffers who have a strong research background may go as far as to undertake a book-length study. However, because the demand on resources is great, and time is often of the essence in lobbying, this is not usually feasible. More modest research reports are common, though, and practically every day in Washington a group releases a short study.

The National Solid Waste Management Association invests significantly in publications that can be used to educate the public, journalists, and policymakers. It issues reports of eight to twelve pages with such titles as "Bioreactor Landfills: A Viable Technology," "Competition in Owning and Operating Solid Waste Systems: Privatization Works Best," and "Municipal Solid Waste Management," which are full of tables and graphs presented in an eye-catching format. The reports clearly strike the right balance between scholarship and readability.[12]

One of the most successful studies ever published by an interest group was conducted by Citizens for Tax Justice, which is supported by organized labor. The group's director, Robert McIntyre, used his background as a tax lawyer to calculate the actual taxes paid by the 250 largest corporations between 1981 and 1983. He found that 17 companies paid no taxes at all for the three years under study, 48 did not have to pay taxes during two of the years, and another 128 firms paid zero taxes in at least one of the years. When the report was sent out to the press, it produced a gusher of publicity. The study was repeatedly cited as evidence that corporate America was not paying its fair share of the tax load.[13] It certainly helped build support for the corporate tax increases that were part of the 1986 tax overhaul passed by Congress.

The success of group-sponsored research is heavily dependent on the quantity and quality of press coverage. The coverage a group receives is based on subjective editorial judgments as to what is "news." The Environmental Working Group published a report in 1995 called "City Slickers," which included a statistical analysis of the geography of farm subsidies. Supporters of these subsidies routinely argue that they help preserve the family farm, which evokes images of hardworking men and women milking cows at dawn and struggling to make ends meet. The report showed that more than $1.2 million in subsidy payments had gone to individuals who lived in Beverly Hills, California. The irony of this led to heavy media coverage and helped recast the issue as one of subsidies of wealthy corporate farms.[14]

A lobbyist's goal is to become known for expertise in a policy area, so that those in government will solicit his or her views and data. Lobbyists want to be known and trusted by the press in the same way. To achieve this recognition, they must be able to offer information not easily available elsewhere. They must also make sure that their own bias does not so color their findings that it will damage their credibility. Given time, lobbyists who are useful sources of information may be able to develop mutually beneficial relationships with reporters. Ideally, a lobbyist wants to be able to take the group's report to a syndicated columnist or to a reporter from the *New York Times* or *Washington*

[12]http://wastec.isproductions.net/webmodules/webarticles/anmviewer.asp?a=478 (accessed Feburary 1, 2006.

[13]Alan Murray, "Trained by Nader, This Populist Tax Lobbyist Takes Aim at Big Business That Avoids Taxes," *Wall Street Journal* May 2, 1985.

[14]Beth L. Leech, Frank R. Baumgartner, Jeffrey M. Berry, Marie Hojnacki, and David C. Kimball, "Organized Interests and Issue Definition in Policy Debates," in *Interest Group Politics*, 6th ed., ed. Allan J. Cigler and Burdett A. Loomis (Washington, DC: CQ Press, 2002).

Post and have that journalist feel confident enough about the source that he or she writes a story using that information. Some lobbyists, such as Michael Jacobson of the Center for Science in the Public Interest and Bob Greenstein for the Center for Budget and Policy Priorities, have made themselves valuable to journalists by providing quick sound bites backed by solid research.[15]

On many issues, however, conflicting research may be provided by groups, and it may be difficult for policymakers to sort out the truth. Advocates for Youth, a nonpartisan, nonprofit group, released two studies in 2005 on the effectiveness of abstinence-only sex education programs, which are partially funded by the national government. The studies concluded that these programs are largely ineffective in delaying sexual activity among teenagers and may contribute to risky sexual behavior by discouraging the use of condoms. However, conservative groups, such as the Family Research Council and the Heritage Foundation, tout studies that show that these programs have a positive effect. In some cases, opposing studies are not of equal quality. However, by issuing a report that contradicts a major study, a group can help weaken the impact of the original study by muddying the waters.

An individual report by an interest group or the effort of a single lobbyist can play a crucial role in the policymaking process, but more often than not it is the cumulative effect of media coverage that is more important in influencing a policy decision. From its inception until the late 1950s, the pesticide industry enjoyed overwhelmingly positive treatment from the nation's press. The vast majority of articles dealt with the economic benefits of pesticides. As one study put it, "Pesticides meant agricultural bounty, an end to hunger, and possibly . . . an end to human diseases borne by insects."[16] Over time, the focus shifted, and by the 1970s the vast majority of stories on pesticides concerned health risks. Scientific discoveries and the independent work of journalists were responsible for some of this negative coverage, but so, too, was the relentless criticism of pesticides by the environmental movement.[17] The environmental groups used their resources to bring the scholarly research to the attention of policymakers and to do what they could to make the general public anxious about the chemicals in their food.

But sometimes the entire point of research is not to convince lawmakers, but to raise doubt about the arguments of the other side. A coalition of industries that oppose stronger pollution controls—petroleum, steel, autos, and utilities—combined in the 1980s to sponsor groups such as the Global Climate Coalition, and the Information Council on the Environment. These new groups sought to raise sufficient doubt about research on global warming to blunt pressure for legislative change. Copying an earlier strategy by tobacco companies confronting research linking smoking to cancer, these groups sought to emphasize that the link between pollution and global warming was not yet proven, and that the scientific community was not unanimous.[18]

[15]Jeffrey M. Berry, *The New Liberalism: The Rising Power of Citizen Groups* (Washington, DC: Brookings Institution, 1999).

[16]Frank R. Baumgartner and Bryan D. Jones, *Agendas and Instability in American Politics* (Chicago: University of Chicago Press, 1993), 110.

[17]Ibid., 113, 184–92.

[18]Sharon Begley, "Global Warming Deniers: A Well-Funded Machine." MSNBC.Com.

Public Relations

When an interest group feels the press is not giving sufficient coverage to an issue or is unsympathetic to its point of view, it may decide to initiate a public relations campaign. By controlling its own copy, a group can bring home to the reader or viewer the terrible consequences it sees if the action it is advocating is not taken.

A particularly controversial public relations campaign was the "Harry and Louise" television advertisements in 1993. After President Clinton unveiled his ambitious proposal to reform the nation's health care system, the Health Insurance Association of America (HIAA) swung into action. HIAA represents small to medium-sized insurance companies, firms that believed they would be hurt by the Clinton plan. Using the same two actors, HIAA spent $14 million to run a series of ads in which a husband (Harry) and wife (Louise) discussed the Clinton proposal and expressed exasperation with the plan's shortcomings. The ads generated considerable publicity about the ads themselves, and many newspaper and TV news stories contemplated the impact that the ads might be having. For all the money spent by HIAA and the controversy engendered by the TV campaign, a survey failed to find any significant impact of the ads on public opinion.[19] However, the ads signaled to members of Congress the resources that the insurance industry was willing to commit to the campaign and may have affected the decisions of some policymakers, even without influencing opinion.

More recently, the AARP mounted a television campaign against President George W. Bush's proposal to change Social Security to create private retirement accounts. Television ads showed a wrecking crew responding to a complaint of a clogged kitchen drain by demolishing a house. The ads tried to persuade citizens that the president's plan was an overreaction to small problems in the financing of Social Security. AARP also bought full-page newspaper ads in cities where Bush was traveling to promote his plan and also bought ads in Spanish-language newspapers and in the magazine *Rolling Stone*, in an effort to reach younger readers.[20]

Unlike the Harry and Louise ads, few public relations campaigns by interest groups are formally evaluated. Most campaigns are too episodic to realistically expect that their impact could be measured. Executives of interest groups must face this problem when contemplating whether to expend their resources on public relations. A lobbyist for the chemical industry put the problem this way: "No one knows what the bottom line is or how to measure it." Because the impact of ads is so uncertain, the enormous costs of public relations loom even larger. A campaign that puts ads in major papers across the country reaches six figures very quickly. A full-page ad in the Sunday *New York Times* alone can run as high as $230,000. Television advertising campaigns can be even more expensive. Altogether, AARP's campaign to change public opinion on Bush's Social Security plan was budgeted at $20 million.

---

[19]Darrell M. West, Diane J. Heith, and Chris Goodwin, "Harry and Louise Go to Washington: Political-Advertising and Health Care Reform," *Journal of Health Policy, Politics and Law* 21 (Spring 1996): 35–68.
[20]Bennett Roth, "AARP Wages Fiery Blitz v. Social Security Plan; Senior Group Pays $20 Million in Ad Blitz," *Houston Chronicle* March 20, 2005, p. Al.

Beyond cost and uncertainty are further problems. TV and print ads must be brief, catchy, and simple. Most policy problems are anything but, and it is often difficult to write ads on complex issues that stand a chance of influencing opinion. An insurance industry lobbyist said his trade group concluded that "our issues are too technical to get them down to a simple, relevant, understandable message." Even if ads have an understandable message, those ads will be seen as just that—ads. Americans face a barrage of advertisements each day and are, understandably, a bit jaded by what Madison Avenue throws at them. Advertisements by interest groups calling for specific policies that will benefit them are going to be interpreted by many people as self-serving political statements. Groups can only hope that the power of their argument makes their case persuasive in spite of this transparency. Finally, by themselves, advertisements will not make things happen. Policymakers are not so easily moved as to change their minds or charge into action because an ad powerfully articulates a group's proposal or grievance. Ads make the most sense when they are part of a larger campaign that involves other tactics as well. Otherwise, they are likely to amount to little more than an expensive means of raising public consciousness.

Lobbying for Values

Political decisions of all kinds are affected by societal values, those deep-seated collective attitudes of Americans on such matters as family life, economic principles, and the purpose of government. Many interest groups that are formed out of social movements have broad agendas linked by core values, such as equality, freedom, and moral traditionalism. Sometimes these groups try to persuade the public that one set of values deserves more attention than it currently receives. In other cases, groups attempt to frame a policy debate as being primarily about one set of values rather than another. As noted in chapter 1, such activity can contribute to *agenda building*. As the attitudes change, the public may come to believe that more attention should be paid to problems that government has minimized or overlooked altogether, or that certain proposals should be rejected or removed from the government agenda.

Journalists and some political scientists refer to a "culture war" over competing sets of values, fought primarily between sets of political activists who are organized into competing interest groups.[21] Most of the continuing struggle over social values has centered on "family values"—gender roles, sexuality, sexual orientation, and abortion. In the 1960s and 1970s, liberal groups sought to liberate men from the materialist values that forced them into jobs that allowed them no creativity, to liberate women to have careers in addition to family roles, and to liberate children to express themselves more and explore their creativity. These groups sought to change the gender role values of men and women, and they worked to change public policy, passing laws to help women overcome discrimination in education and the workplace. Most controversial was an effort to legalize abortion, so that pregnant women could choose whether to become mothers,

---

[21]James Davidson Hunter, *Culture Wars: The Struggle to Define America* (New York: Basic Books, 1992); for another view, see Morris P. Fiorina and Jeremy Pope, *Culture War? The Myth of a Polarized America,* 2nd ed. (New York: Longman, 2006).

which culminated in the Supreme Court decision in *Roe v. Wade*, which overturned all state laws banning abortion.

Conservative groups quickly formed to fight for traditional family values. Eagle Forum and STOP ERA formed to oppose a proposed Equal Rights Amendment (ERA) to the Constitution, guaranteeing women's equality. In many states, competing sets of women lobbied state legislatures on the ERA, which finally failed because it was ratified by too few states. Writing about the bitter conflict, one scholar noted, "The irony in all this is that the ERA would have had much less substantive effect than either proponents or opponents claimed."[22] For both sides, the importance of the fight over the ERA was largely symbolic. For proponents, the ERA symbolized full equality of the sexes and public validation of women's rise from second-class citizenship. Those against the ERA cited many serious issues, such as women and the draft and divorce laws, but underlying these policy arguments was antagonism toward the women's movement and a belief that feminism devalued the role of housewife and mother.

Since the 1980s, Christian Right and "pro-family" groups have advocated a return to traditional values based on their interpretation of biblical precepts. Groups such as Concerned Women for America, Focus on the Family, and the Family Research Council argue that liberal values have eroded the country's moral fiber, as evidenced by increasing divorce rates, high numbers of abortions, the gay rights movement, crime, and drug use. The Traditional Values Coalition describes its agenda: "With an emphasis on the restoration of the values needed to maintain strong, unified families, Traditional Values Coalition focuses upon issues such as education, homosexual advocacy, family tax relief, pornography, the right to life and religious freedom."[23]

As the battle over values has heated up in American politics, the groups themselves have become symbols that help mobilize their opponents. Groups on both sides of values debates spend a good deal of time attacking each other, in communications that are frequently highly inaccurate and inflammatory. Over time, the debates have become increasingly focused on identity politics, with each side attacking the other and misrepresenting its agenda. Christian Coalition leader Pat Robertson argued in a fundraising letter in the 1990s that "the feminist agenda is not about equal rights for women. It is about a socialist, anti-family political movement that encourages women to leave their husbands, kill their children, practice witchcraft, destroy capitalism, and become lesbians."[24] A document on one pro-family group web page warns that " . . . one of the primary goals of the homosexual rights movement is to abolish all age of consent laws and to eventually recognize pedophiles as the 'prophets' of a new sexual order."[25] Meanwhile, liberal groups have argued that the Christian Right wants to destroy democracy to create a theocracy and create a world in which women have few rights.

Research has shown that most Americans are noncombatants in the "culture wars." Most Americans value both freedom and equality, and many value both women's autonomy and fetal life. This means that groups frequently compete to define issues

---

[22]Jane J. Mansbridge, *Why We Lost the ERA* (Chicago: University of Chicago Press, 1986), 2.

[23]http://www.traditional/values.org/about.php (accessed May 4, 2006).

[24]"Equal Rights Initiative in Iowa Attacked," *Washington Post* August 23, 1995, p. A15.

[25]"Homosexual Behavior & Pedophilia," http://us2000.org/cfmc/Pedophilia.pdf. (accessed December 14, 2007).

according to differing values. The most obvious example is the debate over abortion, in which pro-choice forces frame the debate over women's control over their bodies and lives and pro-life forces frame it over the value of fetal life. When the same-sex marriage issue emerged in 2004, many Americans had not yet thought much about the issues. The gay and lesbian rights groups sought to frame the issue as one of basic equality and human rights. Christian Right groups focused on the need to protect heterosexual marriage from the possibility that same-sex couples might wed. Winning the public "framing" debate matters, for it means that people decide on the issue based on the values the interest group prefer.

In 2004, many states amended their constitutions to bar same-sex marriage, suggesting that Christian Right groups won the framing battle in that election. Over the past decade, however, studies have shown that the public has become much more liberal on gay rights issues, as they have come to think of them as matters of equality.[26] In the 2006 election, Arizona became the first state to defeat an anti-gay marriage constitutional amendment, and other states moved to expand protections for same-sex couples.

After the Washington State Supreme Court upheld a ban on same-sex marriage by arguing that the state's marriage law was intended to "promote procreation and to encourage stable families," The Washingon Defense of Marriage Alliance (a gay and lesbian rights group) began collecting signatures for a measure that would limit marriage in the state to couples who were willing and able to have children. The group did not expect its referendum to succeed—indeed, most other gay and lesbian rights groups did not endorse it but the purpose of the gesture was to ridicule the idea that families are defined by procreation, and to reframe the definition of marriage and family in the state.

Some interest groups compete to define values for a particular constituency. The National Organization for Women (NOW) and Concerned Women for America (CWA) both attempt to define values and policies relating to women. NOW argues that women are better off when barriers to equality are lifted and policies are in place that allow women to choose to have careers instead of jobs as homemakers. CWA argues in reply that women are happiest as mothers and housewives and that feminist policies often harm women, children, and families.

Similarly, Focus on the Family and the Sojourners both seek to define key values for evangelical Christians. However, Focus on the Family argues that Christian values suggest low taxes and small government programs, leaving individual families free to practice Christian charity to care for the poor. The Sojourners argue in reply that Christian charity is consistent with government programs to help the poor and disadvantaged, with private charity as a supplement.

The most extensive efforts to activate public values have been in the three-decade battle between pro-life and pro-choice groups over abortion. Surveys show that the public values both fetal life (especially in the late trimesters) and women's autonomy. Interest groups have paid large sums to public opinion research firms to find new ways to

---

[26]Paul Brewer, "The Shifting Foundations of Public Opinion on Gay Rights," *Journal of Politics* 65 (2003); Clyde Wilcox and Barbara Norrander, "Of Moods and Morals: The Dynamics of Opinion on Abortion and Gay Rights," in *Understanding Public Opinion*, 2nd ed., ed. Barbara Norrander and Clyde Wilcox (Washington, DC: CQ Press).

activate one or the other value. Pro-choice groups in the late 1980s mounted a television ad campaign focused on "Who Decides?"—which sought to frame the issue about the power of government to limit women's choices. In recent years, the pro-life movement has sought to disseminate ultrasound images of fetuses, in an effort to focus public attention on fetal rights.

Lobbying for values may seem to be most suited for ideological citizen groups and religious organizations, but corporate America has not shied away from fighting for its values as well. Business plays such a prominent and critical role in society that it is hard to believe that corporate leaders feel that the values underlying our economic system are in jeopardy, yet people in the business world worry about the future of free-market economics. A legacy of the rise of the public interest movement during the 1960s and 1970s and its anticorporate ideology is that business was put on the defensive. Referring to the free-enterprise system, a corporate public affairs official said, "There are popular misconceptions which we must correct." A broad perception is that many people do not understand the position of business on major issues or even understand the role business plays in American society. In the words of one corporate official, "Most people have no idea what free enterprise is all about."

Business has taken a number of steps aimed at enhancing the public's appreciation of free-market principles. Large corporations have used advocacy ads in newspapers and magazines to promote the virtues of capitalism rather than any product or service they sell. Corporations and business leaders have also donated money to colleges and universities to create programs, endow professorships, and sponsor lecture series designed to increase students' understanding of the benefits of capitalism. Likewise, corporations have donated educational materials that promote the virtues of free enterprise on business to school systems across the country. Donations have also been made to conservative think tanks to support research on solutions to our major social problems.

Large corporations, which have the resources to fund such endeavors, understand that it is beneficial to lobby for the long-term interests of business, as well as to lobby on more immediate policy problems. Like other interest groups, corporations recognize the simple truth that ideas are powerful. As one corporate public affairs official put it, "In a democratic society, people vote on ideas." Despite the large sums of money spent by corporations on these kinds of activities, it is hard to know what impact they have had. Nevertheless, corporate leaders can point to the strong pro-business climate that helped elect Ronald Reagan, and later George W. Bush, and helped shape their agendas. It seems likely that the cumulative effect of business's lobbying for values has played at least a small role in influencing the way Americans think. Policies are inextricably tied to prevailing values; when those values are changed, mountains can be moved.

Think Tanks

At one time, think tanks were not considered to be advocacy organizations. Instead, they were thought of as little universities without students. Serious scholars pursued research on public policy questions and hoped that those in government would notice their publications. Their organizations, however, did not generally have a particular political agenda that they wanted to push government to adopt. Typical of the old-style think tank was the sober Brookings Institution, which has long been known for its high-quality analyses of the federal budget and economic policymaking. Although Brookings is known as being closer to the Democratic party's philosophy than the Republicans', the organization has traditionally sought to produce high-quality bipartisan research to inform policymakers.

Though some think tanks still follow the universities-without-students model, a large number of the newer research organizations in Washington are oriented toward advocacy.[27] Advocacy think tanks take a more direct route to trying to influence public policy. These think tanks design more of their projects to cover issues on which congressional or administrative action is imminent; fashion more of their work into shorter, more accessible formats; devote more of their resources to public relations and media outreach; and are more inclined to hire professional staffers who are comfortable with actively trying to influence those in office.

Prototypical of the new advocacy think tanks is the Heritage Foundation, a conservative organization that aggressively seeks a role in the policymaking process. Heritage makes no pretense of ideological neutrality, promising that, "Every day, we cut through the liberal propaganda and reveal the truth about all the major policy issues." The foundation has an annual budget of nearly $40 million. It is less involved in doing research on its own than in drawing on existing research and repackaging the ideas into short position papers. Heritage staffers prepare hundreds of "backgrounders" a year, which rarely exceed twenty pages and synthesize extant research findings that support Heritage's positions.[28] The foundation's web page lists research in thirty-three policy areas. A Heritage executive describes the organization's philosophy this way: "We state up front what our beliefs are and admit that we are combatants in the battle of ideas. We are on one side and we make that clear. We are not just for better government and efficiency, we are for particular ideas."[29] Other advocacy groups, such as the CATO Institute, do not fit neatly into liberal and conservative categories but do promote an ideological agenda (in this case, libertarian).

Some think tanks play an "inside-outside game"—that is, they try to both influence the broader policy debate with research and reports and focus intensely on disseminating their material directly to policymakers, as well as to the broader public or attentive public who follow a particular issue. The American Enterprise Institute (AEI) publishes reports and sponsors book-length scholarship of the sort done by the Brookings Institution, from a conservative perspective. But AEI also has many ties to the George W. Bush administration, including former Bush speechwriter David Frum, Richard Pearle (who is close to former Secretary of Defense Donald Rumsfeld), and Lynne Cheney, wife of the vice president.

However, the press attention to think tank experts does not come about simply because they are knowledgeable—Washington is full of brainy people. Virtually all think

---

[27]See Kent R. Weaver, "The Changing World of Think Tanks," *PS* 22 (September 1989): 563–78; and Bernard Mallee, "Think Tanks Have Broadened Their Influence," *St. Louis Post Dispatch* April 4, 2004, p. B1.

[28]Christopher Georges, "Conservative Heritage Foundation Finds Recipe for Influence: Ideas + Marketing = Clout," *Wall Street Journal* August 10, 1995.

[29]James A. Smith, *The Idea Brokers* (New York: Free Press, 1991), 205.

tanks employ media specialists whose job is to put journalists in touch with the research staff and to gain publicity for studies when they are published. The media staffers pitch stories to journalists much the same way public relations specialists do, but think tanks have considerably more credibility than public relations firms because their *raison d'etre* is policy expertise. This credibility, along with aggresive marketing, has given think tanks considerable success in gaining media attention.

One of the reasons think tanks are so successful in getting their research noticed is that they leave few stones unturned in finding ways to communicate the central findings of their research to people who are unlikely to read the original work. Beyond distributing their actual research reports, said one think tank spokesperson, "We also send out press releases, use talk radio, write op-ed pieces, send mailings to everyone on the Hill or just select committee members." Heritage lists more than twenty employees in its communications and marketing division, and they all help promote the foundation's policy reports. However, in a town full of organizations and people desperately seeking media attention, think tanks cannot succeed on media savvy alone. As an official at one think tank put it, "Sometimes it doesn't matter how aggressive your marketing is. The way to make your work stand out is simply to make your work stand out."

As the think tank population in Washington has grown, specialization has become more evident as each new organization has tried to establish itself in a particular niche. The Center for Equal Opportunity offers a conservative viewpoint on issues of race, ethnicity, and immigration. The Institute for Policy Studies has a decidedly leftist point of view, while the Progressive Policy Institute is emphatic in pursuing what it sees as centrist solutions to policy problems. The Institute for International Economics was started because its founders saw all the economics-oriented think tanks focusing on the domestic American economy. The Washington Institute for Near East Policy publishes a dozen or more monographs a year in the hope that it can influence policy toward Israel and its Arab neighbors. But many small, more specialized institutes have little impact on the policy debate.

Acknowledging the success of conservative think tanks in changing the policy debate, liberal donors have pledged money to start a network of advocacy think tanks. It is too soon to know whether foundations such as the Center for American Progress and the Progressive Legislation Action Network will establish a presence to rival the conservative advocacy groups. At least some of these efforts appear to be aimed at developing winning electoral strategies as much as at building a new liberal policy agenda.[30]

Think tanks are the embodiment of the old Washington saw that information is power. They sell expertise to the public and policymakers, and today's market seems receptive to their product. An interesting trend in Washington is the convergence of think tanks and regular lobbies. The new advocacy-style think tanks, which combine lobbying with their information strategies, are not much different from regular interest groups that try to educate the public at the same time they are lobbying policymakers. For their part, regular interest groups seem to be placing greater emphasis on gathering and disseminating information, which brings them closer to the role played by think tanks.

---

[30]Thomas Edsall, "Rich Liberals Vow to Fund Think Tanks: Aim Is to Compete with Conservatives," *Washington Post* August 7, 2005, p. A1.

Demonstrations and Protests

As Congress considered immigration reform, some interest groups took to the streets to make their positions visible to the media, to the general public, and to lawmakers. In some cities, demonstrators demanded an end to illegal immigration, and greater border security. In many large cities, immigrant groups marched to show their size and organizational strength.

The popularity of political demonstrations is directly rooted in the civil rights movement of the 1960s. Before blacks took to the streets to march, civil rights groups working for legislative remedies to segregation and discrimination made negligible progress. The first and foremost goal of all political protests is the same: to gain media coverage. Like a tree falling in the forest, a protest without media coverage goes unappreciated, no matter how much noise it makes. As E. E. Schattschneider pointed out, when an interest group sees itself at some disadvantage, it is natural for it to want to expand the conflict: "The outcome of every conflict is determined by the *extent* to which the audience becomes involved in it."[31]

Interest groups usually protest because they feel no one will listen to them otherwise. They also reason that, once the injustice about which they are protesting is brought to the attention of a larger audience, enough of the public will side with them to force policymakers into action. However, attracting media attention for a protest is still only one step in a lobbying campaign. Few protests are convincing enough in themselves not to require other tactics as a follow-up. Usually, then, they are part of a larger strategy, in which the protest is designed to bolster direct and other outside lobbying efforts.

The civil rights demonstrations were particularly compelling stories for the media because of the violence that some produced. Evidence from the historical record shows that some of the marches were undertaken with full knowledge that they would provoke outbursts of violence against blacks by antagonistic white policemen. David Garrow writes that Martin Luther King, Jr.'s Southern Christian Leadership Conference (SCLC) consciously decided to "evoke public nastiness and physical violence" from the lawmen who were to confront them at Selma, Alabama.[32] The result was a horrified nation that saw network news coverage of defenseless blacks beaten with nightsticks and chased by mounted policemen. The marches quickly became a symbol of struggle between good and evil, justice and injustice, and Americanism and racism.

Few interest groups that have relied on protest have had anywhere near the success of the SCLC and other civil rights groups. It is not only a matter of authorities' learning that their violence can increase sympathy for protesters but also that few protests are directed toward a point of view that could crumble so easily in the court of public opinion as did racial segregation. Only in the South was there any measurable public support for it, and, when the marches forced the issue to the top of the political agenda, congressional action became inevitable.

---

[31]E. E. Schattschneider, *The Semisovereign People* (Hinsdale, IL: Dryden Press, 1975), 2.
[32]David J. Garrow, *Protest at Selma* (New Haven: Yale University Press, 1978), 54.

Some demonstrations are less focused on protesting current policies than on raising awareness of certain issues. The AIDS Quilt, which contains squares commemorating the lives of those who have died from the disease, was displayed first in Washington, DC, in a public march for gay and lesbian rights in 1987, then traveled to twenty cities. Since then, it has been displayed again in Washington and in other cities. Large public marches, such as those sponsored by pro-life and pro-choice forces, also help mobilize activists, reinvigorate group fundraising, and create opportunities for personal lobbying by group members. Still other public demonstrations and protests are aimed at affecting policies directly. Operation Rescue, a pro-life group that was especially active in the 1980s and 1990s, sought to prevent women from obtaining abortions by physically blockading abortion clinics.

Because few groups can attract thousands of people to a protest, they sometimes resort to histrionics instead. To capture media attention when a conventional demonstration seems unlikely to generate much publicity or when too few protesters are available to put on a credible march, groups may decide on a highly imaginative and unusual protest. Some of these efforts are humorous, as when environmentalists drove through Wisconsin with a fiberglass model of a mutated fish on top of their car.

Conclusion

Lobbying is a multifaceted process and ideally involves the communication of valuable information from the interest group to the policymaker, as well as political pressure applied from the grassroots. In a world of complex policy problems and in a city with thousands of interest groups, lobbies must do more than call on their friends in government. To make a persuasive case, they use their members and activists to lobby from the outside, and they attempt to alter public opinion. This can involve public education, advertising, and attempts to change the mix of values that underpin policy. It can also involve developing policy agendas and attracting attention through demonstrations and protests.

The explosion in the number of interest groups has heightened competition among them. This has pushed Washington offices to search further for means of augmenting the work of their lobbyists; one consequence of this is the growing utilization of members and other followers in advocacy campaigns. Although breakthroughs in communications have facilitated grassroots lobbying, it has always been considered an important part of interest group politics.[33] Washington lobbyists know that their own efforts are aided by a strong show of support from those back home. Activism by rank-and-file citizens adds to the effectiveness of a lobbying campaign by demonstrating to policymakers that people are truly concerned about an issue and that they are waiting to see what policy decisions are going to be made.

High-tech tactics have offered interest groups new ways of involving their members in directly trying to influence their legislators. For interest groups, a key virtue of high-tech politics is that lobbying campaigns can be put in place in a couple of days. Speed is

---

[33]Kay Lehman Schlozman and John T. Tierney, *Organized Interests and American Democracy* (New York: Harper & Row, 1986), 157.

of the essence, and the telecommunications revolution gives lobbies greater opportunities to use their members as players in the process, yet additional tools for speeding the policymaking process are worrisome. The framers of the Constitution envisioned a legislative process built around deliberation in a system that inhibits quick action. Contemporary America is surely a society in need of more reflection and fewer faxes.

All the various means of grassroots lobbying that are available give citizens a chance to participate in politics. Clearly, many people welcome these opportunities and take advantage of them to make their voices heard in the political process. For those able to participate in interest group politics, activism through their lobbies is a way of trying to right the wrongs of government and to fight a personal sense of powerlessness.

Chapter 8

Washington Lobbying

Interest groups vary widely in the extent and variety of their tactics in approaching government in Washington. In the past few decades pro-life groups have lobbied Congress and the president to enact national restrictions on certain late-term abortions, which the movement refers to as "partial birth" abortions, and to make it a double homicide to kill a pregnant woman in the commission of a federal murder. They have pressed Republican presidents to sign executive orders to limit the ability of family planning clinics in the United States and abroad to advise women on abortions, and to nominate federal judges who would reverse *Roe v. Wade*, the decision that overturned national, state, and local laws banning and restricting abortions. They have brought test cases to the federal courts and have filed scores of *amicus curiae* briefs in other cases.

In contrast, some other groups lack the resources to mount this kind of variegated lobbying strategy, yet some are able to achieve their goals with a more narrowly targeted approach. When business interests in Arkansas wanted the national government to pay to pave certain rural roads, they contributed to a PAC affiliated with Alaska representative Don Young (R-AK). He subsequently inserted language into the highway appropriations bill that provided the funds.[1] When the mayor of Tybee, Georgia sought funding to rebuild the town's beach, he posted a plea on YouTube and sent the tape to his local member of Congress.[2]

It might seem best for an interest group to approach a lobbying campaign with a coordinated strategy to influence public opinion, activate group members, and have their lobbyists meet with public officials continually. Such an idealized approach is not generally possible; financial resources are limited, members can be called to action only so many times each year, and most organizations have only a few lobbyists, who must juggle a number of issues simultaneously.

With limited organizational resources, lobbyists must develop advocacy plans with great care. Lobbyists' work is complicated by the ideological differences often found between them and those they wish to influence. Sometimes, neither Congress nor the executive branch gives the group what it wants, and it may turn to the courts, instead. However, going to court is expensive, and issues may be sacrificed because the organization cannot afford to add litigation to its already strained budget.

How do lobbyists and leaders of interest groups make such decisions in planning the structure of lobbying campaigns? After we examine how Washington representatives lobby the three branches of government, we will analyze how interest groups plan their strategy and make their advocacy decisions.

---

[1] Margaret Talev, "Scandal's Glare on Legislators and Their PACs; Leadership Groups Grow, Some with Lobbyists in Charge," *Sacramento Bee* February 20, 2006, p. A1.
[2] Jim Snyder, "Georgia Mayor YouTube's Lobbying Pitch." *The Hill*, June 21, 2007.

Congress

Congress does most of its work in committees, so it is no surprise that most of the work of legislative lobbyists is done there, too. Congressional committees make substantial changes to bills that are referred to them, adding and subtracting provisions in informal negotiations or in committee or subcommittee "markup" sessions. This process provides lobbyists with their best opportunity to alter the content of legislation. Trying to change legislation on the floor of either house through amendments is a chancy strategy. Says one corporate lobbyist, "You have to start at the bottom. You have to start at the subcommittee level. . . . If you wait until it gets to the floor, your efforts will very seldom work."

That Congress relies on its committees works to the advantage of interest groups enabling them to concentrate their lobbyists' work on relatively few legislators and staffers. Since most interest groups employ small professional staffs, communicating effectively with even half of the offices on Capitol Hill may not be possible. Committee-based policymaking is advantageous to interest groups not just because of the committees' more manageable size but also because it facilitates building personal relationships. As one corporate lobbyist noted, "Once you have established a good reputation, they will call on you." In time and with regular contact, lobbyists have the opportunity to prove that their information is reliable and that they can be of help to the committee in developing outside support for pending legislation.

Lobbyists seek to develop good relationships with committee staff, who are more accessible than their bosses and who can put lobbyists' ideas directly into drafts of legislation. Staff members do not act out of line with the general policy preferences of the representatives and senators they work for; however, within this general constraint, their influence can be quite significant. In an interview, a lobbyist for a large manufacturer said bluntly, "If you have a staff member on your side, it might be a hell of a lot better than talking to the member." Another lobbyist described how he circulated his group's research to committee staff, noting that "the staffers, in particular, get to know me. It boosts my credibility. And when an issue comes up that we organize around, the staff recognize me and return my calls."[3]

Some lobbyists make extraordinary efforts to woo staffers. When North American Free Trade Agreement was emerging as a significant political issue, a Mexican business alliance paid for seventy-six congressional aides to go to Mexico to meet with government officials and businesspeople. The business coalition's expectation was that these staffers would influence their bosses' attitudes.[4] Jack Abramoff's lobbying efforts were often concentrated on congressional staff, whom he wined and dined at his own expensive restaurant and provided tickets to concerts and sporting events.[5] Susan Hirschmann,

---

[3]Cited in Christine DeGregorio, "Assets and Access: Linking Lobbyists and Lawmakers in Congress," in *The Interest Group Connection*, ed. Paul S. Herrnson, Ronald G. Shaiko, and Clyde Wilcox (Chatham, NJ: Chatham House, 1998), 150.

[4]Bob Davis, "Mexico Mounts a Massive Lobbying Campaign to Sell North American Trade Accord in U.S.," *Wall Street Journal* May 20, 1993.

[5]Susan Schmidt and Jeffrey H. Birnbaum, "Tribal Money Linked to GOP Fundraising," *Washington Post* December 26, 2004, p. A1.

chief of staff to House Majority Whip Tom DeLay, had ninety days of travel subsidized by interest groups in the two years before she left to become a lobbyist. Most of the time, interest groups paid for her husband, who worked at the Chamber of Commerce, to come along. The total value of her travel was nearly $50,000; interest groups paid an additional $35,000 for her husbands travel.[6] A study by the Center for Public Integrity and North-western University found that over five and one-half years, members and their aides received nearly $50 million in free trips from interest groups, and that three-fourths of these trips were taken by aides.

Often a single committee member can help an interest group in important ways. Interest groups spend considerable time and effort lobbying their friends, trying to per-suade them to become even more involved in supporting their causes.[7] This is especially true in the appropriations process, where the committee processes tens of thousands of member requests for earmarked spending.[8] A single member can often insert an earmark or another provision in a bill, and if there is no organized opposition it may become part of the final legislation.

Although Congressional Democrats had promised to end the secrecy of earmarks, in late summer of 2007 there were still a number of ways around the new rules. One bill to help provide health care for low-income children funneled money to particular hos-pitals, but frequently identified them in obscure ways. For example, the bill singled out "any hospital that is co-located in Marinette, Wisconsin and Menominee, Michigan is deemed to be located in Chicago" for the purpose of Medicare reimbursement. Why pre-tend that the hospital is actually in Chicago? Because hospital wages are higher in Chicago, "relocating" the facility means reimbursing it at a higher rate for services, even though labor costs are lower in Marinette, Wisconsin than in Chicago.[9]

One important part of lobbying involves helping a group's allies achieve their goals. In this way, lobbyists provide a "legislative subsidy" of resources for their congressional ad-vocates in the form of substantive and political information and labor.[10] Thus lobbyists fre-quently work directly with their strongest supporters, helping them pass their bills. Groups also lobby those who are undecided on bills, and they even occasionally provide legislators who oppose them with information that might change their vote on some provisions.

Interest groups may lobby more in one chamber than the other, even if both are con-trolled by the same party. In 2006, Congress considered a wide variety of proposals deal-ing with immigration. Cultural conservatives who wanted to limit immigration and to provide no amnesty to those who had come illegally to work in the United States found

---

[6]"Around the World in 25 Days," Editorial, *Washington Post* June 10, 2006, p. A18.

[7]Richard L. Hall and Frank W. Wayman, "Buying Time: Moneyed Interests and the Mobilization of Bias in Congressional Committees," *American Political Science Review* 84 (1990): 797–820; and Marie Hojnacki and David Kimball, "Organized Interests and the Decision of Whom to Lobby in Congress," *American Political Science Review* 92 (1998): 775–90.

[8]Joseph White, "Making Connections in the Appropriations Process," in *The Interest Group Connection,* 2nd ed., ed. Paul S. Herrnson, Ronald G. Shaiko, and Clyde Wilcox (Washington, DC: CQ Press, 2005), 164–88.

[9]Robert Pear, "Select Hospitals Reap a Windfall Under Child Bill," *New York Times* August 12, 2007. http://www.nytimes.com/2007/-8/12/washington/12health.html?ei=5 (accessed September 20, 2007).

[10]Richard L. Hall and Alan Deardorff, "Lobbying as Legislative Subsidy," *American Political Science Review* 100 (February 2006): 69–84.

friendly committees in the U.S. House of Representatives, whereas business groups that favored guest worker programs and legal status for those already working in the United States found champions in the Senate Judiciary Committee. Since any bill that passes the House and Senate in different language must go to a conference committee to bargain out the differences, both sets of groups were assured some voice in any final deliberations.[11]

In recent years, interest groups have spent more time focused on party leaders, who are often able to intervene in the legislative process by pressuring committee chairs, or by inserting language in the compromise bills created by conference committees. In 1999, for example, financial industry lobbyists worried that House Banking Committee chairman Jim Leach (R-IA) was too committed to bipartisan hearings and open recorded committee votes and that this would result in the delay of a bill they sought to ease regulations on mergers and sales. They met with party leaders to press the urgency of the bill, and they talked with financial reporters in the media to mount a public relations blitz. They pressured party leaders in both chambers to meet privately with Leach and Senate banking committee chairman Phil Gramm (R-TX) to broker a compromise bill that would satisfy an industry that is an important GOP ally.[12]

When interest groups turn from trying to influence a committee to trying to influence a floor vote, they must develop a plan for reaching legislators not regularly dealt with. If a number of interest groups share a point of view, they are likely to divide the task, each group dealing with those members of Congress it is most familiar with. When interest groups cooperated to lobby the U.S. Senate in the spring of 2006 to oppose what they perceived as harsh immigration legislation passed by the U.S. House, Latino groups demonstrated in large cities to get media attention, while lobbyists met with Hispanic lawmakers. Many religious groups lobbied members of both parties. Most decisively, business groups lobbied GOP senators on the committee and in the leadership.

The most visible part of an interest group's effort to influence pending legislation takes place at congressional hearings. On the list of those called to testify at hearings are officials from interest groups involved with the issue at hand. Interest group leaders like to testify because it bestows status on them and their organizations, because it shows members that their group is playing an important part in the legislative process, and because it helps legitimize their further participation.

Virtually every interest group testifies at one time or another. One survey showed that 99 percent of the lobbyists interviewed said their organization had testified before Congress.[13] Participation is high because the costs of testifying are relatively low. Testifying is regarded as window dressing for the more substantive lobbying efforts made by the organization. Congressional testimony can help the group attract new members, raise more money from existing members, and otherwise promote the organization. Groups such as the Sierra Club and the National Rifle Association have transcripts of

[11]In summer of 2007, Congress abandoned efforts to pass immigration reform, after failing to end a Senate filibuster.

[12]Daniel J. Parks, "United at Last, Financial Industry Pressures Hill to Clear Overhaul," *CQ Weekly* October 9, 1999, p. 2373.

[13]Kay Lehman Schlozman and John T. Tierney, *Organized Interests and American Democracy* (New York: Harper & Row, 1986), 150.

congressional testimony prominently displayed on their web pages, and they often e-mail members URLs that lead to particularly strong testimony.

Moreover, hearings offer an opportunity for media coverage, and this can sometimes influence public opinion on the issue. As a consequence, interest groups give a lot of thought to whom they want to put forward to testify. In 1998, when a House Judiciary subcommittee held hearings on a bill to ban certain kinds of second- and third-trimester abortions, a small drama was staged by the interest groups on both sides. The organizations opposing abortion brought forward physicians, who used charts and models of fetuses to demonstrate the inhumanity of the procedures under discussion. Groups trying to protect abortion rights countered with the tearful testimony of a woman who needed a late abortion because her child would have been born with serious deformities and would have died soon afterward.[14]

Interest groups see more potential for influencing public policy by persuading committees to hold hearings in the first place. Even though a group's own testimony may be of little consequence, the hearings themselves can bring a great deal of publicity to an issue. In the early years of the food stamp program, representatives of the hunger lobby helped stimulate congressional hearings designed to bring public attention to the severity of hunger and malnutrition in the United States. The hearings received substantial press coverage, and testimony by doctors and nutritionists helped create public sympathy for expanding the food stamp program. When Republicans took control of Congress in 1994, the National Rifle Association successfully pressed the House leadership for hearings on various gun-related issues. When the Democrats retook control in 2006, consumer groups successfully pressed for hearings on "predatory lending" practices by credit cards companies.

Executive Branch

Few public policies are conclusively settled by legislative action. If an interest group is to maximize effectiveness, it must be skilled in lobbying the executive branch as well. Many interest groups are oriented more toward lobbying a particular agency than they are toward legislative advocacy. The National Association of Broadcasters must constantly monitor the activities of the Federal Communications Commission (FCC), which steadily issues new regulations that can cost stations substantial sums. By comparison, Congress passes broadcast legislation infrequently, and frequently executive branch agencies must decide on important political issues, such as in 2005, when the Food and Drug Administration (FDA) voted to reject over-the-counter sales of the "morning-after pill." In 2006 the agency reversed its position, authorizing sale for women over the age of 18.

When agencies formulate general policies, they usually do so by administrative rule making. Rule making is designed to facilitate public input into the administrative process. Through the notice-and-comment procedure, draft regulations are published in the *Federal Register,* a compendium of all regulations issued each day. Interest groups take advantage of the comment period to write detailed analyses of the proposed administrative regulations. For example, the Endocrine Society is a medical group that is

---

[14]Jerry Gray, "Emotions High, House Takes on Abortion," *New York Times* June 16, 1995.

especially interested in rules regarding Medicare and Medicaid treatment of obesity. These rules usually go through the Department of Health and Human Services, but this is a huge bureaucracy with many branches and bureaus that can issue rules. Before the *Register* was available online, the search for new rules was an exhausting task, but now it is far easier.[15]

Of course, interest groups prefer to help write the regulations rather than to merely comment on them. In one survey, about half the groups in the sample reported that they had helped draft administrative regulations.[16] Another formal means that interest groups use in trying to influence administrative rule making is testifying at fact-finding hearings held by an agency to provide data on regulatory actions it is considering. Interest groups can also file petitions requesting administrative action on a problem. Although the rule-making process has been opened up to a wide range of interest groups, corporations have a substantial advantage in the process, since they seek narrow changes in rules and have substantial resources to obtain them.[17]

Interest groups recognize that, if they are to exert influence on administrative agencies, they must go beyond the formal opportunities available to them. As much as possible, lobbies mobilize political support to buttress their efforts. Groups also try to develop relationships with executive branch policymakers that allow them to express their interests through meetings and phone calls. Most executive branch lobbying is directed at administrative agencies, but some groups also try to influence the White House.

Administrative Agencies

The greatest difference lobbyists see between members of Congress and administrators is that the former are much more worried about the popularity of their actions with constituents back home. A corporate lobbyist describes the differences he sees in his work:

> A good many [in Congress] are idealists, but they have to get elected. They are concerned about their constituency and the media. . . . Agency [administrators] are usually more specialized in their field and they're purists. They are not concerned about the press or a constituency. You bring in your technical experts and you just defend your point of view.

Agency personnel are probably not as callous toward public opinion or interest group concerns as this lobbyist suggests, but lobbying agencies is very different from lobbying Congress. At the highest levels in the federal bureaucracy are the president's appointees, individuals who are strongly interested in the next election. Beneath the top political stratum

---

[15]Scott Furlong, "Exploring Interest Group Participation in Executive Policymaking," in *The Interest Group Connection,* 2nd ed., ed. Paul S. Herrnson, Ronald Shaiko, and Clyde Wilcox (Washington, DC: CQ Press, 2005), 282–97.

[16]Kevin Hula, *Links and Choices: Explaining Coalition Formation Among Organized Interests,* doctoral dissertation, Department of Government, Harvard University, 1995, p. 139. The vast majority of interest groups report participation in some form in administrative rule-making proceedings. See Cornelius M. Kerwin, *Rulemaking* (Washington, DC: Congressional Quarterly, 1994), 195–210.

[17]Jason Webb Yackee and Susan Webb Yackee, "A Bias Towards Business? Assessing Interest Group Influence on the U.S. Bureaucracy," *Journal of Politics* (February 2006): 14–49.

are the career civil servants, who, by virtue of their nonpartisan status, are somewhat more insulated from constituency pressures. Some interest groups find either a hostile or sympathetic ear at both levels, but often groups may have a more favorable hearing with either political appointees or career civil servants. As in working with Congress, lobbyists deal more frequently with staffers than with top officials. The career bureaucrats are not minor functionaries but can hold important positions in order to significantly affect the agency's policies. They are likely to see themselves as technocrats, determined to make up their minds from their own reading of the scientific or social scientific record. Middle-level officials evaluating a drug for the Food and Drug Administration (FDA) have scientific backgrounds and like to think that their decisions are based wholly on the scientific merits of test results and experimental usage, yet FDA evaluators are in regular contact with drug company representatives, on whom they must rely for test data. Indeed, the FDA chief counsel in 2004 was a former litigator for the drug industry.

Although the political independence of civil servants can be troublesome for lobbyists, the worst-case scenario for them is the appointment of high-level administrators who are hostile to their groups. President George W. Bush appointed officials in a variety of agencies who shared his view that industry needed relief from burdensome regulations. Environmentalists found it difficult to gain access to top bureaucrats, or to persuade them with their research. Indeed, scientists for agencies such as the Environmental Protection Agency and National Aeronautics and Space Administration discovered that their research was rewritten or suppressed by political appointees. In some cases, scientists were forbidden from issuing public statements on the results of their research.[18] In March, 2007, the New York Times revealed that in "hundreds of instances in which a White House official who was previously an oil industry lobbyist edited government climate reports to play up uncertainty of a human role in global warming or to play down evidence of such a role." The official, who had no scientific credentials, left government and was immediately hired by Exxon Mobil.[19]

If agencies are hostile toward an interest group's general political philosophy, lobbyists generally can do little to influence top agency administrators directly. They must, instead, try to work through public opinion or, more often, through members of Congress who share their point of view. Legislators on a pertinent committee, especially those high in seniority, can have clout with an agency even if they are of the "wrong" party or ideological persuasion. Agencies want to foster good relations with members of committees that formulate their budgets and oversee their operations. As a result, interest groups on the outs with an agency will prevail upon their congressional allies to intervene in agency policymaking.[20]

Agency officials have strong incentives, however, to cooperate with groups that share at least some of their policy objectives. Administrators need to build outside support for their agencies, and strong clientele support can help them win larger budgets in Congress or protect them from would-be budget cutters at the Office of Management and

---

[18]http://www.msnbc.msn.com/id/6341451/ (accessed April 1, 2006).

[19]Thomas L. Friedman, "How Many Scientists?", *New York Times* March 28, 2007.

[20]Jeffrey M. Berry, *Feeding Hungry People: Rulemaking in the Food Stamp Program* (New Brunswick, NJ: Rutgers University Press, 1984).

Budget. It can also help them win approval for new policy initiatives. At the same time, administrators also value autonomy and balance their desire for outside support with their desire to make decisions themselves.

As with congressional advocacy, lobbyists know that their effectiveness is only as good as their credibility. In their personal presentations to administrators, many lobbyists see their approach being much the same as with legislators or their staffs. A lobbyist for a manufacturing firm said, "There's really not much difference. You are always trying to get them to see things your way." Some indicate, however, that their presentations are even more factual, with more data for administrators than for those on Capitol Hill. "Generally, we have to go into much more detail. . . . We have to go into much more depth," said one lobbyist.

There are times when the "facts" just do not work. Interest group politics is waged largely with competing sets of facts; no group in Washington has cornered the market on the truth. When Department of Treasury officials were formulating a sweeping tax plan in 1986, they were guided by a general principle that special tax advantages given to different groups should be dropped from the tax code, so that all Americans could have their income tax rates reduced. Assistant Secretary of the Treasury Ronald Pearlman agreed to meet with lobbyists from various veterans groups who were concerned about the Treasury's idea to start taxing veterans' disability payments. Their arguments seemed to fall on deaf ears and were taken aback by Pearlman, who asked, "Why should veterans' disability payments be treated differently than any other income?" By the end of the session, Pearlman had not budged, but later the lobbyists were able to get an appointment to see Pearlman's boss, Secretary of the Treasury James Baker. When meeting with Baker, they showed him a copy of a full-page ad they were planning to run in major newspapers. The ad had a large picture of Chad Colley, a Vietnam veteran who is a triple amputee and served as commander of the Disabled American Veterans. Above the picture the ad said, "WHAT'S SO SPECIAL ABOUT DISABLED VETERANS? That's what a top Treasury official said to Chad Colley. . . ." Baker knew the ad was political dynamite, and the offending provision was dropped from Treasury's tax plan.[21]

The ties between interest groups and agencies can become too close. A persistent criticism by political scientists is that agencies regulating business are overly sympathetic to the industries they are responsible for regulating.[22] Critics charge that regulators often come from the businesses they regulate and thus naturally see things from an industry point of view.[23] Even if regulators were not previously involved in the industry, they are often eager to please powerful clientele groups, rather than have them complain to the White House or to the agency's overseeing committees in Congress.

The relationship between agencies and interest groups is influenced by a number of major factors. As noted earlier, the ideology of the administration is a significant variable.

[21]Jeffrey H. Birnbaum and Alan S. Murray, *Showdown at Gucci Gulch* (New York: Random House, 1987), 79–80.

[22]See, for example, Marver H. Bernstein, *Regulating Business by Independent Commission* (Princeton: Princeton University Press, 1955); and Theodore J. Lowi, *The End of Liberalism* (New York: Norton, 1979).

[23]See, *contra*, Paul J. Quirk, *Industry Influence in Federal Regulatory Agencies* (Princeton: Princeton University Press, 1981).

Each interest group's constituency helps determine its ease of access.[24] Citizen groups especially depend on having sympathetic administrators in power to gain meaningful access. The climate of public opinion and the prominence of an agency are also important. Finally, norms of agencies guide civil servants in their interaction with lobbyists.

The White House

As the executive branch has grown, so, too, has White House involvement in cabinet and agency policymaking. A large White House staff gives the president the resources to control an expanding number of policy decisions. One consequence of this is that more and more interest groups find themselves needing access to the inner circle at the White House.

"Contacts" are probably more important for White House lobbying than for any other type of interest group advocacy. The president's aides can be selective with whom they choose to meet. Sometimes the aides prefer not to meet with interest group representatives so as to insulate the president from responsibility for a potentially unfavorable decision. Consequently, contact with someone close to the administration in power is vital for an interest group that wants White House access. A high-ranking administration official who leaves before the president's tenure is up is especially attractive as a lobbyist for groups with serious problems with the government. White House staff can exert influence on the bureaucracy in unexpected ways. In 2007, the White House became involved in Treasury Department rulemaking interpreting a narrow tax break, greatly expanding the scope of the measure, helping ConocoPhillips gain hundreds of millions of dollars in tax relief.

Occasionally, leaders from one sector of society, such as business, labor, or women's groups, are invited to the White House for a pep talk from the president on what the administration is doing for them. This practice can help the president politically by showing a special concern for a particular segment of American society. At times, the president will even call interest group leaders into the Oval Office to give the impression of responsiveness to some constituency. During the height of the civil rights movement, Lyndon Johnson met a number of times with prominent African American leaders, such as Martin Luther King, Jr., and Roy Wilkins of the National Association for the Advancement of Colored People. The photo opportunity for these meetings brought them to the attention of people around the country in their morning newspapers.

One means the White House uses to build support for administration policies is its Office of Public Liaison. First institutionalized in 1970, its job is to reach out to various constituencies and develop good relations with them.[25] Typically, staffers are responsible for a segment of the population, such as Jews, blacks, women, or businesspeople, with whom the White House is concerned. The staffers serve as a point of contact for interest groups representing these constituencies. For lobbyists, the public liaison office is a channel for communicating their interests to the administration. If the administration is generally unsympathetic to the policy demands of the groups, this access to White House liaison staffers may be mostly symbolic.

---

[24]See Anne Schneider and Helen Ingram, "Social Construction of Target Populations: Implications for Politics and Policy," *American Political Science Review* 87 (June 1993): 334–47.
[25]Joseph A. Pika, "Reaching Out to Organized Interests: Public Liaison in the Modern White House," in *The Presidency Reconsidered,* ed. Richard W. Waterman (Itasca, IL: F. E. Peacock, 1993), 195–214.

White House contacts with interest groups extend far beyond the Office of Public Liaison. Many officials seek out contacts with interest groups, either because they feel politically obligated to respond to a group's entreaties or because they seek out a group wanting its support. A White House staffer might try to mobilize support by asking the leaders of certain interest groups to generate a letter-writing campaign among their rank and file directed at members of Congress, in support of a presidential initiative. In 2005, White House political director Karl Rove had frequent contacts with Christian Right groups in an unsuccessful effort to reassure them about the nomination of Harriet Miers for a vacancy on the U.S. Supreme Court, hoping that they would then lobby the Senate on her behalf.

Not all groups have easy access to White House staff. On occasion, the White House invites potentially hostile interest groups to meet in order to defuse their opposition. After Hurricane Katrina hit New Orleans in autumn 2005, President Bush met with civil rights leaders to reassure them of his commitment to rebuilding the city and to explain his policies to encourage faith-based groups to help in the reconstruction. More commonly, White House contacts are with groups that are supportive of administration goals.

The selective access granted by the White House to favored groups is illustrated by the energy task force run by Vice President Dick Cheney for the Bush administration in early 2001. The task force consulted closely with the energy industry, including oil, gas, coal, nuclear power, and ultility companies, but not with environmental and consumer groups. Specific recommendations by industry lobbyists were incorporated into the task force's report verbatim.

The White House restricts access because it cannot handle the onslaught of lobbying that would overwhelm it if access were freely granted. At the same time, it cannot afford to ignore large and important interest groups. The White House task force that developed the Clinton health proposal, which was led by Hillary Rodham Clinton and Ira Magaziner, tried to develop its far-reaching proposal without significant participation by health groups. Given the enormous implications of the proposal for the nation's health care system, health lobbies were quite anxious about what the task force was going to propose and made considerable effort to gain access to Magaziner or Mrs. Clinton. In a ludicrous effort to placate the health lobbies, the White House held a public hearing for groups wanting to offer input to the task force and gave each organization a scant three minutes to speak.[26] Although there are many reasons for the defeat of the Clinton administration's proposal, one of them was the failure of the White House to build a strong, broad interest group coalition to support the plan.

The Courts

If an interest group is to maximize its influence in the policymaking process, it must stand ready to use litigation as one of its lobbying tactics. Because of the high cost of litigation, only the largest interest groups and public interest law firms have substantial legal staffs of their own. For the small Washington offices that predominate, having a skilled litigator

---

[26]Robert Pear, "Clinton Health Team Agrees to Let Public Speak, Quickly," *New York Times* March 25, 1993.

on board is an unaffordable luxury. Furthermore, the lawyers employed full-time by interest groups usually are more experienced in administrative lobbying than in litigation.

Although it is not customary for Washington lobbies to have experienced litigators on their staffs, court suits brought by interest groups are quite common. Most frequently, an outside law firm (usually a Washington firm) is engaged to carry out a group's case. Even if a group has in-house counsel, outside firms are often brought in for cases with high stakes. The major exception is the public interest law firm. Organizations such as the liberal Center for Law and Social Policy and the conservative Center for Individual Rights were created to represent broad classes of people, such as environmentalists, consumers, and taxpayers. Such citizens have important collective interests but, as individuals, they may be able to afford to hire an attorney on their own.

Policy Change

The primary purpose of litigation is to seek a policy change or to stop a change from taking place. After the FDA proposed an ambitious set of regulations designed to stop teenage smoking, cigarette manufacturers immediately sued the agency.[27] When the FDA blocked the distribution of the "morning-after pill," erminist groups immediately sued the agency.[28] Interest groups not only use the courts as an appeals process for adverse decisions by other branches but also litigate when they feel that the political climate makes it fruitless for them to lobby Congress or the executive branch. The courts, though hardly impervious to popular opinion, do not demand the same type of constituency support to institute a policy change as does Congress or an administrative agency.

Civil rights groups have long relied on the courts to fight discrimination. Lawyers from the NAACP litigated against the separate-but-equal doctrine that was subsequently overturned by the Supreme Court in its 1954 decision *Brown v. Board of Education,* which ruled that racially segregated schools were unconstitutional.[29] At the time, strong civil rights legislation had little support in Congress; only the courts offered a reasonable target for lobbying by minority groups. Gay and lesbian rights groups won an important victory in *Lawrence and Garner v. Texas* (2003), which overturned a Texas law barring gay and lesbian couples from having sex in the privacy of their homes. The case was brought by Lambda Legal Defense and Education Fund.

It is hardly unusual for an interest group to be the sponsor of important cases that are decided by the Supreme Court. One study of 306 highly significant constitutional cases found that 163 (53 percent) of them had been sponsored by an interest group. The proportion of significant cases brought by lobbies has increased over time, reflecting the increasing use of the courts by interest groups.[30] Sometimes interest groups go to court

---

[27]Yumiko Ono, "Tobacco Firms Rush to Counterattack Despite Signs of Dissension in Ranks," *Wall Street Journal* August 14, 1995.

[28]http://www.law.com/jsp/article.jsp?id=1137146711572. (accessed April 1, 2006).

[29]*Brown* v. *Board of Education,* 347 U.S. 483 (1954).

[30]Karen O'Connor and Lee Epstein, "The Role of Interest Groups in Supreme Court Policy Formation," in *Public Policy Formation,* ed. Robert Eyestone (Greenwich, CT: JAI Press, 1984), 72–74; Karen O'Connor, "Lobbying the Justices or Lobbying for Justice: The Role of Organized Interests in the Judicial Process," *The Interest Group Connection* 2nd ed., ed. Paul S. Herrnson, Ronald Shaiko, and Clyde Wilcox (Washington, DC: CQ Press), 319–40.

to change the rules under which they can be active. In 2007 Wisconsin Right-to-Life challenged BCRA rules limiting their issue advocacy campaigns all the way to the Supreme Court, where they succeeded in relaxing restrictions.

Part of the rise of interest group litigation comes from citizen groups, which have used legal advocacy as a means to advance their ideological positions. There are a number of reasons for this growing activism. First, as leaders of public interest groups founded during the late 1960s and early 1970s began to look for constructive ways to work for political reform, they were able to find substantial foundation support for public interest litigation. Second, the rules of standing (discussed in the next section) were liberalized during this time, giving citizen groups broader opportunities to bring cases before the federal courts. Third, the success of liberal citizen groups in using litigation has stimulated the formation of conservative citizen groups oriented toward legal advocacy. Sponsored mainly by contributions from corporations and foundations, groups such as the Washington Legal Foundation and the Pacific Legal Foundation have become advocates for a variety of conservative causes.[31] A number of these groups focus on issues involving freedom of religion. The American Center for Law and Justice, with an annual budget of $8 million and a staff of thirteen lawyers, has brought numerous legal actions that have forced schools to allow their facilities to be used by Christian student groups.[32]

For interest groups, the greatest drawback to litigation is its high cost. To see a case through its initial adjudication in a federal court and a subsequent appeal, an interest group must contemplate costs that can easily reach six figures. The Women's Equity Action League lost an important case because, when faced with an appeal, the group could not afford $40,000 for copies of the trial transcript and had to abandon the suit.[33] Interest groups recognize the potential costs and hesitate to enter into litigation unless they see a reasonable chance for success and feel they will be able to carry a suit through an appeal and possibly on to the Supreme Court. Because the cost of litigation is so high, it is the wealthier lobbies, such as the large corporations and trade associations, that are the least likely to be deterred by the price of litigation.[34] But, when substantial damages might be recovered from companies, plaintiffs can often find skilled legal teams willing to take on a case for a share of the award.[35]

Standing

Nearly all public policies are opposed by at least one interest group, but not every group can challenge every policy in court. Groups must show that they have "standing" in

---

[31]Lee Epstein, *Conservatives in Court* (Knoxville: University of Tennessee Press, 1985).

[32]Steven Brown, *Trumping Religion: The New Christian Right, the Free Speech Clause, and the Courts* (Tuscaloosa: University of Alabama Press, 2002); and Hans J. Hacker, *The Culture of Conservative Christian Litigation* (Lanham, MD: Rowman & Littlefield, 2005).

[33]Karen O'Connor, *Women's Use of the Courts* (Lexington, MA: Lexington Books, 1980), 118.

[34]Jack L. Walker, Jr., *Mobilizing Interest Groups in America* (Ann Arbor: University of Michigan Press, 1993), 173.

[35]Wayne V. McIntosh and Cynthia L. Cates, "Cigarettes, Firearms, and the New Litigation Wars: Smoking Guns Behind the Headlines," in *The Interest Group Connection,* 2nd ed., ed. Paul S. Herrnson, Ronald Shaiko, and Clyde Wilcox (Washington, DC: CQ Press, 2005) 341–64.

order to sue. For an interest group to get a case heard before the courts, the group must be an appropriate party to it. The courts' traditional test is that plaintiffs must show some direct injury to have standing. In the mid-1960s, the federal courts began to expand the rules for standing, giving interest groups more latitude to litigate. One major case was *Office of Communication of the United Church of Christ v. FCC* (1965). The church group had filed a petition before the FCC, asking that the license to operate a television station in Jackson, Mississippi, be denied to the current operators because their programming and hiring policies were racist. The FCC denied the petition on the grounds that the station's viewers had not been tangibly injured. A federal court of appeals overturned the FCC denial, saying that standing could not be restricted to those with an economic interest in the case. The court declared that viewers of the station had legitimate standing.[36]

Not only was access expanded for citizen groups, but it was liberalized for corporations and trade associations as well. In another important case, *Association of Data Processing Service Organizations v. Camp* (1970), the Supreme Court considered whether this trade group for data processors could challenge the authority of the Comptroller of the Currency to allow banks to provide data-processing services. The association did not prevail in the lower courts because of legal precedent holding that parties had no standing if their injury was caused by competition. The Supreme Court overturned the decision, setting forth a new doctrine saying there is a valid "zone of interests" for regulated industries that warrants standing in cases where there is a claim of injury, even if that injury has resulted from increased competition.[37] In *NCUA v. First National Bank* (1998), the Court expanded the ability of corporations to sue the government.

These and other cases significantly increased the ability of interest groups to take their grievances before the courts and expanded the range of conflicts between interest groups that the federal courts are called on to adjudicate. The courts, however, can move to make standing more restrictive, too. In recent years, a more conservative Supreme Court has been reluctant to ease the restrictions on standing. In a case brought by the Americans United for Separation of Church and State, the Supreme Court ruled that the group did not have standing to sue to stop the government from giving a surplus army hospital to a small Christian college. The Court ruled that members of the group did not suffer any personal injury other than displeasure with the action and thus did not have the right to fight the property transfer in court.[38] In *Lujan v. Defenders of Wildlife* (1990), the Court ruled that environmental groups cannot merely sue on behalf of nature lovers—they must instead demonstrate that members of the group actually use the land they are suing to protect.

Another means that interest groups use to try to influence the courts is the *amicus curiae* (friend of the court) brief. In suits to which they are not a direct party but have an interest in the outcome, interest groups often file such a document with the court. A group must obtain

---

[36]Office of Communication of the United Church of Christ v. FCC, 359 F.2d 944 (D.C. Cir., 1966).

[37]*Association of Data Processing Service Organizations v. Camp*, 397 U.S. 150 (1970). See Karen Orren, "Standing to Sue: Interest Group Conflict in the Federal Courts," *American Political Science Review* 70 (September 1976): 723–41.

[38]*Valley Forge Christian College v. Americans United for Separation of Church and State*, 454 U.S. 464 (1982).

consent from the parties to the suit or from the court before submitting the brief, though this is not difficult to do, because the courts usually grant such requests. *Amicus curiae* briefs may offer an additional legal interpretation to those being used by the disputants in the case. In the historic case *Regents of the University of California v. Bakke*, (1978), which called on the Supreme Court to rule on affirmative action quotas for the first time, fifty-seven *amicus curiae* briefs were filed.[39] In *Lawrence and Garner v. Texas*, more than twenty groups filed *amicus curiae* briefs, including the Christian Medical and Dental Associations, the Arizona Policy and Pro-Family Network, the American Public Health Association, the American Psychological Association, and Amnesty International, USA. In 2007, the NFL Players Association and the NFL Management Council hired a firm to write an amicus brief arguing for the right of NFL players to receive disability benefits, for two Supreme Court cases.

 Amicus curiae briefs seem most effective when filed prior to the Supreme Court's decision as to whether to consider an issue on appeal or to let the lower court's ruling stand. *Amicus curiae* briefs filed by lobbies at this stage may clarify for judges what is at stake in the case for various interests in society.[40] Once the court agrees to hear a case, it is difficult to discern the impact of *amicus curiae* briefs on how the matter is decided. *Amicus curiae* briefs are occasionally cited by judges in writing opinions, including those concurring or dissenting with the majority.

Appointments

Interest groups also can try to influence the direction of the courts by attempting to affect the selection of federal judges. This task is difficult because the norm is that the Justice Department or administration officials do not meet with interest group representatives to discuss possible selections. Only the American Bar Association, which evaluates the professional qualifications of nominees (and sometimes potential nominees), is consistently active in the selection process. In recent years White House staff have met with and consulted interest group leaders about potential judges.

 Once a nominee is selected, interest groups may decide to try to persuade the Senate not to confirm that person because they regard the nominee as somehow unfit to serve on the bench. Traditionally, the Senate has been reluctant to reject presidential appointees, and interest groups have hesitated to expend their scarce resources opposing candidates they did not like but who were going to be confirmed, anyway. Since the mid-1980s, however, Republican presidents have frequently nominated strongly ideological candidates to federal appeals courts and the U.S. Supreme Court, and this has led to intense opposition by liberal groups and support among conservatives.[41]

 When President Reagan nominated appeals court judge Robert Bork to a seat on the Supreme Court in 1987, liberal groups launched an all-out attack on the highly conservative judge. A newspaper ad sponsored by the National Abortion Rights Action League

---

[39]*Regents of the University of California* v. *Bakke*, 438 U.S. 265 (1978). See Gregory A. Caldeira and John R. Wright, "Organized Interests and Agenda Setting in the U.S. Supreme Court," *American Political Science Review* 82 (December 1988): 1111.

[40]Caldeira and Wright, "Organized Interests and Agenda Setting," p. 1123.

[41]For a general discussion, see Gregory A. Caldeira, Marie Hojnacki, and John R. Wright, "The Lobbying Activities of Organized Interests in Federal Judicial Nominations," *Journal of Politics* 62 (2000): 51–69.

claimed that, as a Supreme Court justice, Bork might try "to wipe out every advance women have made in the twentieth century." People for the American Way paid for anti-Bork TV ads narrated by actor Gregory Peck. Liberal groups also worked hard to galvanize grassroots opposition to Bork, so that senators would hear from large numbers of constituents.[42] The ferocity of the liberal assault on Bork stunned his supporters, and, after his nomination was rejected by the Senate, conservative citizen groups vowed that they would not let this happen to another conservative candidate for the Court.

When Justice Thurgood Marshall announced his retirement in 1991, President Bush nominated Clarence Thomas, whom he had earlier appointed to a federal appeals court, to take Marshall's place. Thomas was very popular on the right because of his fervent conservatism, and citizen groups sympathetic to his candidacy mobilized immediately to make sure his nomination did not get "borked." Liberal citizen groups, however, fearing what Thomas' vote would do on the Court, began looking for ways to discredit him. Two of these groups, the Alliance for Justice and People for the American Way, played a critical role in leading Democratic Senate staffers to Anita Hill, a law professor at the University of Oklahoma who had worked for Thomas at the Equal Employment Opportunity Commission.[43] Hill would eventually come forward and testify at Thomas' Senate confirmation hearings that she had been sexually harrassed by Thomas on numerous occasions. A titantic struggle ensued, and conservative groups went all out to get Thomas confirmed. Some of these conservative groups sponsored television ads that attacked the character of two of the Democratic senators on the Judiciary Committee for their own ethical transgressions. One of the groups, Citizens United, sent 2 million pieces of direct mail in support of Thomas and called its 112,000 members to ask them to call their senators.[44] In a close vote, Thomas was confirmed.

When George W. Bush ran for the presidency (both times), he repeatedly said that there would be no "litmus test" issues for his nominees to the Court but held forth conservative jurist Anton Scalia as a model that he would use in choosing nominees. Republicans remained united behind his first nominee, and, although liberal groups spent money to try to mobilize public support against him, John Roberts was confirmed as chief justice. Bush's second nominee for the court, Harriet Miers, however, came under attack from conservatives who argued that she was not sufficiently committed to pro-life politics and that her legal background gave no evidence that she was fully qualified to serve on the nation's highest court. A number of Christian Right and pro-life groups opposed her confirmation, and eventually her name was withdrawn.[45] In her place, Bush nominated Judge Samuel Alito, whose pro-life credentials on the court were well established. Pro-life groups quickly moved to establish test cases to see if the new judges

---

[42]Stuart Taylor, Jr., "Bork Fight: Tactics Supplant Issues," *New York Times* August 6, 1986; and Stuart Taylor, Jr., "Debate Continues on Accusations of Distortion in Ads Against Bork," *New York Times* October 21, 1987.

[43]Mayer and Abramson, *Strange Justice,* 225–33.

[44]Christine DeGregorio and Jack E. Rossotti, "Campaigning for the Court: Interest Group Participation in the Bork and Thomas Confirmation Processes," in Cigler and Loomis, *Interest Group Politics,* 221; and Mayer and Abramson, *Strange Justice,* 200.

[45]The announcement of opposition by Concerned Women for America was apparently decisive, although secular conservatives had also criticized her nomination strongly. http://www.cwfa.org/articles/9259/MEDIA/misc/index.htm. (accessed April 2006).

would lead the court to overturn *Roe v. Wade*, the 1973 decision legalizing abortion. In early 2006, South Dakota passed a law barring all abortions except to save the life of the mother, a law clearly in conflict with *Roe*, but the law was later overturned by the voters in a referendum. But in 2007 the Court did uphold national and state bans on "partial birth" abortions, a reversal from its earlier decisions.

Liberal groups mobilized more fully to block several of Bush's appointees to federal appeals courts, and Democrats filibustered ten of the most conservative nominees while allowing votes on more than 200. Frustrated Republicans threatened to eliminate the right to filibuster judges through a procedure in which they would claim that this did not constitute a change of rules. This "nuclear option" was avoided when moderate Democrats and Republicans joined together to cut a deal in which Democrats allowed a vote on some nominees but not the entire set. Christian Right groups mounted media events such as "Justice Sunday," in which they claimed that the judges were being filibustered because of their religious faith, and invited religious conservatives to pray that the Senate would allow votes and to financially contribute to the groups' efforts.[46] Senate Majority Leader Bill Frist appeared on the televised event, although he did not echo the claim that the filibusters were based on religion. The Democratic takeover of the U.S. Senate in 2006 makes it less likely that strongly conservative judges will be approved, but wrangling over Court appointments are likely to continue for many years.

Strategic Decision Making

With limited staffs and funds, interest groups must be careful to use their lobbying resources efficiently. As interest groups consider the policy problem at hand, they ask what tactics and longer-term strategies will yield the greatest influence at the lowest cost. Group strategies depend on many things. Lobbyists must assess their available resources and how much money and time a full-blown campaign might cost. They must assess the political environment, including their connections to key policymakers, the party and ideological balance of Congress and key committees, and the likely support or opposition of the president. They must consider the other interest groups that might become involved in the issue, considering which groups might cooperate with them and which might oppose them. They also consider the arena in which the issue will likely be debated, for congressional committees are very different from rulemaking sessions of the bureaucracy, and both are different from arguments before the Supreme Court.

Tactical decision making is also influenced by changes in the political environment. As new opportunities or constraints arise, a group may rethink its basic approach. After Bill Clinton's election, it looked as if some type of reform of the health care system would be enacted. Although philosophically much closer to the Republicans, the Chamber of Commerce vowed cooperation with the new president and said it had an open mind on many key aspects of health care reform. As public support dwindled and the

---

[46]Thomas Edsall, "Conservatives Rally for Justice," *Washington Post* August 15, 2005, p. A2, http://www. washingtonpost.com/wp-dyn/content/article/2005/08/14/AR2005081401036.html. (accessed April 2006).

Clinton plan faltered, the Chamber became openly hostile and abandoned trying to work with the administration.[47] When the GOP took control of Congress in 1994, many groups lost their voice in committee deliberations, while others gained.[48] If Democrats win the presidency in 2008, it is likely that national health insurance will be again on the national agenda, and business groups will need to again choose a strategy.

Many Washington lobbyists are like firefighters, reacting to what is thrust upon them and not able to adhere to plans as to how they are going to allocate their time and effort, yet it is still true that interest groups occasionally try to plot long-term strategy. With little control over how the nation's political agenda develops, an interest group recognizes that its planning is highly problematic. Nevertheless, groups try to implement plans to reorient their strategy toward advocacy. Often issues develop slowly, giving groups plenty of time to consider alternative strategies. George W. Bush announced his preference for private Social Security retirement accounts during his 2000 presidential campaign, so, when he began to promote this actively in 2005, groups such as the American Association of Retired Persons and American Federation of Labor-Congress Industrial Organizations were ready.

A group's approach to judging its influence on government is predicated on the assumption that it can fairly evaluate what works and what does not. When asked directly about this, Washington lobbyists generally indicate that there is little difficulty in determining lobbying success. A lobbyist for a women's group said that she knew her group was effective "when someone gets very angry because you've stepped on his toes." Usually, it is a simple evaluation of whether or not the group got some of what it was after. A farm lobbyist described his group's assessment this way: "If we've decided on eleven policies that we wanted to get through, then we look at those policies at the end of the year. We ask ourselves if we got something accomplished or did we get our butt kicked?" A banking lobbyist answered similarly, "The proof of the pudding is in the results."

While Washington lobbyists express a high degree of certainty in evaluating lobbying success, political scientists are considerably more cautious, finding it very difficult to evaluate the effectiveness of interest groups' advocacy campaigns. In carrying out such analyses, political scientists face formidable obstacles in developing scientifically valid measures of influence. Many actors are always trying to influence the development of a policy. Groups begin lobbying efforts with unequal resources and with significantly different degrees of sympathy on the part of policymakers toward their points of view. Moreover, some policy options are never considered by government officials because they anticipate negative reaction from powerful interests or have come to believe that some policies are outside the proper role of government. Considerable influence may thus be wielded by some sectors of society, though that power is not directly observable in lobbying campaigns.[49] Finally, when research is carried out, it is handicapped by policymakers who are not fully forthcoming about being swayed by interest group pressure.

---

[47]David Rogers, "Business Delivers Another Blow to Health Plan," *Wall Street Journal* February 4, 1994.

[48]James G. Gimpel, "Grassroots Organizations and Equilibrium Cycles in Group Mobilization and Access," in *The Interest Group Connection* 2nd ed., ed. Paul S. Herrnson, Ronald Shaiko, and Clyde Wilcox (Chatham, NJ: Chatham House, 2005), 100–115.

[49]Peter Bachrach and Morton S. Baratz, "Two Faces of Power," *American Political Science Review* 56 (December 1962): 43–54; and John Gaventa, *Power and Powerlessness* (Urbana: University of Illinois Press, 1980).

The rather striking differences between lobbyists' and political scientists' confidence in being able to evaluate advocacy effectiveness can be explained by a number of factors. First, lobbyists probably exaggerate the impact of their own organizations. Despite the many actors who may have been involved, a successful policy outcome is interpreted as validation of the group's effectiveness. A more dispassionate observer would not assume that an outcome matching an interest group's preferences is proof of that group's effectiveness. Second, a lobbyist is likely to define success in terms of what happened to particular alternatives that participants bargained over as a law or regulation was being formulated. Scholars look at a broader context and try to assess the underlying forces that make some alternatives more or less acceptable before the bargaining begins. Third, many topics in political science are subjected to the exacting scrutiny of complex statistical tests or are approached through formal analysis built upon mathematical equations. With such emphasis placed on rigor in the discipline, such indicators as we "stepped on his toes" or we got "our butt kicked" are too vague to impress political scientists.

Conclusion

The diversity of tactics used by interest groups may give the mistaken impression that a wide range of choices are open to a group when it contemplates how it is going to approach government. The issue at hand, the stage it is at in the policymaking process, and the organizational constraints of the group limit the choices. Many such decisions are automatic, and no alternatives other than the tactic eventually used are given serious consideration.

Groups do stop to evaluate whether an approach is working or can work if adopted. Sometimes these questions are asked as part of a broader examination of how the group is doing and whether its fundamental strategy ought to be changed. At other times, it considers the potential of a tactic as it considers whether to take on (or continue with) an issue. For the larger, wealthier groups, the choices are more extensive, while the smaller groups with few lobbyists and a limited budget must restrict themselves to basic, inexpensive advocacy campaigns.

The most valued tactic of all is not so much a tactic as it is a relationship. Lobbyists would prefer not to be the aggressors, bringing pressure to bear on particular targets. The best of all possible worlds is to be in constant contact with policymakers, continually giving them information about the problems facing their group. When issues have to be resolved, it can be done through quiet, informal negotiations between the principals. This type of arrangement requires a great deal of cooperation between lobbies and policymakers. Our next step, then, is to analyze patterns of cooperation and conflict among interest groups and between interest groups and policymakers.

Chapter 9

The Rise of Issue Networks and Coalitions

In early 2001, religious conservatives had formed a small coalition to fight against cloning. The Family Research Council, the Southern Baptist Convention, and the Conference of Catholic Bishops were part of this coalition, as were other groups that focused more narrowly on medical issues. However, as the coalition considered its prospects in influencing national policy, it realized there would be opposition by the scientific community, as well as by large companies that might anticipate big profits from developing cloning techniques in agriculture. The religious conservatives realized that they needed to broaden their base and include other interest groups. Because environmentalists object to the genetic modification of foods and animals, they were a logical coalition partner. As one activist said, "We worry about Frankenstein, they worry about Frankenfood, so there is some common ground. And they have the ear of a very different group of members than we do."

However, there were important barriers to building a larger coalition. Environmentalists were not eager to join in with pro-life forces, and Christian conservatives were wary of working together with more secular green organizations. Although the potential coalition met in a neutral site and conducted negotiations in a meeting cochaired by leaders from both sides, the efforts to build a larger coalition did not ultimately prove successful.[1] However, it is not inevitable that such coalitions fail, for, as we will see, lobbying coalitions create strange bedfellows.

A more successful ad-hoc coalition was formed in the early 2000s when some sixty corporations, including Pfizer and Hewlett-Packard, sought to change the way that federal tax law treated offshore profits. The companies spent $1.6 million in extra lobbying fees, and, when their proposal was written into law, the companies saved collectively more than $100 billion in federal taxes.[2] With such a clear financial incentive to succeed and no real ideological divisions, these companies were able to cooperate in lobbying more easily than the citizen groups.

In 2007, a coalition of more than forty organizations challenged a Bush administration plan to standardize the information provided on state drivers' licenses. Civil rights groups joined with libertarian groups, along with the National Governors Association

---

[1]For a complete account, see Kevin Hula, "Coalitions, Cloning, and Trust," in *The Interest Group Connection,* 2nd ed., ed. Paul S. Herrnson, Ronald Shaiko, and Clyde Wilcox (Washington, DC: CQ Press, 2005) 229–48.
[2]Jeffrey Birnbaum, "Clients' Rewards Keep K Street Lobbyists Thriving," *Washington Post* February 14, 2006, p. A1.

(who objected to the costs the states would pay), and the American Library Association (which argued that the proposal would eventually lead to more intrusions on the privacy of library records).[3]

Interest groups do not operate in a vacuum. In chapter 8, we saw that the partisan and ideological balance of national political institutions has an important impact on the success or failure of interest groups. So, too, does the interest group environment. Although some interest groups lobby alone on most issues, others are members of a number of coalitions and alliances. And some regularly find themselves in opposition to the same groups on most issues. The success of a group's lobbying efforts frequently depends on who supports and who opposes them.

In this chapter, we look at the basis of interest group cooperation and conflict. In particular, we are concerned with the rise of issue networks and the way in which interest group politics has been changed by the emergence of these dense policymaking communities. Moreover, we want to understand the relationship between issue networks and democratic policymaking. Do they enhance or inhibit a broad representation of interests before government? A first step, though, is to examine just why interest groups cooperate in the first place.

Coalitions: Everyday Politics

Coalitions are everywhere in Washington. Lobbyists form them instinctively out of practical necessity. One survey of lobbyists found that approximately 80 percent agreed with the statement "Coalitions are the way to be effective in politics."[4] As one lobbyist put it, "If you're not a good coalition maker, you're not going to survive for long in D.C." Forming a coalition is always a step lobbyists consider in developing an advocacy campaign. Says another lobbyist, "The first thing we do when an issue comes up is sit down and contact people. We find out who our friends are and who our enemies are on the issue and then we form coalitions. I do it every day, on every issue." Although it is difficult to measure the frequency with which groups work in coordination, most lobbyists report that they are more involved in coalitions than ever before. In recent years, the number of coalitions has grown, so that Jeffrey Birnbaum estimates that "By a conservative estimate, Washington has a gazillion coalitions." Birnbaum lists a few of the more specialized business coalitions as:

- LIFO Coalition: opposes repeal of the LIFO (last-in, first-out) inventory accounting method.
- Active Financing Working Group: works to preserve the active financing exception to Subpart F of the Internal Revenue Code, which benefits U.S.-based financial services firms.

---

[3]Spencer Hsu and Darryl Fears, "As Bush's ID Plan Was Delayed, Coalition Formed Against It," *Washington Post* February 25, 2007, A08.
[4]Kevin Hula, *Lobbying Together: Interest Group Coalitions in Legislative Politics* (Washington, DC: Georgetown University Press, 1999).

- Government Withholding Relief Coalition: lobbies to repeal Section 511 of the Tax Increase Prevention and Reconciliation Act, which requires a 3 percent withholding on government payments.
- NAAQS Coalition: lobbies on the Clean Air Act's National Ambient Air Quality Standards.
- Nonqualified Deferred Compensation Working Group: opposes weakening of laws that allow executives to defer part of their salaries.[5]

Coalitions offer a number of advantages. Principally, they offer a means of expanding scarce resources. One interest group may have only two lobbyists; ten interest groups with the same number of lobbyists can provide twenty operatives for the coming battle. The Washington office of an interest group is often stretched thin with a number of issues to follow, so a coalition may enable it to take on a new issue without seriously diminishing its coverage of another. Coalition partners provide other types of resources besides lobbyists. The constituency of each group broadens the coalition's expertise on the issues before policymakers. One group may have access to important committee leaders, another may have a mobilized membership base that will send letters and e-mails, and still another may have technical information that can persuade key policy-makers.

Coalitions also extend the information net. A group added to a coalition is an extra set of eyes and ears and will expand the intelligence gathering that is crucial to any lobbying effort. Finally, a coalition adds to the credibility of an advocacy campaign. The formation of a coalition indicates that a group is not an isolated maverick and that there is some breadth of support for its position. As the Washington representative for a pharmaceutical manufacturer noted, "Your chances for success are really much greater if you [form a coalition]. If you go in to see a congressman or staff member with other people who support your position, it's a lot easier to get their support."

Not all groups enter into coalitions. Some focus on narrow issues, where coalition support is unlikely and unnecessary. Corporations that seek only narrow economic benefits, such as earmarked contracts, may face no opposition among policymakers or interest groups and therefore see no benefits in joining coalitions. Some groups have a narrow issue niche and have no logical allies. In a study of health interest groups, Michael Heaney found that only one was concerned with the regulations surrounding tanning beds.[6] Another scholarly study showed eight separate issues with more than 300 groups lobbying, but that more than 10 percent of issues have only a single organization that lobbies on the issue.[7] Other groups have logical allies but prefer to work alone. Some religious lobby groups prefer to work alone because they do not wish to dilute their moral agenda or to work with those with other beliefs, although, overall, religious

---

[5]Jeffrey Birnbaum, "Lawmakers Feel the Pull of Future Paychecks," *Washington Post* May 22, 2007, p. A13.
[6]Michael T. Heaney, "Outside the Issue Niche: The Multidimensionality of Interest Group Identity," *American Politics Research* 37 (2004): 1–41.
[7]Frank R. Baumgartner and Beth L. Leech, 2001. "Interest Niches and Policy Bandwagons: Patterns of Interest Group Involvement in National Politics," *Journal of Politics* 63 (4): 1191–1213.

groups are more likely than others to join coalitions.[8] Interest groups are more likely to go it alone when they are lobbying an administrative agency, rather than Congress.[9] Regulations are typically narrower in scope and may affect organizations in unique ways.

More commonly, interest groups have the opportunity to join multiple coalitions and alliances. Sometimes groups are invited to join a coalition with a clear understanding that they need not contribute much time or money because the group that is forming the coalition wishes to present its efforts as representing a broad community of interests. At other times, groups may be asked to lobby particular members, to develop a public relations strategy, or to mount a letter-writing campaign on an issue. Some coalitions are temporary, for a single issue. Others are recurring, and still others are permanent coalitions that address a broad range of issues, such as civil rights and economic policy.

The decision to join a coalition is based on many factors.[10] Groups are more likely to join a coalition if they face intense opposition from other groups. They are also more likely to join a coalition if they are interested in the issue at stake more broadly. Although many groups were interested in the Medicare prescription drugs package that passed Congress in 2003, some groups were interested in only small aspects of the bill. One lobbyist for a Washington, DC–based health provider noted that he had not joined into broad coalitions because the interests of his group were narrow and did not line up well with those of the drug companies, the insurance companies, the elderly lobby, or many of the other major players who organized coalitions.

Interest groups are also more likely to join in alliances if they have done so in the past. This may reflect a standing decision by the group's leadership or lobbyists that coalition activity is worthwhile, but it may also reflect growing trust with alliance partners, which lowers the costs of participating in the coalition. Groups that compete for members and resources actually work together frequently—thus, the Sierra Club and Friends of the Earth lobby together, although in some sense each group is competing for the same contributions and activists.

The most common pattern is that an issue will affect a number of groups, and natural allies will be clearly evident to the individual lobbyists. One corporate lobbyist said of advocacy in his industry, "I mostly work in coalitions. . . . In forest products, very seldom do you have an issue that only affects one corporation. An issue might affect just two or three, but not just one." As an issue begins to take shape, the search for coalition partners intensifies. A lobbyist for the National Coal Association describes how he put together a coalition to fight provisions in a bill governing fuel use that could hurt his industry:

> First, I met with gas consumers—they were industrial users—and got their support. If the bill passed, they would get cut off if there was a gas shortage. Second, I met with the railroads. Coal is the railroads' number one product—you

---

[8]Marie Hojnacki, "Interest Groups' Decisions to Join Alliances or Work Alone," *American Journal of Political Science* 41 (1997): 82. For a broader discussion of religious lobbies, see Daniel J. B. Hefrenning, *In Washington but Not of It: The Prophetic Politics of Religious Lobbying* (Philadelphia: Temple University Press, 1995).

[9]Hula, *Lobbying Together: Interest Group Coalitions in Legislative Politics.*

[10]Hojnacki, "Interest Groups' Decisions to Join Alliances or Work Alone," 84.

can't move gas by rail. They have a direct interest in making sure that legislation isn't passed that favors gas over coal. . . . We also brought in labor unions. Gas isn't labor-intensive; coal is a very labor-intensive industry, so labor will support us. I called these meetings separately. There was no reason to include the consumer group with the railroads because their issues are different.

Most coalitions are ad-hoc arrangements. They exist for the specific purpose of working on a single issue and dissolve when that issue reaches a resolution or when the coalition partners no longer feel the effort is worthwhile. When the Justice Department encouraged the Supreme Court to deny legal standing to associations that wish to file suits on behalf of individual members, eight interest groups coalesced to oppose the effort. The American Medical Association, the NAACP, the AFL-CIO, the Chamber of Commerce, the Sierra Club, the Alliance for Justice, the Chemical Manufacturers Association, and the National Association of Manufacturers filed a brief asking the Court not to accede to the Justice Department's request. This unusual partnership of groups was limited to this one issue of standing and did not have a more enduring purpose.[11] Similarly, a broad coalition of religious interests pressed Congress in 1993 to pass the Religious Freedom Restoration Act, which sought to overturn various Supreme Court decisions on certain issues relating to the free exercise of religion. The coalition in this case included some religious bodies that worked together frequently and others that frequently opposed them. They were successful in getting the bill through Congress, although the Supreme Court ultimately declared it to be unconstitutional.

For an ad-hoc coalition that primarily draws on the time and effort of lobbyists, bigger is not always better. Ten groups joined together on an ad-hoc basis is much better than one group working on its own, yet a hundred groups in an ad-hoc coalition may not be much improvement over ten groups. The larger a coalition grows, the more peripheral members it attracts and the more effort is required to manage the coalition. Large coalitions also mean that each group is less accountable for its effort (or lack thereof). In a small coalition, an organization that does little work on that coalition's issues will be conspicuous.

Some ad-hoc coalitions recur at regular intervals. The battles over the confirmation of George W. Bush's nominees for the federal court of appeals and the Supreme Court involved the same groups, but there was no ongoing coalition. Around seventy groups joined together to oppose a handful of Bush's appeals court nominees and to oppose the confirmation of John Roberts and Samuel Alito to the Supreme Court. One young woman in a human rights group referenced the classic movie *Casablanca* in her account of assembling the coalition the first time: "My boss just told me to 'round up the usual suspects' and I knew just who to call." A similar process occurred among conservatives.

Not all coalitions are ad hoc, however. Some are enduring coalitions that groups commit to join and commit resources to maintain. The Leadership Conference on Civil Rights is an unusually large and successful permanent coalition. It was founded in 1950 and has grown to over 192 member organizations. Throughout its history, the Leadership Conference has played a key role in developing strategy over civil rights legislation.

---

[11]Stuart Taylor, Jr., "Coalition Opposes Access Curb," *New York Times* March 19, 1986.

Although the breadth of the coalition is a strength when the member organizations are in agreement, the diversity of the Leadership Conference has also led to considerable internal conflict. Over the years, organizations representing blacks, Hispanics, Jews, labor, and women have quarreled over what issues the coalition ought to pursue.[12]

An example of a looser coalition involved approximately 100 conservative groups assembled by Grover Norquist in the early 1990s. The groups disagree on important issues. It included the Christian Coalition, which is pro-life, but also Republicans for Choice. It included groups that oppose gay rights, and the Log Cabin Republicans (a group of gay and lesbian Republicans). It also included small business groups, home school groups, and many others. The "Wednesday meeting" at the Americans for Tax Reform office has been an important mechanism for the coalition members to communicate and exchange information and for Norquist to attempt to define the agenda. Although Norquist often refered to the group as the "Leave Us Alone Coalition," this reflects more of an effort to create a common ideological framework than an actual unifying theme. It has also been called the "Center-Right" coalition, which may be more appropriate, since some members include Christian conservative groups that advocate for more, not less, government regulation of private conduct.

The coalition still meets, and provides Norquist with additional political clout in Washington. Frequently, the tactics that are debated at coalition meetings are adopted by policymakers, such as Norquist's call to "de-fund the left" by denying funding sources to liberal groups. Soon after this tactic was discussed in the Wednesday meeting, some conservative lawmakers sought to identify and eliminate federal grants to liberal groups. In addition, Norquist first described the strategy of the "K Street Connection" at a Wednesday meeting, and before long it was put into practice by Tom DeLay.

After the 2006 elections, liberal groups formed the "Tuesday group" that meets every other week at the AFL-CIO headquarters. Regular attendees include representatives of the Sierra Club, the League of Conservation Voters, and the American Association for Justice. Its sponsors hope that it will grow into a coalition that will rival Norquist's in influence.

Common Bedfellows, Strange Bedfellows

The old saw "Politics makes strange bedfellows" aptly describes coalition politics among interest groups. Coalitions frequently encompass unlikely sets of partners. The American Civil Liberties Union (ACLU), although often seen as liberal, over the years has worked in alliance with the tobacco industry, the American Bankers Association, and the National Conservative Political Action Committee. Although it joined with the ultraconservative National Rifle Association (NRA) and the National Right-to-Life Committee to oppose the Bipartisan Campaign Reform Act, the ACLU does not support the NRA's interpretation of the second Amendment and supports a woman's right to choose abortion. It joined with the NRA to oppose certain provisions of the Patriot Act. The ACLU even worked with the Christian Coalition to oppose proposed legislation that would have forced the disclosure of grassroots lobbying expenditures, although the

---

[12]Dick Kirschten, "Not Black-and-White," *National Journal* (March 2, 1991): 496–500.

Christian Coalition had recently mailed a fundraising letter that called the ACLU a great threat to American democracy.[13]

In 2007, an unusual coalition formed under the name Alliance for Immigration Reform. This included civil rights and Hispanic groups, religious groups, and also labor and business organizations. The coalition supported a carefully negotiated package with appeal to all members of the coalition.[14]

For all the strange and even bizarre coalitions that form in Washington, the beginning point for any group seeking to form a coalition is still its usual allies. The American Podiatric Medical Association commonly allies with groups representing dentists and psychologists. Repeatedly, these groups have found themselves fighting for inclusion in coverage by insurance plans. The services that podiatrists, dentists, and psychologists provide are not always seen as crucial parts of insurance coverage or worth a more costly premium. Because issues have so often touched upon the common interests of these groups, a pattern of frequent cooperation has developed.

A group's regular allies tend to come from the policy area in which it primarily works; this is where it is most in contact with other lobbies.[15] It is not only that common interests continue to bring the same groups into contact with each other but also that trust and friendships develop over time among lobbyists. As they gain experience working with each other, their contact is likely to increase as they rely on each other to gather information. The lobbyists, legislators, and administrators in a policy area who communicate with each other form an issue network. It is in these networks, which will be discussed more fully later in this chapter, that coalitions breed and multiply. A new coalition effort among frequently teamed partners can easily be initiated with a few phone calls. Thus, the costs of forming a coalition—notably, the lobbyists' time—are kept down.

Many coalitions extend beyond a small circle of friends. Issues can cut across a wide variety of groups, prompting alliances of lobbies from many different policy areas. It is understandable that groups who normally have little to do with each other, but do not work in contradictory ideological directions, can come together to work on an issue. What may be puzzling, however, is when groups that are usually in opposition to each other lay their weapons down and declare a truce while joining together on a particular issue. When the liberal ACLU and the conservative NRA put their differences aside and join together in a coalition, one may wonder if interest groups follow any principles in choosing their allies. Clearly, the norm among interest groups in Washington is that *no one is too evil to work with.* "We may be sworn enemies on one issue and work together on others," said one trade group lobbyist. Chrysler, for example, usually finds itself at odds with environmentalists. However, when the Reagan administration proposed ending fuel economy standards after Chrysler had spent $450 million meeting those standards, the company chose to work with environmental groups to preserve them while

---

[13]Clyde Wilcox and Carin Larson, *Onward Christian Soldiers: The Christian Right in American Politics* (Boulder: Westview, 2006).

[14]Krissah Williams, "Labor Groups, Business Seek Immigration Law Overhaul," *Washington Post* January 20, 2007, p. D01.

[15]John P. Heinz, Edward O. Laumann, Robert L. Nelson, and Robert H. Salisbury, *The Hollow Core* (Cambridge, MA: Harvard University Press, 1994), 254–58.

other car companies fought them. Business groups work with unions to help protect their company or industry from competition but work against them on issues such as pension reform and labor law.

Why is it that interest groups have so little trouble working with their enemies when it suits their needs? Quite simply, it is because lobbying is a profession guided by pragmatism. "We're not fussy [about whom we work with]," a communications industry lobbyist noted bluntly. Short-term results and getting things done, are the day-to-day imperatives. There is not much credit to be gained with the corporate headquarters, member organizations, or rank-and-file members by staying pure in their choice of allies.

To be sure, there are a few exceptions to the no-one-is-too-evil-to-work-with norm. Feminists and conservative Christian groups who are active in the fight against pornography could strengthen their efforts by coalescing, but they have generally worked separately on the issue, rather than together.[16] This is an unusual case, though, and few lobbies have moral qualms about whom they work with. Lobbies are generally much more interested in getting action out of Washington, rather than in reserving a special place in heaven for the pure and righteous. Even feminists and Christian conservatives have worked together in recent years on issues such as sexual trafficking.

However, the example that opened the chapter suggests that there may be limits to the ability of some kinds of citizen groups to cooperate on lobbying. In an era of polarized politics, interest groups demonize their opponents in speeches and direct-mail solicitations. This may not ultimately prevent the ability of professional lobbyists to cooperate, but it may make it harder for interest group leaders to publicly cooperate in a common strategy.

Sharing Resources

Coalitions flourish because they are a means of expanding and coordinating the resources needed for an advocacy effort. A member group enters a coalition with the knowledge that it will be expected to devote some resources to achieving the goals set by the partners. In practical terms, lobbyists must at least cooperate in splitting up the work. In some cases, financial contributions are also expected. Coalitions may also involve meetings—in some cases, many meetings—to hash out strategy and tactics—but groups that enter coalitions believe that the investment will pay off through the extra benefits of sharing the resources of coalition partners.

One resource that coalitions can share is their contacts and their constituency base. A corporate lobbyist says he and his allies divide the contacts this way: "We'll do it based on who knows which member better, who has a facility in his district, [and] the impact of the issue in his district." For large trade groups, the most effective coalition work is internal. If a trade association can mobilize its member companies to participate in a lobbying campaign, it greatly improves its ability to gain access to the offices of many members of Congress. When the American Chemical Council lobbies, it can draw on the 150 member companies that are involved in that industry. These companies are located all over the country and can play a critical role in a lobbying campaign by contacting their own representatives and senators.

---

[16]Jean Bethke Elshtain, "The New Porn Wars," *New Republic* June 25, 1984, pp. 15–20.

Dividing up the lobbying is far easier than deciding to share the costs of a court lawsuit or a research study. Groups do not want to spend money unless an issue is a high priority for them. When there is support for a financial assessment within an ad-hoc coalition, the alliance must decide how to assign contributions. Because ad-hoc coalitions are, by nature, voluntary, informally run groups, only peer pressure can force a group to contribute.[17] In some cases, coalitions are primarily financed by one or two large groups with a strong stake in the policy, which want smaller and less affluent groups to be part of the coalition, both because it helps reduce the overall cost of lobbying and because a broad coalition has more legitimacy on Capitol Hill.

The scarcity of financial resources is not the only reason that groups do not do more to share costs or develop more permanent coalitions. Organizations have identities, which they use to appeal to members and donors, and, the more resources an interest group devotes to coalition activities, the less it has for doing things in its own name. Although interest group leaders can shamelessly claim credit for a policy victory that rightly belongs to a large coalition, few lobbying offices are satisfied with a constant diet of coalition politics. A group's organizational ego makes it want to shine on its own some of the time and to gain the reputation of being able to make things happen in Washington.

In sum, lobbying organizations commonly form coalitions in Washington but are likely to do so under well-defined circumstances. Some coalitions endure for long periods, but others reassemble periodically when an issue repeats itself on the government's agenda. Overall, the chances of success increase when

1. The coalition is clearly intended to be of a temporary, ad-hoc nature.
2. The coalition is limited to one issue.
3. The issue is of some immediacy with a good chance of government action.
4. The coalition is run informally and each group contributes lobbying by its own personnel, rather than giving money to a separate coalition staff.
5. The coalition's members are part of an issue network in which the lobbyists have experience working with each other.
6. Participants believe there is "turn taking" in the leadership for the ad-hoc coalitions that grow from their issue network.
7. The coalition itself is not likely to take on so much public visibility that any successes in lobbying will be entirely credited to it, rather than being shared with the separate member organizations.

From Subgovernments to Issue Networks

Coalitions operate within a broader pattern of interest group interaction. As noted previously, interest groups commonly search for coalition partners among other members

---

[17]See Marie Hojnacki, "Organized Interests' Advocacy Behavior in Alliances," *Political Research Quarterly* 51 (1998): 437–59.

of their issue network. Issue networks, which are characterized by their dense environment of competing interest groups, bear little resemblance to an earlier model of interest group–government relations that was strongly embraced by political scientists. Indeed, few approaches for analyzing the American political system endured as long or as well as that of the policy subgovernment.

In simple terms, a subgovernment consists primarily of interest group advocates, legislators and their aides, and key agency administrators who interact on an ongoing basis and control policymaking in a particular area. Its central belief seems indisputable: Policymaking takes place across institutions. Thus, government decision making can be best understood by looking at how key actors from different institutions and organizations interact with each other.

The subgovernment model can be traced back to Ernest Griffith's description of policy whirlpools in *Impasse of Democracy*.[18] The term *whirlpools* did not have much staying power, but other terms that gained currency include *iron triangles, triple alliances, cozy little triangles,* and *subgovernments*. Whatever the label, the basic idea is the same: A small group of actors dominates the development of policy in a given field. Policymaking is consensual, with quiet bargaining producing agreements among affected parties. Partisan politics does little to disturb these relatively autonomous and stable arrangements. Douglass Cater's description of the sugar subgovernment is instructive:

> Political power within the sugar subgovernment is largely vested within the Chairman of the House Agriculture Committee who works out the schedule of quotas. It is shared by a veteran civil servant, the director of the Sugar Division in the U.S. Department of Agriculture, who provides the necessary "expert" advice for such a complex marketing arrangement. Further advice is provided by Washington representatives of the domestic beet and cane sugar growers, the sugar refineries, and the foreign producers.[19]

The subgovernment model proved popular with political scientists for a number of reasons. First, it provided an escape from the confines of institutional analysis. Research on the Congress or the bureaucracy could not capture the full nature of the policymaking process without going well beyond the boundaries of those institutions. Second, much scholarship in political science focuses on an individual policy domain. To those who wanted to study a particular issue area, the idea of subgovernments offered a conceptual framework to guide their research. Third, the subgovernment idea could be communicated easily to students and scholars alike. The model was based on straightforward, convincing case studies; those who read the relevant works were not required to make leaps of faith or to agree to any problematic assumptions. Fourth, the idea of subgovernments offered a critical perspective on the performance of American government. The closed nature of the policymaking system and the central role played by key interest groups in each area made subgovernments an inviting target for those who found

---

[18]Ernest Griffith, *Impasse of Democracy* (New York: Harrison-Hilton Books, 1939). See John T. Tierney, "Subgovernments and Issue Networks." Paper presented at the annual meeting of the American Political-Science Association, New Orleans, August 1985, p. 28.

[19]Douglass Cater, *Power in Washington* (New York: Vintage Books, 1964), 18.

fault with the direction of public policy. The public interest was not served because not all important interests were represented at the bargaining table.

Because the research on subgovernments was built around case studies, it is not clear how much government policymaking took place in these closed, consensual systems. By the late 1970s, political scientists had begun to doubt that subgovernments characterized the policymaking process. However representative they once were, many subgovernments had crumbled, and a new model of interest group–government relations was needed. An alternative conception was offered by Hugh Heclo, who argued in 1978 that policymaking is best described as taking place within much larger issue networks. If we look "for the closed triangles of control," says Heclo, "we tend to miss the fairly open networks of people that increasingly impinge upon government."[20]

Heclo defines an issue network as "a shared-knowledge group" that ties together large numbers of participants with common technical expertise.[21] Unlike the simple and clearly defined nature of subgovernments, issue networks are difficult to visualize and rather ill defined. Participants move in and out easily, and it is "almost impossible to say where a network leaves off and its environment begins."[22] Networks are not radically different from subgovernments in their membership, because lobbyists, legislators, legislative aides, and agency administrators still make up the vast majority of participants. White House aides, consultants, and prominent, knowledgeable individuals can also be found in their midst, however. Rather, what is distinctive about issue networks is their size and accessibility to new participants. A large network can be made up of dozens and even hundreds of interest groups, a number of executive branch offices, and various congressional committees and subcommittees. Even a smaller network allows for broader and more open participation than does a subgovernment.[23]

A Pattern of Conflict

Despite some evocative imagery, Heclo's model is rather imprecise and does not offer strong empirical evidence on interest group behavior. His model is compelling, however, and, as studies were completed, issue networks gained currency as an alternative to the increasingly discredited subgovernment model. Not all patterns of interest group–government relations fit the issue network model, especially in policy areas that are relatively narrow in focus and involve a limited number of groups.[24] Still, the basic premise of the subgovernment model is now invalid. In other words, *the significant interest groups and key government officials in an issue area do not usually work in a consensual fashion to develop public policy.*

---

[20]Hugh Heclo, "Issue Networks and the Executive Establishment," in *The New American Political System,* ed. Anthony King (Washington, DC: American Enterprise Institute, 1978), 88.

[21]Ibid., 103.

[22]Ibid., 102.

[23]Paul Sabatier has suggested the label "advocacy coalitions" as part of a discussion of change in issue networks. See "An Advocacy Coalition Framework of Policy Change and the Role of Policy-Oriented Learning Therein," *Policy Sciences* 21 (1988): 129–68.

[24]James A. Thurber, "Dynamics of Policy Subsystems in American Politics," in *Interest Group Politics,* 3rd ed., ed. Allan J. Cigler and Burdett A. Loomis (Washington, DC: Congressional Quarterly, 1991), 319–43.

Instead, the research shows that interest groups are typically in open and protracted conflict with other lobbies working in their policy area. One study based on a survey of Washington lobbies found that over 70 percent of the citizen groups and for-profit groups (professional and trade associations) indicated that they face opposition by other lobbies. The figures were around 45 percent for nonprofit groups and 40 percent for organizations with mixed memberships from the profit and not-for-profit sectors.[25] Another study found pervasive conflict between business organizations and citizen groups. Seventy percent of corporations and 66 percent of trade associations said that the growing number of citizen groups had made their lobbying tasks harder. Less conflict was found among business groups themselves.[26]

A third large-scale study found that, in four policy domains, about 75 percent of interest group representatives cited lobbies that were adversaries.[27] The researchers analyzed agriculture, health, labor, and energy policymaking and in each area identified twenty "policy events," such as a committee vote on a bill or the issuance of new regulations by an agency. The typical pattern of interest group alignment for these events was a substantial division among the participating lobbies.[28]

Research also establishes that partisan change is a key factor in determining interest group access to policymakers. Subgovernments were said to be relatively autonomous from the electoral process. Presidents came and went, but subgovernments lived on forever. This is not what Mark Peterson and Jack Walker found in their surveys of interest groups in 1980 and 1985:

> When Reagan replaced Carter in the White House, there was a virtual revolution in the access enjoyed by interest groups in Washington. In the past, many groups may have been able to maintain their contacts with the bureaucratic agencies of the federal government through politically isolated subgovernments or iron triangles, no matter what the outcome of the election, but it was difficult to build such safe enclaves around a group's favorite programs during the 1980s.[29]

Clearly, the Reagan administration profoundly affected the Washington interest group community with its highly ideological agenda and its successful effort to cut budgetary sacred cows. But it is common for presidents to shake up access granted to interest groups. Earlier, the election of Jimmy Carter in 1976 also had significant impact on interest group access to the executive branch. The many liberal citizen groups in Washington were a major beneficiary of his administration. Activists from these organ-

---

[25]Jack L. Walker, *Mobilizing Interest Groups in America* (Ann Arbor: University of Michigan Press, 1991), 129.

[26]Kay Lehman Schlozman and John T. Tierney, *Organized Interests and American Democracy* (New York: Harper & Row, 1986), 283–87.

[27]Heinz et al., *The Hollow Core,* 252.

[28]Ibid., 313–67.

[29]Mark A. Peterson and Jack L. Walker, "Interest Group Response to Partisan Change: The Impact of the Reagan Administration upon the National Interest Group System," in *Interest Group Politics,* 2nd ed., ed. Allan J. Cigler and Burdett A. Loomis (Washington, DC: Congressional Quarterly, 1986), 172.

izations filled important administrative positions and gave generous access to public interest lobbyists. The same groups had found the doors to the Nixon administration's bureaucracies tightly shut.

When Bill Clinton took office after twelve years of Republican control of the executive branch, lobbyists for liberal citizen groups rejoiced because a number of their colleagues were appointed to key agency positions. Environmentalists, for example, cheered the selection of Bruce Babbitt, who had headed the League of Conservation Voters, as Secretary of the Interior. Republican George W. Bush came to office in 2001 and created an even more conservative government than Reagan. Bush's Secretary of the Interior Gale Norton had been active in a legal foundation representing the interests of ranchers, miners, and the timber industry in lawsuits challenging environmental regulations. Environmentalists lost the access they had had to the Interior, and industry gained. The Christian Right applauded the appointment of John Ashcroft as Bush's attorney general, as well as some key appointments that Ashcroft made further down in the department, which gave the group much greater access.

Changes in control of Congress also affect the access of groups to policymakers. Figure 9.1 shows the appearances by environmental groups at congressional committee hearings from 1970 to 2007. Between 1970 and 1982, the number gradually but somewhat erratically increased, peaking during the mid- to late 1980s as the Democratic-controlled House of Representatives (and, after 1986, the Democratic Senate) held

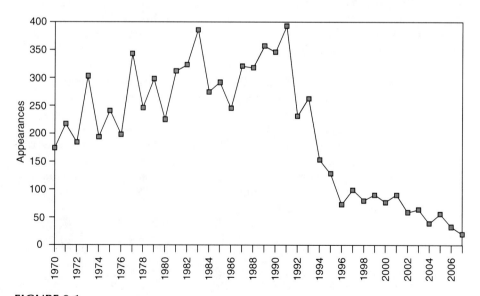

FIGURE 9.1
Appearence at Congressional Committee Hearings by Environmental Groups.
Source: LexisNexis

hearings about the Reagan administration's environmental policies. These appearances dropped during the end of the Bush presidency, but they plummeted after the Republicans took control of Congress in 1994. As Democrats regained control of Congress in 2006, environmental groups were hopeful that their appearances in Congress would increase.

In sum, the simple, stable structure of subgovernments gave way to a much different kind of policy community. Individual lobbying organizations constantly search for coalition partners in an effort to combine resources, so that they can better contend with their interest group adversaries. A lobby's relations with government can be significantly affected by who is in the White House; this is especially true for citizen groups whose ideological character make them vulnerable to changes in administrations. These changes in interest group politics are considerable. Why did they happen?

Again, the Advocacy Explosion

The most important source of change affecting policymaking communities has been the proliferation of interest groups. The arguments in chapter 2 do not need repeating; our goal here is to explore how the growth in the number of lobbies and the increasing diversity of advocacy organizations affected the policymaking process.[30] In this respect, the impact of the advocacy explosion was probably most profound in the way it altered the relations between groups and agencies. For example, the Department of Agriculture, long the bureaucratic center of many subgovernments, was transformed by a "proliferation of groups" that "destabilized the agricultural subsystem."[31] As new groups emerged and demanded to be heard, subgovernments were not able to wall themselves off from those who wanted to be included in policymaking. Subgovernments flourished in the absence of competing interest groups, not in spite of them.

Most new groups approaching subgovernments had resources that made it difficult for the subgovernments to exclude them. Even if an administrative agency was antagonistic to a new group because of its ideological leanings, there were always legislators who held the same views and were willing to help. Particularly notable in this respect was the growth in the number of citizen groups. When these highly conservative or liberal groups found an administrative agency of the opposite persuasion, they worked with allies in Congress to attack agency decisions they disagreed with.[32] One study concluded, "Once these new groups of the Left and Right became permanent fixtures in Washington, the conditions that had nurtured the decenteralized system of subgovernments were fundamentally altered."[33]

---

[30]See Jeffrey M. Berry, "Citizen Groups and the Changing Nature of Interest Group Politics in America," *Annals of the American Academy of Political and Social Science* 528 (July 1993): 30–41.

[31]William P. Browne, "Policy and Interests: Instability and Change in a Classic Issue Subsystem," in Allan J. Cigler and Burdett A. Loomis, ed. *Interest Group Politics,* (Washington: CQ Press, 1983), p. 187.

[32]Jeffrey M. Berry, *Feeding Hungry People: Rulemaking in the Food Stamp Program* (New Brunswick, NJ: Rutgers University Press, 1984).

[33]Thomas L. Gais, Mark A. Peterson, and Jack L. Walker, "Interest Groups, Iron Triangles, and Representative Institutions in American National Government," *British Journal of Political Science* 14 (April 1984): p. 166.

With the growing number of interest groups came a greater variety of interests. The new groups were not just carbon copies of those that already existed. A representative from the National Association of Realtors described the changes for his industry:

> If you go back a few years ago, you would have to say that if the National Association of Realtors and the [National Association of] Home Builders spoke, that was the whole industry speaking. Now there are more groups, such as low income housing groups, real estate developers, residential real estate developers, etc. . . . Members of Congress have to listen to all these groups.

Each new group brings with it a different set of priorities and will aggressively seek out policymakers on its own, as well as frequently enter into coalitions with other groups. The expanding number of advocacy organizations heightens the competition between them because it is difficult for policymakers to find solutions for large numbers of client groups that make all of them winners.

Competition often shades into open conflict. This is most apparent between traditional adversaries, such as business versus labor or business versus liberal public interest groups. Conflict among businesses in the same industry also characterizes a number of policy domains. One important change that has fostered such conflict is the movement toward deregulation. Scholarly analyses of regulatory practices encouraged a view that much of the federal government's regulatory efforts led to inefficiency, unnecessary protection for privileged companies, stifling of competition, and a bad deal for consumers. The hold of industries such as trucking, the airlines, and telecommunications over regulatory policy was shattered by the intellectual appeal of deregulation proposals, nurtured first in academe and in think tanks and then pushed by sympathizers in the legislative and executive branches.[34]

As regulatory barriers that parcel out markets to different types of business enterprises weaken, firms begin to push for further regulatory changes. This has happened in the broad area of financial services. As some regulatory practices have been changed to stimulate competition, various industry sectors have pressed for even more changes. Banks, insurance companies, and brokerage houses all want to encroach on each other's turf. Substantial conflict can exist even within one sector, as in banking. Large money center banks, small banks, and savings and loans do not see eye-to-eye on all issues.

New competition has come not only from traditional segments of the financial services community trying to steal business from each other but also from entirely new players entering the picture. As streaming wireless video becomes more feasible, a variety of companies—including cable television providers, wired and wireless phone providers, Internet stores, movie and television studios, and the makers of handheld digital devices—are lining up to try to gain a piece of the market. Whether there will ever be a big demand to watch movies or television shows on cell phones remains to be seen, but the boundaries of this policy network are difficult to contain.

---

[34]Martha Derthick and Paul Quirk, *The Politics of Deregulation* (Washington, DC: Brookings Institution, 1985).

Recently, firms and broadcasters have argued over the rights to what has been referred to as "white spaces," the unused broadcast channels in between local television channels. The White Spaces Coalition includes Microsoft, Dell, Hewlett-Packard, Google, EarthLink, and Philips Electronics. The Coalition argues that various devices could use these white spaces to expand high-speed Internet access. The National Association of Broadcasters and their engineering group, the Association for Maximum Service Television, argue on behalf of local TV stations stating that mechanical manipulation of those white spaces could interfere with reception of existing channels.[35]

Although the advocacy explosion was the primary reason for the collapse of subgovernments, change in the structure of government contributed to this transformation of interest group politics as well. The institutional arrangements within Congress and the executive branch that helped sustain subgovernments were altered by reforms and changing norms.[36] During the period when subgovernments were declining, the trend in Congress was toward the decentralization of its structure of authority. An important part of this was a growth in the number of subcommittees, which in turn meant more overlapping jurisdictions. For example, at one point 110 committees and subcommittees claimed some jurisdiction over programs of the Environmental Protection Agency.[37] As one observer pointed out, decentralization means that "the scope of conflict changes continually, usually expanding, as legislation passes from one stage to the next. Deals and accommodations devised at one stage cannot be adhered to later because negotiations must be reopened at each stage."[38]

With the Republican control of Congress, after 1994 there was a move to reduce the number of subcommittees and joint referrals of legislation. Moreover, party leaders became increasingly important in the policy process, frequently bypassing committees to rewrite sections of bills, or to insert language in conference committee drafts. This allowed corporations to work alone to insert language into bills, but the much friendlier attitude toward business also encouraged companies to join in coalitions to seek broader cuts in taxes and regulation.

The growth of the executive branch also contributed to the fall of subgovernments. Policymaking became dispersed across more agencies and bureaus, and the authority of many such organizations was reduced as different units began working in the same broad policy area. The autonomy of individual bureaucracies was reduced further as the White House began trying to increase its control over the sprawling executive branch. Recent presidents have used the Office of Management and Budget or other parts of the Executive Office of the President to oversee regulatory policymaking. Over time, the structure of the executive branch and the growth of interest group politics have made agency policymaking more complex and conflictual.

---

[35]Jeffrey Birnbaum, "For the Next Big Bout, Tune in to Channel 41/2," *Washington Post* June 5, 2007, A15.

[36]Jeffrey M. Berry, "Subgovernments, Issue Networks, and Political Conflict," in *Remaking American Politics* ed. Richard A. Harris and Sidney Milkis (Boulder: Westview, 1989), 239–60.

[37]Robert F. Durant, "The Democratic Deficit in America," *Political Science Quarterly* 110 (Spring 1995): 37.

[38]Steven S. Smith, "New Patterns of Decisionmaking in Congress," in *The New Direction in American Politics,* ed. John E. Chubb and Paul E. Peterson (Washington, DC: Brookings Institution, 1985), 221.

The Qualities of Issue Networks

Issue networks are as complex as subgovernments were simple. A network can be defined as "a specific type of relation linking a defined set of persons, objects, or events."[39] In terms of interest groups and government, what does this mean? The "type of relation" is primarily one revolving around the exchange of information.[40] A fundamental axiom of Washington politics is that "information is power," and issue networks provide ways in which information can be gathered and disseminated quickly and inexpensively. As noted in the discussion of coalitions, no one interest group has the means of gathering or monitoring all the information it needs to operate at maximum effectiveness. It is always the case that other groups will have better relationships with some of the key policymakers, have superior knowledge of one aspect of the problem at hand, or will hear about new developments first.[41]

Interest groups develop relationships with other groups in which they freely exchange information under a norm of reciprocity. That is, if one group gives information to a second, the second group is expected to give the first group information when the second acquires it. This does not apply when the groups find themselves on different sides of an issue, as commonly happens to even the best of friends. Information is exchanged in simple and straightforward ways through phone calls, chance meetings (such as those at Capitol Hill receptions), and more formal meetings. Finding out what amendment the subcommittee chair is thinking of offering, or what transpired in a conversation between an agency head and a White House adviser, is information critical to a lobbyist.

The "set of persons, objects, or events" exchange information in a recurring fashion in a particular policy area. The persons are individuals who speak for organizations—notably, interest groups—congressional committees, and executive branch agencies. Not all of these individuals exchange information with all others in their network. Within a large network, there are likely to be clusters of lobbies grouped according to issue focus. People in government are eager to exchange information with lobbyists because it helps them understand what policy alternatives are most politically acceptable and what kind of lobbying strategy is being planned to try to influence them. It is a form of intelligence gathering, and they may gain information that they cannot otherwise acquire at a reasonable cost of time or money.[42] As issues develop, policymakers develop alliances with various groups and keep in touch with them on a regular basis to share information.

It is evident that issue networks are characterized by high degrees of conflict and cooperation. Political scientists have begun to explore the structure of issue networks to see what kinds of cleavages may divide these policymaking communities and to try to identify

---

[39]David Knoke and James Kuklinski, *Network Analysis,* Sage Series on Quantitative Applications in the Social Sciences, no. 28 (Beverly Hills, CA: Sage, 1982), 12.

[40]Karen S. Cook, "Network Structures from an Exchange Perspective," in *Social Structure and Network Analysis,* ed. Peter V. Marsden and Nan Lin (Beverly Hills, CA: Sage, 1982), 177–99.

[41]See, generally, Hula, *Lobbying Together.*

[42]John Mark Hansen, *Gaining Access* (Chicago: University of Chicago Press, 1991); and Hojnacki, "Interest Group Decisions to Join Alliances."

the different kinds of roles groups might play in network politics. Examining the structure of networks is important because it can offer insight into the distribution of power among interest groups.[43] Understanding how individual networks operate is the first step toward comparing networks and building models of the kinds of issue networks that may exist.

Issue networks can be further defined by the following properties:

Hollow cores.   The research that has been done on issue networks shows some common patterns in their internal structure. In their study of four large policy domains, Heinz and his colleagues found that none of the four had a central lobbying group that acted as a broker among most of the other groups in the network. In the energy field, for example, there is no one trade association or large corporation that is at the center of all communication among energy groups. No one lobby coordinates all the major interest group activity; hence, there is a "hollow core" in the middle of the network.[44] This is the case not only because policy differences and ideological divisions exist within a network but also because there are so many issues and organizations that no one group could provide such consistent leadership.

Multiple niches.   Another structural characteristic of networks is that most individual groups are narrowly focused. They generally operate within issue niches, interacting primarily with those groups representing similar interests.[45] For example, one agricultural lobbyist commented, "In agriculture it tends to be commodity groups working closely together. We have to. We're not all that different." These different groups, representing dairy, soybean, peanut, wheat, cotton, cattle, and other such interests, rely largely on each other. Sometimes the politics of niches may change, however. In 2007, an alliance of specialty crop growers (primarily vegetables and fruit) were lobbying for a bigger slice of the federal pie in competition with many of the groups listed above.

The importance of being expert.   Much of the glamour and glitz of Washington lobbying is generated by the handful of lobbyists who have unusual access to those in power because of their high-powered reputations or political connections. For the foot soldiers of the lobbying profession, however, having extensive knowledge about one's issue area is critical to ongoing access to policymakers. It is not that being an expert in earlier times was not helpful. Rather, as policymaking has become more complex and competition from other interest groups in the same area has increased, expertise has become a more significant means by which lobbyists qualify themselves as participants in the policymaking process.

Expertise is something more than familiarity with the issues. All lobbyists have a sound knowledge of the issues they work on. Expertise is a very high degree of knowledge about a policy area, including enough technical sophistication to gain the respect of those in government who are themselves specialists in the policy area.

[43]David Knoke, *Political Networks: The Structural Perspective* (New York: Cambridge University Press, 1990), 1–27; and Barry Wellman, "Structural Analysis: From Method and Metaphor to Theory and Substance," in *Social Structures: A Network Approach,* ed. Barry Wellman and S. D. Berkowitz (New York: Cambridge University Press, 1988), 19–61.

[44]Heinz et al., *The Hollow Core,* 275–308.

[45]William P. Browne, "Organized Interests and Their Issue Niches: A Search for Pluralism in a Policy-Domain," *Journal of Politics* 52 (May 1990): 477–509.

A lobbyist on issues such as toxic wastes, nuclear energy, and acid rain cannot get far without some working knowledge of the scientific issues at the root of the controversies.

Sloppy boundaries.   One criticism that can be made of the issue network model is that the lack of precisely defined boundaries can make a network seem like an amorphous blob. The membership and overall shape of networks are fluid; a new organization can enter a network by developing a relationship with just one other organization already in it. Becoming a critical player in a network may be difficult, but finding other organizations to exchange information with is not. Boundaries are sloppy because issue areas overlap considerably and because there is no central authority capable of excluding new participants.

Even within these broad generalizations, there is reason for caution. As the case study of telecommunications in the next section will demonstrate, networks do not always operate by the norms of well-defined niche politics. Although the research demonstrating that issue networks have hollow cores is very persuasive, the research was restricted to rather large policy domains. It is conceivable that, in smaller networks, centrally located groups play more of a consistent leadership role.

Continuity and Change in Issue Networks

Some issue networks remain relatively static over long periods of time. Although there have been changes in the network of groups and actors who make agricultural policy, the network has remained relatively stable for decades. In contrast, other issue networks change dramatically. Sometimes this change is gradual, as when health groups became involved in tobacco policy, transforming the issue from one of agriculture to one of public health. In other cases, the transformation is more rapid. The pro-life and pro-choice camps have been locked in a protracted and very static political battle for three decades, and there have been little in the way of new arguments or new issues. But, in the early 2000s, the issue networks became more complex over a new issue—the use of stem cells from embryos in medical research that seeks to cure diseases such as Parkinson's and Alzheimer's. The issue split the pro-life camp and brought in new actors, such as biotechnology companies that seek the profits that might come from medical breakthroughs, science groups that want to use embryonic stem cells without limitations, and public health groups advocating for research to find cures for these diseases.

Sometimes new issues create new coalitions, which then move beyond those issues. Evangelical Christian churches and groups became involved in the issue of opposing the persecution of Christians across the world and, in the process, formed alliances with a variety of other groups, including Catholics, Jews, Buddhists, African Americans, and feminists. In forging the coalition, however, evangelicals found their agenda inevitably expanding to include a much broader range of human rights issues.[46] As a result, the

---

[46]Allen D. Hertzke, *Freeing God's Children: The Unlikely Alliance for Global Human Rights* (Lanham, MD: Rowman & Littlefield, 2004).

National Association of Evangelicals has recently been involved in lobbying on issues such as AIDS programs in Africa, global warming, and the use of torture in interrogating prisoners.

Sometimes the causes of the changes are complex. Consider the case of telecommunications. At a hearing of the House Telecommunications Subcommittee in 1976, freshman Representative Tim Wirth (D-CO) was surprised at the large turnout for the session. He asked the witness from AT&T who was testifying to identify his colleagues sitting in the audience. After five minutes, the AT&T executive had identified those in only one corner of the room. A reporter noted that a frustrated Wirth asked, "Will everyone associated with AT&T just stand up?" Everyone in the audience stood up, all 150 of them."[47]

At one time, the Bell monopoly was extensive. Anyone who wanted to have phone service, or even to buy a telephone, dealt with AT&T. The power of the phone monopoly was symbolized by comedian Lily Tomlin's routine as a phone operator, in which she would frequently snigger the line "We don't care; we don't have to. We're the phone company." Legal action eventually broke up the Bell system monopoly. In the 1960s, the FCC ruled that other companies could sell telephones, that a rival company could offer long-distance service, and that AT&T was required to rent access to local lines. The Justice Department filed an antitrust suit against AT&T in 1974, charging it with monopolizing various parts of the telecommunications industry. AT&T counterattacked with an effort to get Congress to pass a law that would forbid competition in the long-distance business. Despite an extraordinary effort by AT&T, the bill did not come close to passage. In January 1981, the case of *United States v. American Telephone and Telegraph* began in the courtroom of federal district judge Harold Greene. AT&T then unsuccessfully lobbied the White House to get the Justice Department to drop the case and finally entered into negotiations with the Justice Department to break up the Bell system.

In an out-of-court agreement, AT&T agreed to give up local telephone service. Seven new regional companies ("Baby Bells"), such as Pacific Telesis in the West and NYNEX in the Northeast, were created to take over local phone service. AT&T retained long-distance services, although it had to face competition from other companies. AT&T was also able to keep control of two of its prized possessions—Bell Labs, its research arm, and Western Electric, its manufacturing division. AT&T also won the right to enter the computer industry, an important goal of the company. It had long had the technological know-how, but as a regulated monopoly it had not been allowed to sell computers. This substantially sweetened the deal for AT&T, which was losing three-quarters of its assets in the settlement.

One of the political consequences of the AT&T breakup and the competition that had earlier come to the phone industry was a spectacular growth in telecommunications advocacy. Just about anybody with expertise on telecommunications could land a lucrative position with one of the newly established Washington offices of firms in the industry. All seven regionals set up lobbying offices to protect their interests against AT&T. The one part of AT&T that did not shrink was its political arm: After reorganizing its Washington

---

[47]Monica Langley, "AT&T Sends a Horde of Lobbyists to Fight a Phone-Bill Proposal," *Wall Street Journal* November 4, 1983.

operations in the wake of the breakup, it had fifty-five lobbyists on board.[48] For lawyers with the right experience, the AT&T breakup was a cause for celebration. "Washington D.C.'s 'telecommunications bar' boomed like a Nevada silver town."[49]

Today the telecommunications issue network has grown much more complex. With technology changing rapidly, basic phone service can now be obtained through wired lines, a variety of types of wireless devices, and Internet providers. Home Internet service can be provided by cable companies, phone companies, and satellite companies, and cell phone providers now offer wireless Internet access worldwide for various notebook computers and handheld devices. Potentially more important are the various music and video services that can be provided to various home and handheld devices, as evidenced by the recent introduction of the iPhone by Apple. Many companies already compete to sell music and video that can be downloaded to personal computers, and a number of companies anticipate a booming market to download video and music to cell phones and various handheld players.[50]

The range of companies that are involved in telecommunications has increased dramatically, and as a result there are now many peripheral issues that have created webs of groups with special interests in small portions of telecommunications policy. Content providers, such as record companies, have worked hard in Congress and the courts to protect their investment in various types of content, pushing to pass and enforce laws to prevent the sharing of music over the Internet. Movie studios are also part of this debate, as are privacy groups and consumer advocacy groups. Content providers have sought to increase the fees for satellite radio stations, and this has brought counter lobbying from that industry. A variety of groups have spent millions lobbying over "net neutrality" legislation that would forbid those who provide Internet service to homes and other networks from privileging the information packets sent by clients who pay a higher rate.

Another peripheral issue brought education and public interest groups into telecommunications issue networks. In the late 1990s, the FCC created a program that taxed telecommunications providers and used the funds to subsidize Internet access for schools and public libraries. When phone companies and antitax groups mobilized to fight the program, a countermobilization by education associations and other citizen groups emerged to support it.[51]

Conclusion

In surveying the relationship of interest groups to other lobbies and government policymakers, both stability and change can be observed. Interest groups still coalesce with

---

[48]Michael Wines, "Ma Bell and Her Newly Independent Children Revamp Lobbying Networks," *National Journal* January 28, 1984, pp. 148–52.

[49]Steve Coll, *The Deal of the Century* (New York: Atheneum, 1986), 365.

[50]Yuki Noguchi, "TV When—and Where—You Want It: New Video Technologies Free Viewers from the Couch," *Washington Post* February 12, 2006, p. A1.

[51]Shoko Kiyohara, "Changes in the Telecommunications Political Process in the United States: The Impact of the Establishment of an E-Rate." Presented at the annual meeting of the Northeastern Political Science Association, November 2004.

each other for the same reasons they always have. They need to share resources (staff, money, and contacts) because each group is limited in the amount of advocacy it can engage and its ability to influence the federal government. Coalitions also enhance the credibility of a group's position.

Change has come as well in the way lobbies interact with others in their political environment. For years, political scientists argued that policymaking through subgovernments was characteristic of the way Washington worked. This may have been true of an earlier time, but it is not accurate today. With the sharp increase in the number of interest groups, policymaking communities changed dramatically. One way to conceive of the interaction of large numbers of interest groups and government officials is to think of these organizations and people as a network. Issue networks facilitate communication between people working in the same policy area.

The decline of subgovernments and the rise of issue networks raise some important questions for political scientists and how they view interest group politics. When the subgovernment model was widely accepted, political scientists were highly critical of the relationships at the core of the policymaking process. To scholars, subgovernments suggested a privileged position for a small number of groups in each policy area. For the political scientists who thought that pluralist theory offered a far too generous assessment of American democracy, the subgovernment model offered a considerably different view of interest groups. At the heart of pluralist thinking is the belief that democratic ends are reached through the bargaining and compromise of affected interests in an open political system. Subgovernments represented agency capture by clientele groups, highly restricted participation, stability that preserves the status quo, and centralized decision making. Subgovernments were evidence that a group-based policymaking system is deeply flawed and does not promote democratic government.

Issue networks suggest something else entirely. The policymaking process is seen as more open, more decentralized, more conflictual, more dynamic, and more broadly participatory. In short, issue networks come much closer to fulfilling the pluralist prescription for democratic politics. This is not to say that they are a perfect mechanism for promoting true pluralist democracy. Despite their expanded participation, issue networks do nothing to ensure that all affected interests are represented at the bargaining table. Lacking a centralized decision-making process, issue network politics may also favor the status quo by making compromise more difficult to achieve when there are sharply divergent views. In the last analysis, though, issue networks come closer to fitting our expectations of democratic policymaking than do subgovernments.

Chapter 10

Bias and Representation

The central issue of interest group politics is the bias of representation. Because some sectors of society are better represented by lobbies than others, we must ask if the advantages gained by such representation are a threat to the integrity of the democratic process. How great is the bias of the interest group society, and what are the consequences of this?

The sector of American society that is best represented by interest groups is big business. Controversy has long surrounded the involvement of business in the political process, and claims of undue corporate influence are a continuing refrain in American political debate. The charges against business are quite serious. Political journalist William Greider, for example, says that the increasing political activity of business "is the centerpiece in the breakdown of contemporary democracy."[1] In his masterful *Politics and Markets*, social scientist Charles Lindblom concluded, "The large private corporation fits oddly into democratic theory and vision. Indeed, it does not fit."[2]

Judging whether or not business possesses a level of influence that is inimical to democracy is extremely difficult because we have no agreed-upon standard for measuring interest group power. Defining power in academic journals is one thing; trying to apply the definition in the real world of Washington politics is quite another. Indeed, political scientists have generally shied away from trying to resolve the thorny measurement issues involved in calculating how much political power is exercised by groups in a policy conflict.[3]

Even without the ideal measuring instruments, there is much to be gained by trying to determine what kinds of advantages are held by business and by other types of interest groups. Such an analysis can help us clarify the types of issues that members of Congress must address in writing legislation that regulates interest group behavior. This includes such policies as campaign finance, lobbying laws, and the policymaking procedures that facilitate or hinder interest group access to government. In this chapter, we look at three questions about interest groups and the bias of representation. First, what kinds of resources are available to business, and how do those resources compare with other sectors of the interest group universe? Second, does business have a special relationship with government, allowing it to influence public policy in ways not available to other interest groups? Third, are there ways that other types of interest groups are advantaged

---

[1]William Greider, *Who Will Tell the People?* (New York: Simon and Schuster, 1992), 331.
[2]Charles E. Lindblom, *Politics and Markets* (New York: Basic Books, 1977), 356.
[3]See Jeffrey M. Berry and Kevin Hula, "Interest Groups and Systemic Bias." Paper delivered at the annual meeting of the American Political Science Association, Washington, DC, August 1991.

in the contemporary American political system? The chapter closes with some thoughts on how the biases in interest group representation might be reduced.

Corporate Wealth and Political Advocacy

The resources available to business are so immense that it is easy to conclude that corporations can dominate any policy issue if they choose to use those resources, yet equating wealth and status with political power is dubious. In the words of one scholar, "One cannot *assume* that the disproportionate possession of certain resources (money, organization, status) leads to the disproportionate exercise of political power. Everything depends on whether a resource can be converted into power, and at what rate and at what price."[4] How does business try to convert its wealth into power? What resources does it draw upon in trying to influence public policy?

Representation

Washington lobbying is very much a day-to-day activity; influence is achieved through continuous work in the trenches. Simply being in Washington, monitoring what is going on, is important. In this sense, business is greatly advantaged because, in terms of who is represented by Washington lobbyists, the bias toward business is overwhelming. An analysis by Kay Schlozman and John Tierney of 6,600 organizations that maintained some presence in Washington in the 1980s is revealing. Of those interest groups that maintain an office in Washington, approximately half are corporations or business trade associations. When organizations that are represented by a law firm, public relations firm, or other hired hands are added to the pool, the tilt toward business is even more evident. Roughly 70 percent of all the organizations having representation in Washington through an office of their own or through hired representatives were corporations (including foreign companies) or business trade groups.[5] A more recent study based on new lobby registrations concluded that "the extent of business predominance in the group system is greater than previously reported."[6] Studies of interest groups in state politics confirm the dominance of business interests.[7]

At the very least, keeping a lobbyist in Washington puts a company in the information loop of the policymaking process and reduces its uncertainty about what actions government might take.[8] If a corporate office is just a small listening-post operation, company executives will still be kept abreast of developments and, as the need arises,

---

[4]James Q. Wilson, "Democracy and the Corporation," in *Does Big Business Rule America?*, ed. Ronald Hessen (Washington, DC: Ethics and Public Policy Center, 1981), 37.

[5]Kay Lehman Schlozman and John T. Tierney, *Organized Interests and American Democracy* (New York: Harper & Row, 1986), 67.

[6]Frank R. Baumgartner and Beth L. Leech, "Interest Niches and Policy Bandwagons: Patterns of Interest Group Involvement in National Politics," *Journal of Politics* 63 (2001): 1195.

[7]David Lowery, Virginia Gray, and Matthew Fellowes, "Sisyphus Meets the Borg: Economic Scale and Inequalities in Interest Representation," *Journal of Theoretical Politics* 17 (2005): 41–74.

[8]John P. Heinz, Edward O. Laumann, Robert L. Nelson, and Robert H. Salisbury, *The Hollow Core* (Cambridge, MA: Harvard University Press, 1993), 1–3.

can hire more help from the pool of lobbyists-for-hire in Washington. However, lobbyists are more than passive conveyors of Washington intelligence. In the daily interaction of issue network politics, lobbyists help create expectations about acceptable policy alternatives, exchange studies and other information that influence the way problems are defined, and create the coalitions that may negotiate with government officials.

The value of representation is obvious. What is important is not simply that there are more lobbyists for business than for other parts of society but that large corporations are represented in so many important ways. We noted in chapter 6 that Microsoft had sixteen lobbyists and retained twenty lobby firms to represent the company. Microsoft is also a member of various trade associations and belongs to various business peak associations. It uses its executive personnel in lobbying and raises money to contribute to campaigns.

Microsoft is not a typical American corporation. The largest American companies are most advantaged in the degree to which they are represented in Washington. Small and midsize firms are represented primarily by trade groups. Some very large firms do not have their own offices in Washington, preferring to work with trade groups, keeping lawyers or other lobbyists on retainer or hiring them when the occasion arises, and sending personnel from headquarters to Washington when an issue heats up. Nevertheless, whether it has a Washington office or not, the large American corporation speaks loudly with many tongues in the policymaking process.

Deep Pockets

Microsoft "backstops" the Washington office with help from headquarters. Resources are made available as needed, avoiding unnecessary staffing in Washington and promoting a close working relationship between top corporate executives and government affairs specialists. Says one lobbyist for a different corporation, "I have all the backup I could want. I have everything I need. If I call headquarters and say I need something, I'll usually get it." A lobbyist from a telecommunications company emphasized the cooperation between Washington and headquarters: "If we need additional employees, the only question is, 'Who?' If we need money, they say go ahead and spend it."

One advantage in having headquarters personnel backstop lobbying campaigns is that it helps maximize the use of technical expertise in advocacy endeavors. Executives brought to Washington to talk to legislators or their staffers or to administrators can speak with great authority about the consequences of policy alternatives. The use of executives in lobbying also helps keep the Washington office talking to corporate headquarters about what the company needs and what is politically possible in Washington. One corporate lobbyist noted, "As legislation froths up to the top, we need substantial interplay with senior management [who might] say, 'Section 7 kills us in our strategic plan,' and I wouldn't know that."

It is best to conceive of the Washington offices of a large business as a coordinating mechanism for the parent corporation's advocacy. It utilizes executives from corporate offices when their efforts can be useful; it helps direct campaign contributions if the company has a PAC; it draws on corporate funds to make donations to ad-hoc coalitions and other advocacy groups; it hires law firms and public relations firms as the need arises; it works with trade associations to which the parent company belongs; it may donate corporate funds in the form of "soft money" to one or both of the two major political parties; and it may contribute money to think tanks and other organizations that are doing research seen as favorable to the company's interests. Hence, the size of a corporation's Washington office may bear little relationship to the resources it has at its disposal. Stated another way, if an environmental citizen group has an annual budget of $500,000 for its lobbying office, that is basically what it has available for advocacy. If a Washington office of a major corporation has an annual budget of $500,000, that is just the starting point. Rather, it has an elastic budget covered by the deep pockets of its corporate parent.

The advantage that business has in being able to purchase multiple forms of representation is illustrated by the magnitude of the coordinated efforts of drug companies to influence public policy. The drug industry uses all of the tools described in earlier chapters. They contribute money through PACs and bundled individual contributions. In 2004, they gave an estimated $17 million to federal candidates, including nearly $1 million to George W. Bush and more than half that amount to John Kerry. The industry has more than 1,200 lobbyists in Washington and has spent more than $800 million since 1998 in lobbying national government. Senator Charles Grassley, chairman of the Senate Finance Committee, noted, "You can hardly swing a cat by the tail in that town [Washington] without hitting a pharmaceutical lobbyist."[9] Several hundred of those lobbyists are former lawmakers, including Billy Tauzin, a former legislator who chaired the House Energy and Commerce committee that drafted portions of the Medicare prescription drug law in 2003 (which provided prescription drugs for the elderly with few cost controls) and now chairs the industry trade association. The drug industry also spent nearly $50 million in 2003 and 2004 alone lobbying state governments.[10] The financial power of the drug industry is not fully reflected in its obvious lobbying and contributing, because the industry also sponsors foundations and research to help bolster its goals.

The industry won a great victory with the passage of the Medicare prescription drug bill. Although many other lobbies, including those for the elderly, and many unions joined to lobby on behalf of the final bill, the provisions that would have affected the industry most involved details settled earlier. The industry beat back a series of proposals for containing the costs of prescription drugs, and expects to be a player in any national discussion about national health insurance in the near future.

A Special Relationship

In the wake of business's expanded influence during the 1970s, the election of Ronald Reagan in 1980 brought an administration into power that was unusually sympathetic to corporate interests. For twelve years, the Reagan and Bush administrations pushed policies that greatly benefited business. After two years of Democrat Bill Clinton, the Republican capture of the Congress in the 1994 elections promised more pro-business

---

[9]In Jim Drinkard, "Drugmakers Go Furthest to Sway Congress," *USA Today* April 25, 2005, p. A1.
[10]Center for Public Integrity, http://www.publicintegrity.org/rx/report.aspx?aid=794 (accessed April 8, 2006).

and antiregulatory policies. When George W. Bush was elected in 2000, pro-business forces controlled the presidency and both branches of Congress. One lobbyist in a firm with mostly corporate clients described the early years of the Bush administration in the early 2000s as "better than my wildest dream."

Some would argue, however, that to focus on what business gets out of one administration over another is to miss the point. Business, in Charles Lindblom's words, enjoys a "privileged position" in American politics. Business prosperity is so vital to the nation's well-being that corporate America maintains unique advantages in the political system. Lindblom says that, for governmental officials, "businessmen do not appear simply as the representatives of a special interest, as representatives of interest groups do. They appear as functionaries performing functions that government officials regard as indispensable."[11] Even though business does not win every battle, it always wins the war because, if it does not get its way, Lindblom concludes, "Recession or stagnation is a consequence."[12] Thus, both legislators and the administration in power are especially eager to please those in the business community because they do not want to suffer the electorate's wrath after an economic downturn. Of course, individual businesses seek to maximize profit, not to help the overall economy, but Lindblom argues that collectively they play a vital role in maintaining the nation's economic well-being.

Lindblom's notion of a "privileged position" goes to the heart of the question concerning the power of business. Should business be viewed simply as a strong set of interest groups with the most lobbyists and the most money to use? Or, as Lindblom claims, does business's critical importance to our well-being give it unique advantages in the governmental process? This question can be addressed from many directions, but the analysis here will be limited to two lines of inquiry. First, we will examine the type of access business leaders have to government officials. Second, we will turn to the question of whether America is ruled through a power elite led by an inner circle of business leaders.

Access

It has already been established that business is unusually well represented and that the presence of so many lobbyists in the employ of business is significant in the everyday policymaking of Washington. Organizations with representatives in issue networks help shape policy over the long term. But a fair evaluation of representation in Washington would go beyond counting lobbyists. An underlying question is "Who gets to see whom?" There is a qualitative difference between seeing a middle-level bureaucrat about a particular regulation and having a private audience with the assistant secretary responsible for that broad policy area. Most lobbyists have good access to congressional staffers, but they cannot always get to see party leaders and committee and subcommittee chairs when they needed.

This may seem to be a pretty low-level test for assessing business influence. If business is truly a dominant power, need it be concerned about getting better access to

---

[11]Lindblom, *Politics and Markets,* 175.
[12]Ibid., 187.

subcommittee chairs and party leaders? The answer is an unequivocal yes—it is significant. Access beyond what normally accrues to Washington representatives is a critical measure of influence because it indicates that an interest group gets a hearing not available to others. If business as a class consistently gets more access to high-ranking government officials, then it does have a special relationship that places its policy concerns at a higher level of importance than the concerns of others. The vast sums of money that PACs donate to congressional campaigns are an indication of the high premium some interest groups place on access. In the real world of Washington politics, special access is what interest groups strive for.[13]

By this criterion, business does well. Although the wealth of corporations may give them the most lobbyists along with deep pockets for backstopping Washington offices, their access is built on more than that. The high status of companies, their importance to the welfare of the district or state, and the personal connections of their executives yield a high degree of access to key policymakers. In a survey of leaders from various segments of American society, respondents were asked if they had talked to a member of Congress a few times a year or more. Among business leaders, who were primarily corporate executives rather than lobbyists, fully 86 percent talked to a member of Congress at least a couple of times a year. Thus, almost all the corporate leaders in the sample were able to converse directly to legislators on at least an intermittent, if not regular, basis. It is important to point out, however, that the figures were relatively high for the leaders of other sectors of the interest group community, too. The comparable figures were 75 percent for black leaders, 68 percent for labor leaders, 62 percent for farm leaders, and 57 percent for feminist leaders. For the public at large, only 15 percent reported talking to a member of Congress at least a couple times a year.[14] The door to the office of a member of Congress is generally open to leaders of important constituencies, but it is open a tad wider to business.

Among those who gave at least $200 to a congressional candidate in 1996, a significant majority was a member of a business group, and many others were members of professional groups that often include business leaders. Figure 10.1 shows the percentage of donors who belong to various types of groups, by partisanship. Note that, among Republicans, business and professional groups are dominant and, that among Democratic donors, there are almost as many donors who are members of business groups as are members of environmental groups: only a tiny portion of donors are union members. More than 75 percent of donors who were members of business groups had contacted a member of Congress about a policy issue, compared to just over half of other donors. Among those who were members of neither business nor professional groups, the number dropped to 45 percent—a large number but much lower than that for business group members.

After the Republicans captured Congress in 1994, the majority staffers on committees not only gave business lobbyists an unusual amount of access but actually had them write some of the legislation that was being proposed. When the Senate Judiciary

---

[13]For a different view, see Stephen Ansolabehere, John DeFiguerido, and James Snyder, "Why Is There So Little Money in Politics," *Journal of Economic Perspectives* 17 (2003): 105–30.

[14]Sidney Verba and Gary Orren, *Equality in America* (Cambridge, MA: Harvard University Press, 1985), 69.

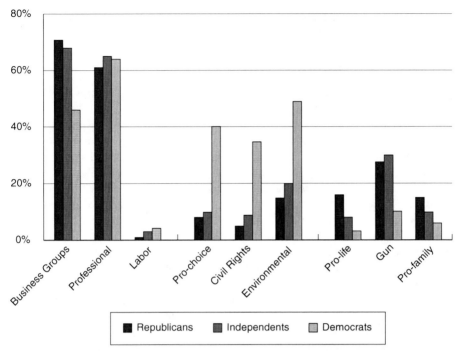

FIGURE 10.1
Membership in Types of Groups among Congressional Donors.
Source: Congressional Donor Survey 1996.

Committee took up the task of rewriting some key environmental laws, it turned much of the job over to Hunton & Williams, a law firm with a specialty in representing electric utilities before regulatory agencies. Hunton & Williams wrote much of one bill, and, when Democrat staffers were briefed, the firm's lawyers had to explain it to them because GOP staffers did not appear to know the specifics of what had been put into the legislation.[15] As noted in chapter 8, energy providers wrote key elements of the energy plan adopted by the Bush administration in 2001. Energy lobbyists drafted elements of the proposal, mindful of their impact on company profits.

Republicans reject criticism of this kind of coziness by saying it is no different from the access granted by the Democrats to liberal groups, such as organized labor and environmental lobbies. There is some truth to this. When the Democrats control the White House, they appoint their interest group allies to key agency policymaking positions and ensure access for the groups that support the party. When Democrats gained control of Congress in 2006, environmental groups had far easier access to policymakers. A key difference is that the Democrats give much better access to business than the Republicans give to labor and liberal citizen groups. The reason, again, is that business

---

[15]Stephen Engelberg, "Business Leaves the Lobby and Sits at Congress's Table," *New York Times* March 31, 1995.

is different: The Democrats cannot ignore the needs of private enterprise, but the Republicans usually feel they can disregard workers and liberal groups.

A Business Monolith?

If business has enormous advantages in resources and access, this still does not guarantee that business will win all of its battles. If the business community is united, then it should have considerable advantages over its opponents; however, if business is fragmented and unable to agree on key elements of policymaking, then business victories may be less likely. After all, businesses seek to maximize profits for their shareholders, and this may not be consistent with helping another company win a special benefit from Congress.

Some argue that, although businesses may disagree over the details of policy, the interlocking ownership of many companies guarantees cooperation on key issues. Michael Useem, in *The Inner Circle,* attempts to show the dominance of a small ruling class of business elites in the United States and Britain. For Useem, an "inner circle" of business elites "gives coherence and direction to the politics of business."[16] These corporate leaders are people who are on the boards of several major corporations and thus form an interlocking network. Their most important interaction does not concern what one company can do to help another. Rather, when not discussing the company on whose board they sit, they turn to broader business developments and governmental activity affecting business.

Members of the inner circle are distinguished from other business executives in that they have an abiding concern for the health of business generally and do not confine their political activities to working on behalf of their own companies' narrow interests. If all corporate leaders directed their political efforts only toward helping their own companies' immediate needs, their parochialism could damage the broader, long-term interests of all large corporations. Through their communication with other corporate leaders, this inner circle is able "to enter politics on behalf of consensually arrived at classwide interests."[17] There is no formal consensus, of course, but through the interlocking ties the communication that flows back and forth educates the inner circle as to the areas of agreement and concern.

In a more recent, and very careful, study, Mark Mizruchi argues that the nature of business unity is conditional. He finds statistical evidence of many of Useem's claims, including the notion that interlocking directorates, overlapping financial patterns of ownership, and other forms of economic and social networks produce even more business unity than exists among firms in the same industry.[18] He finds evidence of an inner circle of business leaders who exert strong influence on business political behavior. He documents that, when business leaders testify before Congress, they agree with one another four times as often as they disagree, yet he does find disagreement among even firms that are linked through several networks and identifies companies that are not part of the larger business networks.

---

[16]Michael Useem, *The Inner Circle* (New York: Oxford University Press, 1984), 3.
[17]Ibid., 58.
[18]Mark S. Mizruchi, *The Structure of Corporate Political Action* (Cambridge, MA: Harvard University Press).

With considerable resources and energetic advocacy, the Chamber of Commerce, the National Association of Manufacturers, and the Business Roundtable are certainly organizations whose leadership qualifies as part of an ostensible inner circle. These organizations work on broad issues facing business and try to educate those in government about the long-term needs of the free-enterprise system. At the same time, these groups can be immobilized on policy debates because their broad memberships are divided. The 1986 tax reform bill is a case in point. The sweeping reform legislation was initially intended to create a "level playing field" by eliminating special tax provisions that helped some industries but not others. Many such provisions were left in the tax code, but the new law did remove or reduce some major tax advantages, such as ending the investment tax credit. These changes hurt heavy manufacturing industries, such as aluminum, steel, and machine tools. At the same time, many service industries, such as retailing, which did not enjoy major tax preferences, were helped by the law because it lowered the general corporate tax rate. Because it hurt some industries while helping others, the tax reform bill created a bitter split among big business leaders. Even the Business Roundtable, symbol of the clout of big business during the Reagan years, was fractured. "Part of the group went in one direction, part went in the other direction, and both lost," said Irving Shapiro, former DuPont CEO and past chair of the Roundtable. The National Association of Manufacturers and the Chamber of Commerce were immobilized as well.[19] Nothing could be more fundamentally important to business than an overhaul of the tax code, but on this issue the inner circle sat on the sidelines.

It would be too severe a test to demand absolute unanimity by big business on behalf of broad policy decisions. Nevertheless, if the advocacy efforts of business can be taken as a measure of the pursuit of classwide objectives, substantial unity is commonly absent. Nor do we see evidence of an inner circle of elites who consistently promote classwide interests against other sets of business leaders. Different areas of policy divide the top business elite in different ways. If decisions ultimately favor long-term classwide interests, these decisions may reflect one set of elites and their organizations prevailing over another set more than they reflect a cohesive inner circle working its will. Frequently, business groups are actively opposed to one another, as in recent battles over who will control access to and the content of the wireless media market.

Even if business is unified, it is not always successful. Mark Smith argues that the conditions that allow for business unity also allow for substantial mobilization by groups opposed to business.[20] His research suggests that business wins only when it has public support. Thus, public opinion constrains the success even of a unified business community. Further research is needed to specify the relationship between business interests and public opinion, since much of what business seeks is not salient to the public, and business has considerable resources to try to swing public opinion. But there are important limits to business power, and business does not always win.

---

[19]Alan S. Murray, "Lobbyists for Business Are Deeply Divided, Reducing Their Clout," *Wall Street Journal* March 25, 1987.

[20]Mark A. Smith, *American Business and Political Power: Public Opinion, Elections, and Democracy* (Chicago: University of Chicago Press, 2000).

Beyond Business

Although business is uniquely favored in the American political system, other interest group sectors are not without their own distinctive advantages. The governmental process is structured by many social, economic, and political divisions and biases that work to support the advocacy of some groups but not others.

Power of the People

The traditional counterweight to the resources of business is the power of the people. If policymakers have to choose between the equally intense preferences of business leaders and of ordinary citizens, they will most likely choose the option favored by ordinary citizens. The reason is simple: There are more ordinary citizens than business leaders and thus more votes to be gained. In the real world, issues are not so starkly drawn, and ordinary citizens do not usually form a coherent, unified political force.

Nevertheless, the power of numbers works in favor of some important interest group constituencies. It is not merely that large interest group constituencies have many voters to cast ballots in the next election but also that they are sources of workers in campaigns. As noted in Chapter 3, organized labor has traditionally provided Democratic candidates with campaign workers to staff the phone banks and walk the precincts. Although organized labor has shrunk in size, it is still an extraordinarily important resource for Democrats. Christian Right and pro-family groups give little money directly to the Republicans, but many recent GOP candidates have staffed their campaign organizations with volunteers from the local chapters of those groups.

When an interest group has a large number of members with impassioned views and has built an effective organizational structure that can quickly mobilize the rank and file, it is greatly respected (and maybe even feared) by politicians. This is why the American Association of Retired Persons has been so effective over the years. It can mobilize a huge number of senior citizens who are deeply concerned about Social Security and Medicare. Business, while it can contribute valuable campaign money through its PACs, does not have the same kind of energy or broad commitment by its employees. Middle managers at IBM are not going to organize to work on behalf of a congressional candidate on the basis of his or her views on the future of the computer industry. Not many interest groups have this kind of power of the people, but those who do are endowed with an extraordinary political resource.

Citizen groups may lack the resources of corporations, but they represent often hundreds of thousands or even millions of voters who care deeply about issues. These groups also have access to Congress. In one study of citizen groups in national politics, Jeffrey Berry reported that citizen groups offered fully one-third of all congressional testimony in the early 1990s.[21] Citizen groups were cited by media stories fully ten times more than their numbers would suggest.

---

[21]Jeffrey M. Berry, *The New Liberalism: The Rising Power of Citizen Groups* (Washington, DC: Brookings Institution, 1999), 20.

Berry also found that liberal groups outnumbered conservative groups in congressional lobbying by a wide margin. He argued that liberal groups have key resources, including a large membership base, media visibility, and perceived credibility on key issues. Conservative citizen groups were less successful in advancing their agenda in his study, which ended shortly after Republicans first won control of Congress in 1994. Indeed, Berry even found that environmental groups defeated business groups on a series of key measures in the new GOP Congress, in part because the Republican bills sought more radical change than was possible.[22]

A decade later, citizen groups remain powerful and liberal groups retain significant resources. Although the Bush administration has spent considerable effort pushing Congress to approve oil drilling in the Arctic National Wildlife Refuge, environmentalists have blocked this for years. Environmental groups have done better within Congress (where public opinion matters, and many Democrats and moderate Republicans have power) than within the agencies of the executive branch. The U.S. political system makes it easier for groups to protect the status quo than to change it, and environmental groups did their best to block changes. Over the first six years of the Bush administration, however, environmentalists lost with increasing frequency. The White House used its discretion repeatedly to relax regulations and open up public lands for exploitation. Clearly, there are limits on the power of liberal citizen groups, just as there are limits on the power of business. As liberal citizen groups have pressed the new Democratic Congress to enact more environmental regulations, they now find that business groups can use these same rules to protect the status quo.

Meanwhile, conservative citizen groups have been disappointed in their successes with the Bush administration. Although Bush was initially seen as a likely savior for the Christian conservative agenda, he spent most of his political resources on tax cuts and the deregulation of business, as well as on the Iraq war. Although citizen groups pushed him to back a constitutional amendment banning same-sex marriage, Bush dropped the issue after his reelection. Once again, these groups have sought to change the status quo, which is more difficult than to protect it. In 2007, gay and lesbian rights groups are pushing the Congress to enact more protections, and are similarly finding it difficult to implement change.

Even if citizen groups have the power to offset business, however, it is important to remember that not all positions on issues are represented by powerful groups. There is a substantial lobby to end all abortions, and another substantial lobby to protect abortion rights, but only a few small groups advocate allowing absorptions in some but not all circumstances, even though surveys show that many Americans hold this positions.

Reform

We end where we began, with Madison's dilemma. Our form of government allows people to organize and lobby for their own selfish interests, even if the policies they advocate are contrary to the general well-being of the country. The increasing prominence

---

[22]Ibid., 110–14.

of lobbying organizations in the governmental process has focused attention on the problems associated with interest group politics. If the system is ailing, why not fix it? Madison's warning in *Federalist* No. 10 is sobering. Efforts to cure the "mischiefs of faction," warns Madison, could end up "destroying" our political freedom:

> Liberty is to faction what air is to fire, an aliment without which it instantly expires. But it could not be a less folly to abolish liberty, which is essential to political life, because it nourishes faction than it would be to wish the annihilation of air, which is essential to animal life, because it imparts to fire its destructive agency.[23]

Madison believed that the size and diversity of the country and the structure of our government would prevent any particular faction from oppressing all others. Madison's solution certainly has worked to make it harder for any one set of groups to dominate American politics. Nevertheless, his solution is not entirely adequate. At times in our history, the government has stepped in to limit the power of groups, and recent calls for lobbying reform strike a familiar chord in American politics. Lobbies are always a target for those frustrated with the performance of government. One might think that the public's high level of alienation from government would have prompted serious reform years ago. Concern about interest group politics has stimulated an ongoing debate in Congress over a stream of bills designed to reform our campaign finance and lobbying laws.

In the summer of 2007, Congress passed a lobby reform bill, which was generally greeted with praise by the reform community. The bill bars members of the Senate and House from accepting gifts from lobbyists or their clients. It limits lobby-sponsored trips to one day, and effectively bars the use of corporate jets to carry members and aides. Trips must be approved in advance, and disclosed to the public. The bill also requires lobbyists who bundle more than $15,000 to disclose this activity, and requires members of Congress to disclose information about earmarked spending. It is too early to know how this new legislation will work, although we noted earlier that some members are evading the disclosure of earmarked spending. Reformers lamented the failure to create an independent office to help enforce the rules.

Meanwhile, the Supreme Court left the reach of important elements of the BCRA campaign finance reforms in doubt at a critical time in the 2008 election cycle. Students of campaign finance warned that the presidential public financing system was in danger of becoming irrelevant.

Beyond the dilemma outlined in *Federalist* No. 10 and the partisan and ideological differences that are brought to the debate in Congress, there is an additional reason that it is so hard to agree on interest group reforms. What are the principles that should guide what is allowable interest group activity? And what is so harmful that we must violate *Federalist* No. 10's warnings and restrict the freedom of groups? Madison speaks of the ultimate consequence of faction-based politics as "oppression." This is a rather extreme condition, and surely a government must not wait to take action until circumstances suggest that such disaster looms. What principles, then, should be followed in deciding

---

[23]*The Federalist Papers* (New York: New American Library, 1961), 78.

whether the regulation of interest groups is just or an unwarranted violation of personal freedom? There appear to be three commonsense standards for regulating interest groups.

First, government should be vigilant in ensuring that interest group spending does not play an undue role in the political process. In the abstract, few disagree with this. Controversy comes from efforts to set specific limits on spending by groups. Still, government has long regulated what lobbies could spend money on. If corporations could donate unlimited amounts of their general revenues to political candidates, these contributions would so dominate campaign spending that the contributions by others would become largely symbolic. Just as free speech is no longer free speech if someone owns all the newspapers and TV stations, interest group politics is not fair when money spent by one sector crowds out the participation of others. Congress passed the Bipartisan Campaign Reform Act in 2002, and this has reduced the flow of corporate treasury funds into elections, but current campaign finance rules give candidates an incentive to spend all of their fundraising efforts courting wealthy interests, not average citizens. Cities have experimented with reforms that match small contributions by as much as 4 to 1, giving candidates an incentive to interact with the less affluent. These laws might provide a model for federal legislation.

Second, government should protect the integrity of the political system. No one would take issue with this, but the devil is in the details. The new lobby rules go far toward reforming the connections between lobbyists and lawmakers. Now we must see whether Congress has the will to enforce these provisions.

Third, government should ensure that disadvantaged sectors of society that are inadequately represented by interest groups receive support to improve their representation in the political process. For the poor, minorities, and the disabled, there are interest groups active on their behalf, but they are few in number and do not have the resources to fund the kind of advocacy efforts they need. Over the years, the government has taken steps through grants and contracts to help groups for the disadvantaged to organize, develop programs, and train leaders. Such efforts reduce the inequities that are inevitable in any society. Despite their good intentions, these programs are controversial because they have partisan implications. Republicans perceive, correctly, that such programs help empower constituencies partial to the Democrats. The GOP has repeatedly made efforts to "defund the left" by trying to reduce the federal money available for advocacy organizations.[24] Not every such program may be worthwhile, but Congress must rise above partisan and ideological considerations. Interest group politics is only defensible when all significant constituencies are represented by viable lobbying organizations.

The lobbying world is, by and large, an adversarial one.[25] Groups are aligned against each other, and the type of prohibitions and rules described earlier is designed to keep policy fights reasonably fair. Another way of trying to structure interest group politics

---

[24]Michael S. Greve, "Why 'Defunding the Left' Failed," *Public Interest* 89 (Fall 1987): 91–106; Jeff Shear, "The Ax Files," *National Journal* April 15, 1995, pp. 924–27; and Keith Bradsher, "House Seeking Data on Nonprofit Groups," *New York Times* September 27, 1995.

[25]See Jane J. Mansbridge, *Beyond Adversary Democracy* (New York: Basic Books, 1980).

is to make it "cooperationist," rather than adversarial.[26] If ways can be found to develop policy through mediation of interest group differences, many of the problems of interest group politics will be diminished. One such approach is negotiated rule making. This procedure is used by the government in some cases, and it allows agencies to turn over the formulation of regulations to panels of interest group representatives. The Negotiated Rulemaking Act requires that these panels be balanced in their makeup, and that all interests who "will be significantly affected" by the regulations will be represented.[27] This is a particularly useful procedure when protracted conflict between business and citizen groups would otherwise prevail.[28] It makes policymaking efficient and requires consensus among interest group participants.

Government can nurture cooperationist policymaking in other ways, and efforts should be made to develop additional procedures that encourage groups with different views to work together in a publicly spirited search for policy solutions. At the same time, we should recognize that no set of government reforms is going to eliminate conflict in politics. Even though people may not be as inherently selfish as Madison assumed, self-interest will always be a part of politics. Thus, government must always be ready to maintain the balance between personal freedom and the need to prevent interest groups from seriously damaging the democratic process. This cannot easily be done by enacting reforms hastily during political crises. The current wave of lobbying scandals and continued problems in campaign finance provide the opportunity for thoughtful and deliberate reform. Whether it occurs remains to be seen.

---

[26]Steven Kelman, "Adversary and Cooperationist Institutions for Conflict Resolution in Public Policymaking," *Journal of Policy Analysis and Management* 11 (1992): 178–206.

[27]*Negotiated Rulemaking Act of 1989,* 101st Congress, 1st session, 1989, Senate Report 101–97, p. 16.

[28]Jeffrey M. Berry, "Citizen Groups and the Changing Nature of Interest Group Politics in America," *Annals of the American Academy of Political and Social Science* 528 (July 1993): 30–41.

Bibliography

Aberbach, Joel, and Bert Rockman. "Bureaucrats and Clientele Groups." *American Journal of Political Science* 22 (November 1978): 818–32.

Abramson, Jill, and Timothy Noah. "In GOP Controlled Congress, Lobbyists Remain as Powerful as Ever—And Perhaps More Visible," *Wall Street Journal,* April 20, 1995.

Adams, Greg D. "Abortion: Evidence of Issue Evolution." *American Journal of Political Science* 41 (July, 1997): 718–37.

Aldrich, Howard, and Udo Staber. "How American Business Organized Itself in the Twentieth Century." Paper delivered at the annual meeting of the American Political Science Association, Washington, DC, August 1986.

Aldrich, John, and David W. Rohde. "The Consequences of Party Organization in the House: The Role of the Majority and Minority Parties in Conditional Party Government." In *Polarized Politics: Congress and the President in a Partisan Era,* edited by Jon R. Bond and Richard Fleisher. Washington, DC: CQ Press, 2000.

American Political Parties: Decline or Resurgence? Edited by Jeffrey E. Cohen, Richard Fleisher, and Paul Kantor. Washington, DC: CQ Press, 2001.

"Americans Taking Abramoff, Alito, and Domestic Spying in Stride." Pew Research Center for the People & the Press, Jan 11, 2006.

Ansolbehere, Stephen, John DeFigueiredo, and James Snyder. "Why is There So Little Money in Politics?" *Journal of Economic Perspectives* 17 (2003): 105–30.

Appollonio, D. E., and Raymond J. La Raja. "Who Gave Soft Money? The Effect of Interest Group Resources on Political Contributions." *Journal of Politics,* 66(4): 1134–54, 2004.

Bachrach, Peter, and Morton S. Baratz. "Two Faces of Power." *American Political Science Review* 56 (December 1962): 947–52.

Baer, Denise L., and Julie A. Dolan. "Intimate Connections: Political Interests and Group Activity in State and Local Parties." *American Review of Politics* 15 (Summer 1994): 257–89.

Baran, Jan Witold. "Can I Lobby You? Don't Let One Bad Abramoff Spoil the Whole Bunch." *The Washington Post,* Sunday January 8, 2006, p. B01.

Barasko, Maryann. *Governing NOW: Grassroots Activism in the National Organization for Women.* Ithaca: Cornell University Press, 2004.

Barnes, Fred. "The Parasite Culture of Washington," *New Republic,* July 28, 1986, p. 26.

Bauer, Raymond A., Ithiel de Sola Pool, and Lewis Anthony Dexter. *American Business and Public Policy.* New York: Atherton, 1963.

Baumgartner, Frank R. "The Growth and Diversity of U.S. Associations: 1956–2004: Analyzing Trends Using the Encyclopedia of Associations." Working paper, March 29, 2005.

Baumgartner, Frank R., and Beth L. Leech. "Interest Niches and Policy Bandwagons: Patterns of Interest Group Involvement in National Politics." *Journal of Politics* 63 (2001): 1195.

Baumgartner, Frank R., and Bryan D. Jones. *Agendas and Instability in American Politics.* Chicago: University of Chicago Press, 1993.

Beamish, Rita, "Environmental Critics Got EPA Grants." *AP Breaking News,* December 29, 2005.

Bedlington, Anne H. "The Realtors Political Action Committee: Covering All Contingencies." In *After the Revolution: PACs, Lobbies, and the Republican Congress,* edited by Robert Biersack, Paul S. Herrnson, and Clyde Wilcox. Boston: Allyn and Bacon, 1999.

Bednar, Nancy L., and Allen D. Hertzke. "The Christian Right and Republican Realignment in Oklahoma." *PS* 28 (March 1995): 11–15.

Bee, Margaret Talev. "Scandal's Glare on Legislators and Their PACs; Leadership Groups Grow, Some with Lobbyists in Charge." *Sacramento Bee,* February 20, 2006, p. A1.

Begley, Sharon. "Global Warming Deniers: A Well-Funded Machine." *MSNBC.com*

Bennett, James T., and Thomas J. DiLorenzo. *Destroying Democracy.* Washington, DC: Cato Institute, 1985.

Bentley, Arthur. *The Process of Government.* Chicago: University of Chicago Press, 1980.

Berke, Richard. "GOP Seeks Foe's Donors, and Baldlly," *The New York Times,* June 17, 1995.

Bernstein, Marver H. *Regulating Business by Independent Commission.* Princeton: Princeton University Press, 1955.

Berry, Jeffrey. *The New Liberalism.* Washington, D.C.: Brookings Institution Press, 1999.

Berry, Jeffrey M. *Lobbying for the People.* Princeton: Princeton University Press, 1977.

———. *Feeding Hungry People: Rulemaking in the Food Stamp Program.* New Brunswick, NJ: Rutgers University Press, 1984.

———. "Beyond Citizen Participation: Effective Advocacy Before Administrative Agencies." *Journal of Applied Behavioral Science* 17 (October 1981): 463–77.

———. "Citizen Groups and the Changing Nature of Interest Group Politics in America." *Annals of the American Academy of Political and Social Science* 528 (July 1993): 30–41.

———. "On the Origins of Public Interest Groups: A Test of Two Theories." *Polity* 10 (Spring 1978): 379–97.

———. "Public Interest vs. Party System." *Society* 17 (May–June 1980): 42–48.

———. "Subgovernments, Issue Networks, and Political Conflict." In *Remaking American Politics,* edited by Richard A. Harris and Sidney M. Milkis. Boulder: Westview, 1989.

———. "The Dynamic Qualities of Issue Networks." Paper delivered at the annual meeting of the American Political Science Association, New York, September 1994.

———. "Who Will Get Caught in the IRS's Sights?" *Washington Post*, November 21, 2004, p. B03.

———. *The New Liberalism: The Rising Power of Citizen Groups*. Washington, DC: Brookings Institution, 1999.

Berry, Jeffrey M., and David F. Arons. *A Voice for Nonprofits*. Washington, DC: Brookings Institution, 2003.

Berry, Jeffrey M., and Kevin Hula. "Interest Groups and Systemic Bias." Paper delivered at the annual meeting of the American Political Science Association, Washington, D.C., August 1991.

Berry, Jeffrey M., and Deborah Schildkraut. "Citizen Groups, Political Parties, and the Decline of the Democrats." Paper delivered at the annual meeting of the American Political Science Association, Chicago, September 1995.

Berry, Jeffrey M., Kent E. Portney, and Ken Thomson. *The Rebirth of Urban Democracy*. Washington DC: Brookings Institution, 1993.

Biersack, Robert, Paul S. Herrnson, and Clyde Wilcox, eds. *Risky Business?* Armonk, NY: M. E. Sharpe, 1994.

———. 1993. "Seeds for Success: Early Money in Congressional Elections." *Legislative Studies Quarterly* 18 (1993): 535–52.

Birnbaum, Jeffrey. "GOP Freezes Jobs List, a Vestige of the K Street Project," *The Washington Post*, January 26, 2006, p. A02.

———. "Don't Cry for Republican Lobbyists." *The Washington Post*, November 13, 2006, D1.

———. "Study Finds Missed Messages on Capital Hill." *The Washington Post*, October 2, 2006, D1.

———. "The Humane Society Becomes a Political Animal." *The Washington Post*, January 30, 2007.

———. "Lawmakers Feel the Pull of Future Paychecks." *The Washington Post*, May 22, 2007, A13.

———. "For the Next Big Bout, Tune in to Channel 41/2." *The Washington Post*, June 5, 2007.

Birnbaum, Jeffrey, and Alan S. Murray. *Showdown at Gucci Gulch*. New York: Random House, 1987.

Birnbaum, Jeffrey, and Thomas Edsall. "For lobbyists, big spending means big presence," *The Washington Post*, July 28, p. A1.

Birnbaum, Jeffrey H. "Clients' Rewards Keep K Street Lobbyists Thriving." *The Washington Post*, February 14, 2006, p. A1.

———. "Lobbyists Making Themselves at Home on the Hill." *The Washington Post*, July 24, 2007, A3.

———. "Immigration Pushes Apart GOP, Chamber," *The Washington Post*, December 14, 2005, p. A01.

———. "The Forces That Set the National Agenda," *The Washington Post*, April 24, 2005, p. B1.

———. "The Road to Riches Is Called K Street: Lobbying Firms Hire More, Pay More, Charge More to Influence Government," *The Washington Post,* June 22, 2005, p. A1.

Birnbaum, Jeffrey H., and Dan Balz. "Case Bringing New Scrutiny to a System and a Profession." *Washington Post,* January 4, 2006, p. A1.

Boatright, Robert G., Michael J. Malbin, Mark J. Rozell, and Clyde Wilcox. "Interest Groups and Advocacy Organizations After BCRA." In *The Election After Reform: Politics and the Bipartisan Campaign Reform Act,* edited by Michael J. Malbin. Lanham, MD: Rowman & Littlefield, 2006.

Boerner, Christopher, and Jennifer Chilton Kallery. *Restructuring Environmental Big Business.* Occasional Paper No. 146, Center for the Study of American Business, Washington University, December 1994.

Bond, Joh R., and Richard Fleisher, eds. *Polarized Politics: Congress and the President in a Partisan Era.* Washington, DC: CQ Press, 2000.

Bosso, Christopher J. *Pesticides and Politics.* Pittsburgh: University of Pittsburgh Press, 1987.

———. "The Color of Money: Environmental Groups and the Pathologies of Fund Raising." In *Interest Group Politics,* 4th ed., edited by Allan J. Cigler and Burdett A. Loomis. Washington, DC: Congressional Quarterly, 1995.

Bosso, Christopher J., and Michael Thomas Collins. "Just Another Tool? How Environmental Groups Use the Internet." In *Interest Group Politics,* 6th ed., edited by Allen J. Cigler and Burdett Loomis. Washington, DC: CQ Press, 2002.

Box-Steffensmeir, Janet. "A Dynamic Analysis of the Role of War Chests in Campaign Strategy." *American Journal of Political Science* 40 (1996): 352–71.

Bradsher, Keith. "House Seeking Data on Nonprofit Groups," *New York Times,* September 27, 1995.

Brainard, Lori. "Citizen Organizing in Cyberspace: Illustrations from Health Care and Implications for Public Administration." American Review of Public Administration. 33, No. 4, 384–406.

Brewer, Paul. "The Shifting Foundations of Public Opinion on Gay Rights." *Journal of Politics* 65 (2003): 61–78.

Brewer, Paul, and Clyde Wilcox. "Trends: Same-Sex Marriages and Civil Unions." *Public Opinion Quarterly;* 69, no. 4 (2005): 599–616.

Broder, David S. *The Party's Over.* New York: Harper & Row, 1972.

Brown, Kirk F. "Campaign Contributions and Congressional Voting." Paper delivered at the annual meeting of the American Political Science Association, Chicago, September 1983.

Brown, Steven. *Trumping Religion: The New Christian Right, the Free Speech Clause, and the Courts.* Tuscaloosa: University of Alabama Press, 2002.

Brown v. Board of Education, 347 U.S. 483 (1954).

Browne, William P. *Cultivating Congress.* Lawrence: University Press of Kansas, 1995.

———. "Mobilizing and Activating Group Demands: The American Agriculture Movement." *Social Science Quarterly* 64 (March 1983): 19–34.

———. "Organized Interests and Their Issue Niches: A Search for Pluralism in a Policy Domain." *Journal of Politics* 52 (May 1990): 477–509.

————. "Policy and Interests: Instability and Change in a Classic Issue Subsystem."
In *Interest Group Politics,* 2nd ed., edited by Allan J. Cigler and Burdett A.
Loomis. Washington DC: Congressional Quarterly, 1986.

————. *Private Interests, Public Policy, and American Agriculture.* Lawrence:
University Press of Kansas, 1988.

Burger, Timothy J. "The Lobbying Game: Why the Revolving Door Won't Close."
Time Magazine Online Edition, February 16, 2006. *http://www.time.com/time/
nation/article/0,8599,1160453,00.html.* Accessed 2/28/06.

Burnham, Walter Dean. *Critical Elections and the Mainsprings of American Politics.*
New York: Norton, 1970.

Burnstein, Paul, and April Linton. "The Impact of Political Parties, Interest Groups,
and Social Organizations on Public Policy." *Social Forces* 81 (2002): 380–408.

Caldeira, Gregory A., Marie Hojnacki, and John R. Wright. "The Lobbying Activities
of Organized Interests in Federal Judicial Nominations." *Journal of Politics* 62
(2000): 51–69.

Caldeira, Gregory A., and John R. Wright. "Organized Interests and Agenda Setting in
the U.S. Supreme Court." *American Political Science Review* 82 (December
1988): 1111.

Campaign Finance Institute. "So the Voters May Choose . . . Reviving the Presidential
Matching Fund System." 2005. *http://www.cfinst.org/.*

Campbell, Andrea Louise. "Participatory Reactions to Policy Threats: Senior
Citizens and the Defense of Social Security and Medicare." *Political Behavior*
25 (2003): 29–49.

Campbell, David E., and J. Quinn Monson. "The Religion Card: Gay Marriage and the
2004 Presidential Election." Presented at conference on the 2004 election, Ohio
State University, January, 2006.

Cantor, David. "The Sierra Club Political Committee." In *After the Revolution: PACs,
Lobbies, and the Republican Congress,* edited by Robert Biersack, Paul S.
Herrnson, and Clyde Wilcox. Boston: Allyn and Bacon, 1999.

Caro, Robert. *The Path to Power.* New York: Random House, 1982.

Cater, Douglass. *Power in Washington.* New York: Vintage, 1964.

Center for Public Integrity, *http://www.publicintegrity.org/rx/report.aspx?aid = 794.*
Accessed 4/8/06.

Chubb, John E. *Interest Groups and the Bureaucracy.* Stanford, CA: Stanford
University Press, 1983.

Cigler, Allan J., and Burdett A. Loomis, eds. *Interest Group Politics,* 4th ed.
Washington, DC: Congressional Quarterly, 1995.

Cillizza, Chris. "Emily's List Celebrates Clout as It Turns 20." *The Washington Post,*
October 18, 2005, p. A13.

Clark, Peter B., and James Q. Wilson. "Incentive Systems: A Theory of
Organizations." *Administrative Science Quarterly* 6 (September 1961): 129–66.

Clawson, Dan, Alan Neustadtl, and Denise Scott. *Money Talks.* New York: Basic
Books, 1992.

Clovis, Debora, and Nan Aron. "Survey of Public Interest Law Centers." Alliance for
Justice, Washington, D.C., n.d.

Cochran, John. "Interest Groups Make Sure Lawmakers Know the 'Score.'" *CQ Weekly Report,* April 19, 2003.

Coll, Steve. *The Deal of the Century.* New York: Atheneum, 1986.

"Communicating with Congress: How Capitol Hill is Coping with the Surge in Citizen Advocacy," *http://www.cmfweb.org/cwcsummary.asp#ft1.* Accessed 3/4/06.

"Communication and the Congress." Washington, DC: Burson-Marsteller and the Institute for Government Public Information Research, 1981.

Conger, Kimberly H, and John C. Green. "Spreading Out and Digging In: Christian Conservatives and State Republican Parties." *Campaigns & Elections* 23 (2002): 59–61.

Conybeare, John C., and Peverill Squire. "Political Action Committees and the Tragedy of the Commons." *American Politics Quarterly* 22 (April 1994): 154–74.

Cook, Karen S. "Network Structures from an Exchange Perspective." In *Social Structure and Network Analysis,* edited by Peter V. Marsden and Nan Lin. Beverly Hills, CA: Sage, 1982.

Costain, Anne N. *Inviting Women's Rebellion.* Baltimore: Johns Hopkins University Press, 1992.

———. "Representing Women: The Transition from Social Movement to Interest Group." *Western Political Quarterly* 34 (March 1981): 100–113.

Costain, Anne N., and W. Douglas. "Interest Groups as Policy Aggregators in the Legislative Process." *Polity* 14 (Winter 1981): 249–72.

Cusack, Bob, Jeff Dufour, Geoff Earle, Josephine Hearn, Jonathan E. Kaplan, Megan Scully, Jim Snyder, and Jeffrey Young. "Top Lobbyists: Hired Guns," *The Hill,* April 27, 2005; and "K Street Spread," *The Hill,* April 20, 2005.

Cushman, John H., Jr. "Short of Cash, N.A.A.C.P. Stops Paying Its Employees," *New York Times,* November 2, 1994.

Dahl, Robert A. *Dilemmas of Pluralist Democracy.* New Haven, CT: Yale University Press, 1982.

———. "Further Reflections on 'The Elitist Theory of Democracy.' " *American Political Science Review* 60 (June 1966): 296–305.

———. "The Concept of Power." *Behavioral Science* 2 (July 1957): 201–15.

———. A *Preface to Democratic Theory.* Chicago: University of Chicago Press, 1956.

———. A *Preface to Economic Democracy.* Berkeley: University of California Press, 1985.

———. *The New American Political (Dis)Order.* Berkeley: Institute for Governmental Studies, 1994.

———. *Who Governs?* New Haven, CT: Yale University Press, 1961.

Dalton, Russell J. *The Green Rainbow.* New Haven, CT: Yale University Press, 1994.

Dalton, Russell J., and Manfred Kuechler, eds. *Challenging the Political Order.* NewYork: Oxford University Press, 1990.

Davis, Bob. "Mexico Mounts a Massive Lobbying Campaign to Sell North American Trade Accord in U.S.," *Wall Street Journal,* May 20, 1993.

DeGregorio, Christine. "Assets and Access: Linking Lobbyists and Lawmakers in Congress." In *The Interest Group Connection,* edited by Paul S. Herrnson, Ronald G. Shaiko, and Clyde Wilcox. Chatham, NJ: Chatham House, 1998.

DeGregorio, Christine, and Jack E. Rossotti. "Campaigning for the Court: Interest Group Participation in the Bork and Thomas Confirmation Processes." In *Interest Group Politics,* edited by Allan J. Cigler and Burdett A. Loomis. Washington, DC: Congressional Quarterly, 1986.

Delaney, Kevin J., and Amy Schatz. "Google Goes to Washington with Own Brand of Lobbying." *Wall Street Journal,* July 20, 2007, A1.

Derthick, Martha, and Paul J. Quirk. *The Politics of Deregulation.* Washington, DC: Brookings Institution, 1985.

Dexter, Lewis Anthony. *How Organizations Are Represented in Washington.* Indianapolis: Bobbs-Merrill, 1969.

————. *The Sociology and Politics of Congress.* Chicago: Rand McNally, 1969.

Dowie, Mark. *Losing Ground.* Cambridge: MIT Press, 1995.

Downs, Anthony. *An Economic Theory of Democracy.* New York: Harper & Row, 1957.

Drinkard, Jim. "Drugmakers Go Furthest to Sway Congress." *USA Today,* April 25, 2005. p. A1.

Drinkard, Jim, and William M. Welch. "AARP Accused of Conflict of Interest." *USA Today,* November 21, 2003, p. 11A.

Durant, Robert F. "The Democratic Deficit in America." *Political Science Quarterly* 110 (Spring 1995), p. 37.

Duverger, Maurice. *Political Parties.* New York: John Wiley, 1963.

Eastman, Hope. *Lobbying: A Constitutionally Protected Right.* Washington, DC: American Enterprise Institute, 1977.

Editorial, "The Lobbying-Industrial Complex."August 26, 2005, p. A18.

Edsall, Thomas B. "College Republicans' Fundraising Criticized; Front Organizations Were Used in Direct-Mail Campaign That Collected Millions." *The Washington Post,* December 26, 2004.

————. "Two Top Unions Split from AFL-CIO: Others Are Expected to Follow Teamsters." *The Washington Post,* July 26, 2005, p. A01.

————. "Soros-Backed Activist Group Disbands as Interest Fades." *The Washington Post,* August 3, 2005, p. A3.

————. "Rich Liberals Vow to Fund Think Tanks: Aim Is to Compete with Conservatives." *The Washington Post,* August 7, 2005, p. A1.

————. "Conservatives Rally for Justice," *The Washington Post,* August 15, 2005, p. A2. *http://www.washingtonpost.com/wpdyn/content/article/2005/08/14/AR200508140 1036.html.* Accessed April 1, 2006.

Elshtain, Jean Bethke. "The New Porn Wars." *New Public,* June 25, 1984, pp. 15–20.

Engelberg, Stephen. "Business Leaves the Lobby and Sits at Congress's Table," *New York Times,* March 31, 1995.

Engleberg, Stephen. "GOP and lobbies passed Contract; Success marks a new partnership, era," *The Houston Chronicle,* April 17, 1995, p. A6.

————. "100 Days of Dreams Come True for Lobbyists in Congress," *New York Times,* April 14, 1995.

Epstein, Edwin M. "Business and Labor under the Federal Election Campaign Act of 1971." In *Parties, Interest Groups, and Campaign Finance Laws,* edited by Michael J. Malbin. Washington, DC: American Enterprise Institute, 1980.

Epstein, Lee. *Conservatives in Court.* Knoxville, TN: University of Tennessee Press, 1985.

"Equal Rights Initiative in Iowa Attacked." *The Washington Post,* August 23, 1995, p. A15.

Erikson, Robert S., and Thomas R. Palfrey. "Equilibria in Campaign Spending Games: Theory and Data." *American Political Science Review* 94 (September 2000): 595–609.

Evans, Diana. "PAC Contributions and Roll-Call Voting: Conditional Power." In *Interest Group Politics,* 2nd ed., ed. Allan J. Cigler and Burdett A. Loomis. Washington, DC: Congressional Quarterly, 1986.

Evans, Sara. *Personal Politics.* New York: Knopf, 1979.

"Ex-Malaysian Leader Says He Paid Abramoff," *http://www.washingtonpost.com/wpdyn/content/article/2006/02/21/AR2006022100259.html.* Accessed 2/26/06.

Faison, Seth. "U.S. and China Sign Accord to End Piracy of Software, Music Recordings and Film." *New York Times,* February 27, 1995.

Federalist Papers. New York: New American Library, 1961.

Fiorina, Morris, Samuel J. Abrams, and Jeremy C. Pope. *Culture War? The Myth of a Polarized America.* New York: Longman, 2004.

Fowler, Linda L. "How Interest Groups Select Issues for Voting Records of Members of the U.S. Congress." *Legislative Studies Quarterly* 7 (August 1982): 401–13.

Francia, Peter L. *The Future of Organized Labor in American Politics.* New York: Columbia University Press, 2006.

Franz, Michael M., Joel Rivlin, and Kenneth Goldstein. "Much More of the Same: Television Advertising Pre- and Post-BCRA." In *The Election After Reform: Money, Politics, and the Bipartisan Campaign Reform Act,* edited by Michael J. Malbin. Lanham, MD: Rowman & Littlefield, 2006.

Freeman, Richard B., and James L. Medoff. *What Do Unions Do?* New York: Basic Books, 1984.

Friedman, Thomas L. "How Many Scientists?" *The New York Times,* March 28, 2007.

Furlong, Scott. "Exploring Interest Group Participation in Executive Policymaking." In *The Interest Group Connection,* 2nd ed., edited by Paul S. Herrnson, Ronald Shaiko, and Clyde Wilcox. Washington, DC: CQ Press, 2005.

Gais, Thomas L., Mark A. Peterson, and Jack L. Walker. "Interest Groups, Iron Triangles, and Representative Institutions in American National Government." *British Journal of Political Science* 14 (April 1984): 161–85.

Gamson, William. *Power and Discontent.* Homewood, IL: Dorsey Press, 1968.

———. *The Strategy of Social Protest.* Homewood, IL: Dorsey Press, 1975.

Garrow, David J. *Protest at Selma.* New Haven, CT: Yale University Press, 1978.

Garson, G. David. *Group Theories of Politics.* Beverly Hills, CA: Sage, 1978.

Gaventa, John. *Power and Powerlessness.* Urbana, IL: University of Illinois Press, 1980.

Gelb, Joyce, and Marian Lief Palley. *Women and Public Policies,* rev. ed. Princeton, NJ: Princeton University Press, 1987.

Georges, Christopher. "Conservative Heritage Foundation Finds Recipe for Influence: Ideas + Marketing = Clout," *Wall Street Journal,* August 10, 1995.

Gimpel, James G. "Grassroots Organizations and Equilibrium Cycles in Group Mobilization and Access." In *The Interest Group Connection,* edited by Paul S. Herrnson, Ronald Shaiko, and Clyde Wilcox. Washington, DC: CQ Press, 2005.

Goldin, Davidson. "A Law Center Wages Fight Against Political Correctness," *New York Times,* August 13, 1995.

Goldstein, Amy. "GOP Leaders Embrace Business Campaign to Defeat Health Care Measures." *Washington Post,* November 5, 1997, p. A14.

Goldstein, Kenneth M. *Interest Groups, Lobbying, and Participation in America.* New York: Cambridge University Press, 1999.

Goodliffe, Jay. "The Effect of War Chests on Challenger Entry in U.S. House Elections." *American Journal of Political Science* 45 no. 4 (2001): 830–44.

Gormley, William T., Jr. *The Politics of Public Utility Regulation.* Pittsburgh: University of Pittsburgh Press, 1983.

Gray, Jerry. "Emotions High, House Takes on Abortion," *New York Times,* June 16, 1995.

Green, Donald P., and Jonathan S. Krasno. "Salvation for the Spendthrift Incumbent: Reestimating the Effects of Campaign Spending in House Elections." *American Journal of Political Science* 32 (November 1988): 884–907.

Green, John C., Mark J. Rozell, and Clyde Wilcox. *Marching to the Millennium: The Christian Right in American Elections 1980–2000.* Washington, DC: Georgetown University Press, 2003.

Green, Mark. "Political PAC-Man," *New Republic,* December 13, 1982, p. 24.

Greenstone, J. David. *Labor in American Politics.* New York: Knopf, 1969.

Greider, William. *Who Will Tell the People?* New York: Touchstone, 1993.

Grenzke, Janet M. "PACs in the Congressional Supermarket: The Currency Is Complex." *American Journal of Political Science* 33 (February 1989): 1–24.

Greve, Michael, and James Keller. *Funding the Left: The Sources of Financial Support for "Public Interest" Law Firms.* Washington, DC: Washington Legal Foundation, 1987.

Greve, Michael S. "Why Defunding the Left Failed." *Public Interest* 89 (Fall 1987): 91–106.

Griffith, Ernest. *Impasse of Democracy.* New York: Harrison-Hilton Books, 1939.

Guth, James L., John C. Green, Lyman A. Kellstedt, and Corwin E. Smidt. "Onward Christian Soldiers: Religious Activist Groups in American Politics." In *Interest Group Politics,* 4th ed., edited by Allan J. Cigler and Burdett A. Loomis. Washington, DC: Congressional Quarterly, 1995.

Hacker, Hans J. *The Culture Of Conservative Christian Litigation.* Lanham MD: Rowman & Littlefield, 2005.

Hall, Richard L. "Buying Time: Moneyed Interests and the Mobilization of Bias in Congressional Committees." *American Political Science Review* 84 (September 1990): 797–820.

Hall, Richard L., and Alan Deardorff. "Lobbying as Legislative Subsidy." *American Political Science Review* 100 (February 2006): 69–84.

Hall, Richard L., and Frank W. Wayman. "Buying Time: Moneyed Interests and the Mobilization of Bias in Congressional Committees." *American Political Science Review* 84 (1990): 797–820.

Hall, Robert, and Robert Van Houweling. "Campaign Contributions and Lobbying on the Medicare Modernization Act of 2003." September, 2006.

Hamm, Keith E. "Patterns of Influence Among Committees, Agencies, and Interest Groups." *Legislative Studies Quarterly* 8 (August 1983): 379–426.

Hansen, John Mark. "The Political Economy of Group Membership." *American Political Science Review* 79 (March 1985): 79–96.

———. *Gaining Access.* Chicago: University of Chicago Press, 1991.

Harris, Richard A. *Coal Firms Under the New Social Regulation.* Durham, NC: Duke University Press, 1985.

Hayes, Michael T. *Lobbyists and Legislators.* New Brunswick, NJ: Rutgers University Press, 1981.

Heaney, Michael T. "Outside the Issue Niche: The Multidimensionality of Interest Group Identity." *American Politics Research* 37 (2004): 1–41.

Heclo, Hugh. "Issue Networks and the Executive Establishment." In *The New American Political System,* edited by Anthony King. Washington, DC: American Enterprise Institute, 1978.

Hefrenning, Daniel J. B. *In Washington But Not Of It: The Prophetic Politics of Religious Lobbying.* Philadelphia: Temple University Press, 1995.

Heinz, John P., Edward O. Laumann, Robert L. Nelson, and Robert H. Salisbury. *The Hollow Core.* Cambridge, MA: Harvard University Press, 1993.

Henriquez, Diana B., and Andrew Lehren. "Religious Groups Granted Millions in Pet Projects." *The New York Times,* May 13, 2007, A1.

Herman, Edward S. *Corporate Control, Corporate Power.* New York: Cambridge University Press, 1981.

Herrnson, Paul S. *Party Campaigning in the 1980s.* Cambridge, MA: Harvard University Press, 1988.

———. "The National Committee for an Effective Congress: Liberalism, Partisanship, and Electoral Innovation." In *Risky Business?,* edited by Robert Biersack, Paul S. Herrnson, and Clyde Wilcox. Armonk, NY: M.E. Sharpe, 1994.

Hertzberg, Hendrik. "Abramoffed." *http://www.newyorker.com/talk/content/articles/060116ta_talk_hertzberg.* Accessed 1/16/06.

Hertzke, Allen D. *Representing God in Washington.* Knoxville: University of Tennessee Press, 1988.

———. *Freeing God's Children: The Unlikely Alliance for Global Human Rights.* Lanham, MD: Rowman & Littlefield, 2004.

Hinds, Michael deCourcy. "Advocacy Units Seek New Funds," *New York Times,* January 9, 1982.

Hirschman, Albert O. *Exit, Voice, and Loyalty.* Cambridge: Harvard University Press, 1970.

Hojnacki, Marie, "Interest Groups' Decisions to Join Alliances or Work Alone." *American Journal of Political Science* 41 (1997): 61–87.

———. "Organized Interests Advocacy Behavior in Alliances." *Political Research Quarterly* 51: 437–59.

Hojnacki, Marie, and David Kimball. "Organized Interests and the Decision of Whom to Lobby in Congress." *American Political Science Review* 92 (1998): 775–90.

"Homosexual Behavior & Pedophilia," *http://us2000.org/cfmc/Pedophilia.pdf*.

Howard, Marc Morje. *The Weakness of Civil Society in Post-Communist Europe.* NewYork: Cambridge University Press, 2003.

Hrebner, Ronald J., and Ruth K. Scott. *Interest Group Politics in America,* 2nd ed. Englewood Cliffs, NJ: Prentice Hall, 1990. *http://www.referenceforbusiness.com/ industries/Service/Direct-Mail-Advertising-Services.html*. Accessed 1/21/06.

Hsu, Spencer, and Darryl Fears. "As Bush's ID Plan was Delayed, Coalition Formed Against It." *The Washington Post,* February 25, 2007, A08.

Hula, Kevin. "Coalitions, Cloning, and Trust." In *The Interest Group Connection*, 2nd ed., edited by Paul S. Herrnson, Ronald Shaiko, and Clyde Wilcox, Washington, DC: CQ Press, 2005.

———. "Dolly Goes to Washington: Coalitions, Cloning, and Trust." In *The Interest Group Connection: Electioneering, Lobbying, and Policymaking in Washington,* edited by Paul S. Herrnson, Ronald G. Shaiko, and Clyde Wilcox. Washington, DC: CQ Press, 2005.

———. *Lobbying Together: Interest Group Coalitions in Legislative Politics.* Washington, DC: Georgetown University Press, 1999.

———. *Links and Choices: Explaining Coalition Formation Among Organized Interests.* Doctoral dissertation, Department of Government, Harvard University, 1995.

Hunter, Floyd. *Community Power Structure.* Chapel Hill, NC: University of North Carolina Press, 1953.

Imig, Douglas. *Poverty and Power: The Political Representation of Poor Americans.* Lincoln: University of Nebraska Press, 1996.

Jackson, Brooks. *Honest Graft.* New York: Knopf, 1988.

Jackson, David J., and Steven T. Engel. "Friends Don't Let Friends Vote for Free Trade: The Dynamics of the Labor PAC Punishment Strategy over PNTR." *Political Research Quarterly* 56 (2003): 442–48.

Jacobson, Gary C. *Money in Congressional Elections.* New Haven, CT: Yale University Press, 1980.

———. "The Effects of Campaign Spending in House Elections: New Evidence for Old Arguments," *American Journal of Political Science* 34 (May 1990): pp. 334–62.

———. *A Divider, Not a Uniter: George W. Bush and the American People.* NewYork: Longman, 2006.

Johnson, Paul E. "How Environmental Groups Recruit Members: Does the Logic Still Hold Up?" Paper delivered at the annual meeting of the American Political Science Association, Chicago, September 1995.

———. "Interest Group Recruiting: Finding Members and Keeping Them." In *Interest Group Politics,* 5th ed., edited by Allan J. Cigler and Burdett Loomis. Washington, DC: CQ Press, 1998.

Kady, Martin II. "Party Unity: Learning to Stick Together." *CQ Weekly Report,* January 9, 2006, p. 92.

Kelman, Steven. "Adversary and Cooperationist Institutions for Conflict Resolution in Public Policymaking." *Journal of Policy Analysis and Management* 11 (1992): 178–206.

Kerwin, Cornelius M. *Rulemaking.* Washington, DC: Congressional Quarterly, 1994.

Key, V.O., Jr. *Politics, Parties, and Pressure Groups,* 5th ed. New York: Crowell, 1964.

Kilborn, Peter T. "Militant Is Elected Head of A.F.L-C.I.O., Signaling Sharp Turn for Labor Movement," *New York Times,* October 26, 1995.

Kingdon, John W. *Agendas, Alternatives, and Public Policies.* Boston: Little, Brown, 1984.

———. *Congressmen's Voting Decisions,* 2nd ed. New York: Harper & Row, 1981.

Kirschten, Dick. "Not Black-and-White." *National Journal,* March 2, 1991, pp. 496–500.

Kiyohara, Shoko. "Changes in the Telecommunications Political Process in the United States: The Impact of the Establishment of an E-Rate." Presented at the annual meeting of the Northeastern Political Science Association, November 2004.

Knoke, David. *Political Networks: The Structural Perspective.* New York: Cambridge University Press, 1990.

Knoke, David, and James Kuklinski. *Network Analysis.* Beverly Hills, CA: Sage, 1982.

Knoke, David, and Edward O. Laumann. "The Social Organization of National Policy Domains." In *Social Structure and Network Analysis,* edited by Peter V. Marsden and Nan Lin. Beverly Hills, CA: Sage, 1982.

Knoke, David, and James W. Wood. *Organized for Action.* New Brunswick, NJ:Rutgers University Press, 1981.

Kollman, Ken. *Outside Lobbying: Public Opinion & Interest Group Strategies.* Princeton, NJ: Princeton University Press. 1998.

Kotz, Nick, and Mary Lynn Kotz. *A Passion for Equality.* New York: Norton, 1977.

Krasno, Johnathan S., and Donald Philip Green. "Preempting Quality Challengers in House Elections." *Journal of Politics,* 50 no. 4 (1988): 920–36.

Krasno, Johnathan S., Donald Philip Green, and Johnathan A. Cowden. "The Dynamics of Campaign Fundraising in House Elections," *Journal of Politics,* 56 no. 2 (1994): 459–74.

Kumar, Martha Joynt, and Michael Baruch Grossman. "The Presidency and Interest Groups." In *The Presidency and the Political System,* edited by Michael Nelson. Washington, DC: Congressional Quarterly, 1984.

Ladd, Jr., Carll Everett, with Charles D. Hadley. *Transformations of the American Party System,* 2nd ed. New York: Norton 1978.

Langley, Monica. "AT&T Sends a Horde of Lobbyists to Fight a Phone-Bill Proposal." *Wall Street Journal,* November 4, 1983.

Larson, Carin. "An Uphill Climb: The Christian Right and the 2004 Election in Colorado." In *The Values Campaign? The Christian Right in the 2004 Elections,* edited by John C. Green, Mark J. Rozell, and Clyde Wilcox. Washington, DC: Georgetown University Press, 2006.

Laumann, Edward O., and David Knoke. *The Organizational State*. Madison: University of Wisconsin Press, 1987.

Leech, Beth L., Frank R. Baumgartner, Jeffrey M. Berry, Marie Hojnacki, and David C. Kimball. "Organized Interests and Issue Definition in Policy Debates." In *Interest Group Politics*, 6th ed., edited by Allan J. Cigler and Burdett A. Loomis. Washington, DC: CQ Press, 2002.

Lester, James P., and W. Douglas Costain. "The Evolution of Environmentalism." In *The New American Politician*, edited by Bryan D. Jones. Boulder: Westview, 1995.

Liebman, Robert C., and Robert Wuthnow. *The New Christian Right*. New York: Aldine, 1983.

Light, Paul. *Artful Work*, 2nd ed. New York: McGraw-Hill, 1995.

Lindblom, Charles E. *Politics and Markets*. New York: Basic Books, 1977.

Lipset, Seymour Martin, Martin Trow, and James Coleman. *Union Democracy*. Garden City, NY: Doubleday Anchor Books, 1956.

Lipsky, Michael. "Protest as a Political Resource." *American Political Science Review* 62 (December 1968): 1144–58.

Lowery, David, Virginia Gray, and Matthew Fellowes. "Sisyphus Meets the Borg: Economic Scale and Inequalities in Interest Representation." *Journal of Theoretical Politics* 17 (2005): 41–74.

Lowery, David, Virginia Gray, Jennifer Anderson, and Adam J. Newmark. "Collective Action and the Mobilization of Institutions." *The Journal of Politics 66*, (August 2004), 684–705.

Lowi, Theodore J. *The End of Liberalism*. New York: Norton, 1979.

Luker, Kristin. *Abortion and the Politics of Motherhood*. Berkeley: University of California Press, 1984.

Lundstrom, Marjie. "Planned Parenthood Volunteers Seek to Be Election Force." *Sacramento Bee,* July 17, 2004, p. A3.

Lusterman, Seymour. *Managing Federal Government Relations*. New York: Conference Board, 1988.

———. *The Organization & Staffing of Corporate Public Affairs*. New York: Conference Board, 1987.

Luttbeg, Norman R., and Harmon Zeigler. "Attitude Consensus and Conflict in an Interest Group." *American Political Science Review* 60 (September 1966): 655–66.

MacKenzie, G. Calvin, ed. *The In-and-Outers*. Baltimore: Johns Hopkins University Press, 1987.

Madland, David Lawrence. "A Wink and a Handshake: Why the Collapse of the U.S. Pension System has Provoked Little Protest." Doctoral dissertation, Georgetown University, 2007.

Mallee, Bernard. "Think Tanks Have Broadened their Influence," *St. Louis Post Dispatch* B1, April 4, 2004.

Manley, John F. "Neo-Pluralism: A Class Analysis of Pluralism I and Pluralism II." *American Political Science Review* 77 (June 1983): 368–83.

Mansbridge, Jane. "Does Participation Make Better Citizens?" Paper presented at the PEGS Conference, February 11–12, 1995. *http://www.cpn.org/crm/contemporary/participation.html.* Accessed 2/14/06.

Mansbridge, Jane J. *Beyond Adversary Democracy.* New York: Basic Books, 1980.
————. *Why We Lost the ERA.* Chicago: University of Chicago Press, 1986.
Markus, Gregory B. "Civic Participation in America." Report of the Civic Engagement Study. Ann Arbor: University of Michigan, 2002.
Marsh, David. "On Joining Interest Groups." *British Journal of Political Science* 6(July 1976): 257–72.
Martin, Cathie Jo. "Nature or Nurture? Sources of Firm Preference for National Health Reform." *American Political Science Review* 89 (December 1995): 898–913.
Maxwell, Carol. *Pro-Life Activists in America: Motivation and Meaning.* New York: Cambridge University Press, 2002.
Mayhew, David. *Divided We Govern.* New Haven: Yale University Press, 1991.
McAdam, Doug. *Political Process and the Development of Black Insurgency.* Chicago: University of Chicago Press, 1982.
McCann, Michael W. *Taking Reform Seriously.* Ithaca, NY: Cornell University Press, 1986.
McCarry, Charles. *Citizen Nader.* New York: Saturday Review Press, 1972.
McConnell, Grant. *Private Power and American Democracy.* New York: Knopf, 1966.
————. "100 Days of Dreams Come True for Lobbyists in Congress," *New York Times,* April 14, 1995.
————. *Common Cause.* Chatham, NJ: Chatham House, 1984.
————. *Cooperative Pluralism.* Lawrence: University Press of Kansas, 1993.
————. "Interest Groups and the Policymaking Process: Sources of Countervailing Power in America." In *The Politics of Interests,* edited by Mark P. Petracca. Boulder: Westview, 1992.
McGrath, Phyllis S. *Redefining Corporate-Federal Relations.* New York: Conference Board, 1979.
McIntosh, Wayne V., and Cynthia L. Cates. "Cigarettes, Firearms, and the New Litigation Wars: Smoking Guns Behind the Headlines." In *The Interest Group Connection,* 2nd ed., edited by Paul S. Herrnson, Ronald Shaiko, and Clyde Wilcox. Washington, DC: CQ Press, 2005.
McQuaid, Kim. "The Roundtable: Getting Results in Washington." *Harvard Business Review* 59 (May–June 1981): 114–23.
Meckle, Laura. "GOP Group to Air Pro-Nader TV Ads," *The Washington Post,* October 27, 2000.
Meier, August, and Elliott Rudwick. *CORE: A Study in the Civil Rights Movement.* New York: Oxford University Press, 1973.
Meredith, Todd. "Open the Envelope: Getting People to Look at the Direct Mail They Receive." *Campaigns & Elections* December 2004; Encyclopedia of American Industries, "Direct Mail Advertising Services."
Meyer, David S., and Douglas Imig. "Political Opportunity and the Rise and Decline of Interest Group Sectors." *Social Science Journal* 30 (July 1993): 253–70.
Michels, Robert. *Political Parties.* New York: Free Press, 1958. Originally published in 1915.
Milbank, Dana. "For Would-Be Lobbying Reformers, Money Habit Is Hard to Kick." *The Washington Post,* January 26, 2006, p. A06.

Miller, Paul A. President of the American League of Lobbyists. Testimony before the United States Senate Committee on Homeland Security and Governmental Affairs On Lobbying Reform: Proposals and Issues, Wednesday, January 25, 2006. *http://www.alldc.org/pdf/millertestimony012506.pdf*. Accessed 2/26/06.

Mills, C. Wright. *The Power Elite.* New York: Oxford University Press, 1956.

Mizruchi, Mark S. *The Structure of Corporate Political Action.* Cambridge: Harvard University Press, 1992.

Moe, Terry M. *The Organization of Interests.* Chicago: University of Chicago Press, 1980.

———. "A Calculus of Group Membership." *American Journal of Political Science* 24 (November 1980): 593–632.

———. "The Devolutionary Era: A New Phase of Activism Linking Religious and Secular Conservatives in the 104th Congress." Paper delivered at the annual meeting of the New England Political Science Association, Portland, Maine, May 1995.

———. "Toward a Broader View of Interest Groups." *Journal of Politics* 43 (May1981): 531–43.

Moen, Matthew C. *The Transformation of the Christian Right.* Tuscaloosa: University of Alabama Press, 1992.

Moore, W. John. "The Gravy Train," *National Journal,* October 10, 1992, p. 2295.

Mucciaroni, Gary. *Reversals of Fortune.* Washington, DC: Brookings Institution, 1995.

Müller-Rommel, Ferdinand. "New Political Movements and 'New Politics' Parties in Western Europe." In *Challenging the Political Order* edited by Dalton and Kuechler, p. 216.

Mundo, Philip A. *Interest Groups: Cases and Characteristics.* Chicago: Nelson-Hall, 1992.

Murray, Alan. "Trained by Nader, This Populist Tax Lobbyist Takes Aim at Big Business That Avoids Taxes," *Wall Street Journal,* May 2, 1985.

Murray, Alan S. "Lobbyists for Business Are Deeply Divided, Reducing Their Clout," *Wall Street Journal,* March 25, 1987.

Mutz, Diana C. "Cross-cutting Social Networks: Testing Democratic Theory in Practice." *American Political Science Review* 96 (2002): 111–26.

Negotiated Rulemaking Act of 1989. 101st Congress, 1st session, 1989, Senate Report 101–97, p. 16.

Nie, Norman H., Sidney Verbay and John R. Petrocik. *The Changing American Voter.* Cambridge: Harvard University Press, 1976.

Noguchi, Yuri. "TV When—and Where—You Want It: New Video Technologies Free Viewers from the Couch." *The Washington Post,* February 12, 2006, p. A1.

Norris, Pippa, and Joni Lovenduski. *Political Recruitment: Gender, Race, and Class in the British Parliament.* Cambridge, England: Cambridge University Press, 1995.

Nownes, Anthony J., and Allan J. Cigler. "Public Interest Groups and the Road to Survival," *Polity* 27 (Spring 1995): 379–404.

Nugent, Margaret Latus. "When Is a $1,000 Contribution Not a $1,000 Contribution?" *Election Politics* 3 (Summer 1986): 13–16.

O'Brien, David J. *Neighborhood Organization and Interest Group Processes.* Princeton, NJ: Princeton University Press, 1975.

O'Connor, Karen. "Lobbying the Justices or Lobbying for Justice: The Role of Organized Interests in the Judicial Process." In *The Interest Group Connection* 2nd ed., edited by Paul S. Herrnson, Ronald Shaiko, and Clyde Wilcox. Washington, DC: CQ Press, 2005.

———. *Women's Organizations' Use of the Courts.* Lexington, MA: Lexington Books, 1980.

———. "The Role of Interest Groups in Supreme Court Policy Formation." In *Public Policy Formation,* edited by Robert Eyestone. Greenwich, CT: JAI Press, 1984.

O'Connor, Karen, and Lee Epstein. "The Rise of Conservative Interest Group Litigation." *Journal of Politics* 45 (May 1983): 478–89.

Office of Communication of the United Church of Christ v. FCC, 359 F. 2d 944 (D.C.Cir., 1966).

Olson, Mancur, Jr. *The Logic of Collective Action.* New York: Schocken, 1968.

———. *The Rise and Decline of Nations.* New Haven, CT: Yale University Press, 1982.

Ono, Yumiko. "Tobacco Firms Rush to Counterattack Despite Signs of Dissension in Ranks," *Wall Street Journal,* August 14, 1995.

Orren, Karen. "Liberalism, Money, and the Situation of Organized Labor." In *Public Values and Private Power in American Politics,* edited by J. David Greenstone. Chicago: University of Chicago Press, 1982.

———. "Standing to Sue: Interest Group Conflict in the Federal Courts." *American Political Science Review* 70 (September 1976): 723–41.

Parks, Daniel J. "United at Last, Financial Industry Pressures Hill to Clear Overhaul." *CQ Weekly,* October 9, 1999, p. 2373.

Parrish, Michael. "EPA Rule on Ethanol Overturned," *Boston Globe,* April 29, 1995.

Patterson, Kelly D. "Political Firepower: The National Rifle Association." In *After the Revolution: PACs, Lobbies, and the Republican Congress,* edited by Robert Biersack, Paul S. Herrnson, and Clyde Wilcox. Boston: Allyn and Bacon. 1999.

Pear, Robert. "Clinton Health Team Agrees to Let Public Speak, Quickly," *New York Times,* March 25, 1993.

———. "Select Hospitals Reap a Windfull Under Child Bill." *The New York Times,* August 12, 2007.

Peterson, Mark A. "The Presidency and Organized Interest Groups: White House Patterns of Interest Group Liaison." *American Political Science Review* 86 (September 1992): 612–25.

Peterson, Mark A., and Jack L. Walker. "Interest Group Responses to Partisan Change." In *Interest Group Politics,* 2nd ed., edited by Allan J. Cigler and Burdett A. Loomis. Washington, DC: Congressional Quarterly, 1986.

Peterson, Paul. "The Rise and Fall of Special Interest Politics." In *The Politics of Interests,* edited by Mark P. Petracca. Boulder: Westview, 1992.

Petracca, Mark P., edited by *The Politics of Interests.* Boulder: Westview, 1992.

Pika, Joseph A. "Reaching Out to Organized Interests: Public Liaison in the Modern White House." In *The Presidency Reconsidered,* ed. Richard W. Waterman. Itasca, IL: F.E. Peacock, 1993.

Piven, Frances Fox, and Richard Cloward. *Poor People's Movements.* New York: Pantheon, 1978.

Policy Studies Journal. Symposium on Interest Groups and Public Policy 11 (June 1983).

Polsby, Nelson W. *Consequences of Party Reform.* New York: Oxford University Press, 1983.

———. *Community Power and Political Theory.* New Haven: Yale University Press, 1980.

———. "Interest Groups and the Presidency." In *American Politics and Public Policy,* edited by Walter Dean Burnham and Martha Wagner Weinberg. Cambridge, MA: MIT Press, 1978.

Pratt, Henry J. *The Gray Lobby.* Chicago: University of Chicago Press, 1976.

Public Affairs Offices and Their Functions. Boston: Boston University School of Management, 1981.

Public Interest Law: Five Years Later. New York: Ford Foundation, 1976.

Putnam, Robert D. *Making Democracy Work: Civic Traditions in Modern Italy.* Princeton, NJ: Princeton University Press, 1993.

Quirk, Paul J. *Industry Influence in Federal Regulatory Agencies.* Princeton, NJ:Princeton University Press, 1981.

———. "Food and Drug Administration." In *The Politics of Regulation,* edited by James Q. Wilson. New York: Basic Books, 1980.

Raney, Rebecca Fairley. "Cheap Online Fundraising Is a Boon to Political Groups." *The New York Times,* November 23, 1999.

Rauch, Jonathan. *Demosclerosis.* New York: Times Books, 1994.

Regents of the University of California v. *Bakke,* 438 U.S. 265 (1978).

Ricci, David M. *The Transformation of American Politics.* New Haven, CT: Yale University Press, 1993.

Richardson, Jeremy J., ed. *Pressure Groups.* New York: Oxford University Press, 1993.

Rochon, Thomas, and Daniel Mazmanian. "Social Movements and the Policy Process." *Annals of the American Academy of Political and Social Science* 538 (July 1993): 75–87.

Rogers, David. "Business Delivers Another Blow to Health Plan," *Wall Street Journal,* February 4, 1994.

Rosenbaum, Walter A. "Public Involvement as Reform and Ritual: The Development of Federal Participation Programs." In *Citizen Participation in America,* edited by Stuart Langton. Lexington, MA: D.C. Heath, 1978.

Roth, Bennett. "AARP Wages Fiery Blitz v. Social Security Plan; Senior Group Pays $20 Million in Ad Blitz." *Houston Chronicle* March 20, 2005, p. A1.

Rothenberg, Lawrence S. *Linking Citizens to Government.* New York: Cambridge University Press, 1992.

Rozell, Mark J., and Clyde Wilcox. *Second Coming: The Christian Right in Virginia Politics.* Baltimore: Johns Hopkins University Press. 1996.

Rozell, Mark J., Clyde Wilcox, and David Madland. *Interest Groups in American Campaigns: The New Face of Electioneering,* 2nd ed. Washington, DC: CQ Press, 2006.

Sabatier, Paul. "An Advocacy Coalition Framework of Policy Change and the Role of Policy-Oriented Learning Therein." Policy Sciences 21 (1988): 129–68.

Sabato, Larry J. *The Rise of Political Consultants.* New York: Basic Books, 1981.

Sale, Kirkpatrick. *SDS.* New York: Vintage, 1974.

Salisbury, Robert H. "Are Interest Groups Morbific Forces?" Paper delivered to the Conference Group on the Political Economy of Advanced Industrial Societies, Washington, DC, August 1980.

———. "An Exchange Theory of Interest Groups." *Midwest Journal of Political Science* 13 (February 1969): 1–32.

———. "Interest Groups." In *Handbook of Political Science,* Vol. 4, edited by Fred I. Greenstein and Nelson W. Polsby. Reading, MA: Addison-Wesley, 1975.

———. "Interest Representation: The Dominance of Institutions." *American Political Science Review* 78 (March 1984): 64–76.

———. "Washington Lobbyists: A Collective Portrait." In *Interest Group Politics,* 2nd ed., edited by Allan J. Cigler and Burdett A. Loomis. Washington, DC: Congressional Quarterly, 1986.

———. "Why No Corporatism in America?" In *Trends Toward Corporatist Intermediation,* edited by Philippe C. Schmitter and Gerhard Lehmbruch. Beverly Hills, CA: Sage, 1979.

Salisbury, Robert H., John P. Heinz, Edward O. Laumann, and Robert L. Nelson. "Who Works with Whom?" *American Political Science Review* 81 (December 1987): 1217–34.

Sarafini, Marilyn Webber. "Senior Schism." *National Journal,* May 6, 1995, p. 1093.

Sarasohn, Judy. "A Marriage Group's 'Interesting' Union." *The Washington Post,* June 2, 2005, p. A23.

———. "India, Pakistan Sign with US Lobby Shops," *The Washington Post,* September 15, 2005, p. A31.

Schattschneider, E. E. *The Semisovereign People.* Hinsdale, IL: Dryden Press, 1975.

Schlozman, Kay Lehman. "Representing Women in Washington: Sisterhood and Pressure Politics." In *Women, Politics, and Change,* edited by Louise A. Tilly and Patricia Gurin. New York: Russell Sage, 1990.

Schlozman, Kay Lehman, and John T. Tierney. *Organized Interests and American Democracy.* New York: Harper & Row, 1986.

Schmidt, Susan, and Jeffrey H. Birnbaum. "Tribal Money linked to GOP Fundraising," *The Washington Post* December 26, 2004, p. A1.

Schneider, Anne, and Helen Ingram. "Social Construction of Target Populations: Implications for Politics and Policy." *American Political Science Review* 87 (June 1993): 334–47.

Shaiko, Ronald. "Greenpeace, U.S.A.: Something Old, New, Borrowed." *Annals of the American Academy of Political and Social Science* 538 (July 1993): 88–100.

———. "Making the Connection: Organized Interests, Political Representation, and the Changing Rules of the Game in Washington Politics." In *The Interest Group Connection* 2nd ed., edited by Paul S. Herrnson, Ronald G. Shaiko, and Clyde Wilcox. Washington, DC: CQ Press, 2005.

Shames, Shauna L., and Greg Weiner. "Raising Money, Raising Hackles: Analyzing Interest Group Responses to Supreme Court Decisions Through Direct Mail Solicitations." Paper presented at the annual meeting of the Southern Political Science Association, Atlanta, 2006.

Shear, Jeff. "The Ax Files." *National Journal,* April 15, 1995, pp. 924–27.

Sinclair, Barbara. *Unorthodox Lawmaking: New Legislative Processes in the U.S. Congress.* Washington, DC: CQ Press, 2000.

Smith, James A. *The Idea Brokers.* New York: Free Press, 1991.

Smith, Mark A. *American Business and Political Power: Public Opinion, Elections, and Democracy.* Chicago: University of Chicago Press, 2000.

Smith, Martin J. *Pressure, Power, and Policy.* Pittsburgh: University of Pittsburgh Press, 1993.

Smith, Steven S. "New Patterns of Decisionmaking in Congress." In *The New Direction in American Politics,* edited by John E. Chubb and Paul E. Peterson, 221. Washington, D.C.: Brookings Institution, 1985.

Sorauf, Frank J. *Inside Campaign Finance.* New Haven, CT: Yale University Press, 1992.

———. *Money in American Politics.* Glenview, IL: Scott, Foresman/Little, Brown, 1988.

Stewart, Joseph Jr, and Edward V. Heck. "The Day-to-Day Activities of Interest Group Lawyers." *Social Science Quarterly* 64 (March 1983): 173–82.

Stone, Alan. *Public Service Liberalism.* Princeton, NJ: Princeton University Press, 1991.

Stone, Peter H. "The Big Harvest," *National Journal* (July 30, 1994): 1790–93.

Stratmann, Thomas. "What Do Campaign Contributions Buy? Deciphering the Causal Effects of Money and Votes." *Southern Economics Journal* 57 (1991): 606–20.

———. "Can Special Interests Buy Congressional Votes? Evidence from Financial Services Legislation." *Journal of Law and Economics* 45 (2002): 345–74.

Tarrow, Sidney. *Power in Movement.* New York: Cambridge University Press, 1994.

Taylor, Paul. "The Death of Withholding, or How the Bankers Won a Big One," *The Washington Post,* July 31, 1983.

Taylor, Stuart, Jr. "Coalition Opposes Access Curb," *New York Times,* March 19, 1986.

———. "Bork Fight: Tactics Supplant Issues," *New York Times,* August 6, 1986.

———. "Debate Continues on Accusations of Distortion in Ads Against Bork," *New York Times,* October 21, 1987.

The Public Interest Law Firm. New York: Ford Foundation, 1973.

Thomas, Clive, and Ronald Hrebenar. "Changing Patterns of Interest Group Activity: A Regional Perspective." In *The Politics of Interests,* edited by Mark P. Petracca. Boulder: Westview, 1992.

Thomas, Evan. "Peddling Influence," *Time,* March 3, 1986.

Thurber, James A. "Dynamics of Policy Subsystems in American Politics." In *Interest Group Politics,* 3rd ed., edited by Allan J. Cigler and Burdett A. Loomis. Washington, DC: Congressional Quarterly, 1991.

Tierney, John T. "Organized Interests and the Nation's Capitol." In *The Politics of Interests,* edited by Mark P. Petracca. Boulder: Westview, 1992.

———. "Subgovernments and Issue Networks." Paper presented at the annual meeting of the American Political Science Association, New Orleans, August 1985, p. 28.

Tocqueville, Alexis de. *Democracy in America.* edited by J.P. Mayer. Garden City, NJ: Doubleday, 1969.

Toward a More Responsible Two-Party System. Report by the American Political
    Science Association's Committee on Political Parties. New York: Rinehart, 1950.
Truman, David B. *The Governmental Process,* 2nd ed. New York: Knopf, 1971.
Uchitelle, "Battle for Presidency of A.F.L.-C.I.O. Emerges After Kirkland Withdraws
    from Race," *New York Times,* June 11, 1995.
Useem, Michael. *The Inner Circle.* New York: Oxford University Press, 1984.
Uslaner, Eric. *The Moral Foundations of Trust.* New York: Cambridge University
    Press, 2002.
Valley Forge Christian College v. *Americans United for Separation of Church and
    State,* 454 U.S. 464 (1982).
VandeHei, Jim. "GOP Monitoring Lobbyists' Politics; White House, Hill Access May
    Be Affected." *The Washington Post,* June 10, 2002, p. A01.
Verba, Sidney, and Gary Orren. *Equality in America.* Cambridge, MA: Harvard
    University Press, 1985.
Verba, Sidney, Kay Lehman Schlozman, and Henry E. Brady. *Voice and Equality.*
    Cambridge, MA: Harvard University Press, 1995.
Vogel, David. *Fluctuating Fortunes.* New York: Basic Books, 1989.
————. "How Business Responds to Opposition: Corporate Political Strategies
    During the 1970s." Paper delivered at the annual meeting of the American
    Political Science Association, Washington, DC, September 1979.
————. "The New Political Science of Corporate Power." *Public Interest* 87
    (Spring 1987): 63–79.
————. "The Public-Interest Movement and the American Reform Tradition."
    Political Science Quarterly 95 (Winter 1980–81): 607–28.
————. *Lobbying the Corporation.* New York: Basic Books, 1978.
Vose, Clement. *Caucasians Only.* Berkeley, CA: University of California Press, 1949.
Walker, Jack L. *Mobilizing Interest Groups in America.* Ann Arbor: University of
    Michigan Press, 1991.
Walker, Jack L., Jr. "A Critique of the Elitist Theory of Democracy." *American
    Political Science Review* 60 (June 1966): 285–95.
————. "The Origins and Maintenance of Interest Groups in America." *American
    Political Science Review* 77 (June 1983): 390–406.
Warren, Mark E. *Democracy and Association.* Princeton, NJ: Princeton University
    Press, 2001.
Warren, Mark R. *Dry Bones Rattling: Community Building to Revitalize American
    Democracy.* Princeton, NJ: Princeton University Press, 2001.
Wattenberg, Martin. *The Decline of American Political Parties, 1952–1996,*
    Cambridge: Harvard University Press, 1998.
Wayne, Leslie, and Melody Petersen. "A Muscular Lobby Rolls Up Its Sleeves."
    New York Times, November 4, 2001, p. 1.
Weaver, Kent R. "The Changing World of Think Tanks." *PS* 22 (September 1989):
    563–78.
Weisman, Jonathan. "Closed-Door Deal Makes $22 Billion Difference: GOP
    Negotiators Criticized for Change In Measure on HMOs," *The Washington Post,*
    January 24, 2006, p. A1.

Weisman, Jonathan, and Charles Babcock. "K Street's New Ways Spawn More Pork," *The Washington Post,* January 27, 2006, p. A1.

Weissman, Steve, and Ruth Hassan. "527 Groups and BCRA." In *The Election After Reform: Money, Politics, and the Bipartisan Campaign Reform Act,* edited by Michael J. Malbin. Lanham, MD: Rowman & Littlefield, 2006.

Weissman, Stephen R., and Kara D. Ryan. "Soft Money in the 2006 Election and the Outlook for 2008: The Changing Nonprofits Landscape." Report prepared for the campaign Financial Institute *http://www.cfirst.org/books_reports/pdf/NP_softmoney_06-08.pdf,* Accessed 9/13/07.

Wellman, Barry. "Structural Analysis: From Method and Metaphor to Theory and Substance." In *Social Structures: A Network Approach,* edited by Barry Wellman and S.D. Berkowitz. New York: Cambridge University Press, 1988.

Welch, William M., and Jim Drinkard. "Social Security fight gets personal," *USA TODAY,* February 28, 2005, p. 1A.

West, Darrell M., Diane J. Heith, and Chris Goodwin. "Harry and Louise Go to Washington: Political Advertising and Health Care Reform." *Journal of Health Policy, Politics and Law* 21 (Spring 1996): 35–68.

White, Joseph. "Making Connections in the Appropriations Process." In *The Interest Group Connection,* 2nd ed., edited by Paul S. Herrnson, Ronald G. Shaiko, and Clyde Wilcox. Washington, DC: CQ Press, 2005.

Wilcox, Clyde. "The Christian Right in Virginia: A Mixed Blessing for Democracy." Presented at the Conference on Civil Society in the United States, Georgetown University, June 1999.

———. "Coping with Increasing Business Influence: The AFL-CIO's Committee on Political Education" In *Risky Business?,* edited by Robert Biersack, Paul S. Herrnson, and Clyde Wilcox. Armonk, NY: M. E. Sharpe, 1994.

Wilcox, Clyde, and Carin Larson. *Onward Christian Soldiers: The Christian Right in American Politics,* 3rd ed. Boulder: Westview, 2006.

Wilcox, Clyde, and Barbara Norrander. "Of Moods and Morals: The Dynamics of Opinion on Abortion and Gay Rights." In *Understanding Public Opinion,* 2nd ed., edited by Barbara Norrander and Clyde Wilcox. Washington, DC: CQ Press, 2004.

Williams, Krissah, "Labor Groups, Business Seek Immigration Law Overhaul." *The Washington Post,* January 20, 2007, D01.

Wilson, Graham K. *Business and Politics.* Chatham, NJ: Chatham House, 1985.

———. *Interest Groups.* Oxford: Basil Blackwell, 1990.

———. *Unions in American National Politics.* London: Macmillan, 1977.

Wilson, James Q. *Political Organizations.* New York: Basic Books, 1973.

———. "Democracy and the Corporation." In *Does Big Business Rule America?* edited by Ronald Hessen. Washington, DC: Ethics and Public Policy Center, 1981.

Wines, Michael. "Ma Bell and Her Newly Independent Children Revamp Lobbying Networks." *National Journal,* January 28, 1984, pp. 148–52.

Wright, John R. *Interest Groups and Congress.* Boston: Allyn & Bacon, 1996.

———. "Contributions, Lobbying, and Committee Voting in the U.S. House of Representatives." *American Political Science Review* 84 (June 1990): 417–38.

———. "PACs, Contributions, and Roll Calls: An Organizational Perspective." *American Political Science Review* 79 (June 1985): 400–14.

Yackee, Jason Webb, and Susan Webb Yackee. "A Bias Towards Business? Assessing Interest Group Influence on the U.S. Bureaucracy." *Journal of Politics* (February 2006).

Zeigler, Harmon, and Michael Baer. *Lobbying.* Belmont, CA: Wadsworth, 1969.

Index